365 Life Lessons from Bible People

A Life Application® Devotional

365
LIFE LESSONS
from BIBLE PEOPLE

A LIFE APPLICATION® DEVOTIONAL

EDITORS:
Michael Kendrick
Daryl Lucas

CONTRIBUTORS:
Jack Crabtree
Mark Fackler
Michael Kendrick
Mary Ann Lackland
Daryl Lucas
Neil Wilson
Len Woods

Tyndale House Publishers, Inc.
Wheaton, Illinois

Developed for Tyndale House by the Livingstone Corporation. Dr. James C. Galvin, Daryl Lucas, and Michael Kendrick, project staff.

Some of the *365 Life Lessons from Bible People* are adapted from the Personality Profiles found in the *Life Application Bible,* copyright © 1988, 1989, 1990, 1991 by Tyndale House Publishers, Inc.

Life Application is a registered trademark of Tyndale House Publishers, Inc.

All Scripture quotations, unless otherwise indicated, are taken from the *Holy Bible,* New International Version®. Copyright © 1973, 1978, 1984 by International Bible Society. Used by permission of Zondervan Publishing House. All rights reserved. The "NIV" and "New International Version" trademarks are registered in the United States Patent and Trademark Office by International Bible Society. Use of either trademark requires permission of International Bible Society.

Scriptures marked NCV are taken from the *New Century Version,* copyright ©1987, 1988, 1991 by Word Publishing, Dallas, Texas 75039. Used by permission.

Scripture quotations marked NRSV are taken from the New Revised Standard Version of the Bible, copyrighted, 1989 by the Division of Christian Education of the National Council of the Churches of Christ in the United States of America, and are used by permission. All rights reserved.

Scripture verses marked TLB are taken from *The Living Bible,* copyright © 1971 owned by assignment by KNT Charitable Trust. All rights reserved.

Library of Congress Cataloging-in-Publication Data

365 life lessons from Bible people : a life application devotional /
    editors, Michael Kendrick, Daryl Lucas ; contributors, Jack Crabtree . . . [et. al.].
       p. cm.
    Includes indexes.
    ISBN 0-8423-3799-7 (SC : alk. paper)
     1. Bible—Biography—Meditations.   2. Bible—Meditations.
  I. Kendrick, Michael, date.   II. Lucas, Daryl.   III. Crabree, Jack, date.
BS571.A18   1996
242′.5—dc20   95-44518

Printed in the United States of America

01 00 99 98 97 96
7   6   5   4   3   2

INTRODUCTION

Biographies continue to fascinate us. Take a look at the nonfiction best-seller list, and you'll undoubtedly find a few life stories of celebrities or historical greats. We are curious to learn how these people think and behave. We want to know about their personal habits. In short, we want to understand what lifts them beyond the ordinary.

This book is a collection of short episodes from the lives of men and women who played a role in the unfolding of God's plan. More than a retelling of facts, each reading is designed to illustrate a principle that can be applied to one's own spiritual life. The book covers a wide range of personalities—from humble people who obeyed God wholeheartedly to kings and rebels whose evil was their undoing. Each story concludes with Scripture references for further study.

This book can be used in several ways. The 365 readings make it an ideal yearly devotional, one that can be used by itself or with other Scripture reading plans. The concise format also makes it suitable for family devotions. Teachers and small group leaders as well can use the book as a resource for developing more extensive studies of prominent Bible people. However you choose to use this book, we hope that it will help you develop the character God wants to create in you.

CONTENTS

Failure, Frustration—and Hope

ADAM

I heard you in the garden, and I was afraid because I was naked;
so I hid. (Genesis 3:10)

It is almost impossible to imagine what Adam's life was like. He was first and one-of-a-kind: no childhood, no parents, no schooling, no guilt, close contact with God, perfect world, only one rule to follow. Life today is vastly different.

Yet we can identify with Adam's struggles: (1) He's embarrassed to admit mistakes and wants to avoid confronting his problems; (2) his kids get into big trouble, spoiling many of his dreams for their future; (3) he works harder and gets less done as life goes on; and (4) as an older adult, all his labors have little to show except a small farm and scattered grandchildren.

Yet even Adam had hope. Genesis 3:15 is God's first piece of good news: Satan will be defeated; a Savior will come. That promise gave Adam hope and still lifts us from the pits to the heavens, from "What's the use?" to "Praise the Lord!" When life seems barren and pointless, remember that even Adam had this hope.

Jesus has come, salvation is won, and the Bible promises another (the Second) coming at the end of time, when all of our tears will be wiped away. Whenever you're discouraged, remember that.

Each new day is another chapter in the unfolding promise of
deliverance and life.

Adam's story is told in Genesis 1:26–5:5. Adam is also mentioned in 1 Chronicles 1:1; Luke 3:38; Romans 5:14; 1 Corinthians 15:22, 45; and 1 Timothy 2:13-14.

Following Dangerous Desires

EVE

The woman was convinced. How lovely and fresh looking it was! And it would make her so wise! (Genesis 3:6, TLB)

We know very little about Eve, the first woman in the world, yet she is the mother of us all. She was the final piece in the intricate and amazing puzzle of God's creation. As her descendants, we have inherited her propensity for sin, particularly when it comes to questioning God's sufficiency in our lives.

Eve was vulnerable to Satan's line of attack, for he knew her weakness: lack of contentment. How could she be happy when she was not allowed to eat from one of the fruit trees? Eve fell for the idea that the one item that was not within her reach would make her happy. And Eve was willing to accept Satan's insinuations without checking with God.

Sound familiar? How often is our attention drawn from the much we possess to the little that we don't? We get that I've-got-to-have-it feeling. We open ourselves to envy, greed, and all kinds of selfish behavior in order to satisfy our longings. And when we follow through on our impulses, the satisfaction we find is hollow and vanishes quickly.

God has given us all we need to be happy. Why waste our time pursuing something that's second-rate?

Focus on all God has given you, not on the little you lack.

Eve's story is told in Genesis 2:19–4:2.

Passing the Buck

EVE

Then the Lord God said to the woman, "What is this you have done?" The woman said, "The serpent deceived me, and I ate." (Genesis 3:13)

Adam and Eve's fall into sin provides the first instance in history of people who "passed the buck." When God asked Adam about his sin, Adam blamed Eve. Eve said, in effect, "Don't look at me—it was the serpent's fault." And if God had inquired of the serpent, he certainly would have passed the blame back to the woman and man. How relieved Eve must have been when God turned to the serpent and announced his punishment! Her relief was short lived, however. God refused to accept her rationalization and held her responsible for her wrongdoing.

The consequences of Eve's rebellion are well known, and humans have followed her example ever since. It is so easy to excuse our sin by blaming someone else. It is a way of avoiding the pain of getting right with God and other people. But God knows the truth! And he holds each of us responsible for what we do. Admit your sin and confess it to God. Don't make matters worse by blaming someone else.

Blaming someone else for our wrongdoing only increases the consequences of our sin.

Read more about Eve in Genesis 2:19–4:2.

Full Pardon Is Available

CAIN

The Lord said to Cain, "Where is your brother Abel?" "I don't know,"
he replied. "Am I my brother's keeper?" (Genesis 4:9)

Among his other distinctions, Cain is the first to offer the world an
unforgettable quotation. These famous words have come to stand
for excuse making, disregard for loved ones, and outright lying. A
rough man, strong and impetuous, Cain despised weakness and
had little patience for those whose work he judged inferior. He
paid little heed to God. Independent and strong-willed, he was not
above asking for a break when he knew he was beaten (4:13).

After Cain murdered Abel, God gave him a mark. It was a sign
to keep hooligans away from him, but it was also a reminder that
God still cares for even the worst of criminals.

Cain's story teaches us never to give up on anybody. God's love
and mercy reach to people who do not deserve them, whose personalities are toughened and resistant. God never quits on anybody.

When you have opportunities to help toughened people,
remember that God was merciful to Cain. If you are a prisoner or
ex-con, remember that the very first criminal was still under God's
care. If you are a victim of crime, hard as it may be, let God do the
judging and sentencing so that your heart may be free to forgive
and live again.

God takes control of the most sorry, desperate circumstances and
keeps us in his watchful care.

Cain's story is told in Genesis 4:1-17. Cain is also mentioned in
Hebrews 11:4; 1 John 3:12; and Jude 11.

Giving Your Best to God

ABEL

Abel brought the fatty cuts of meat from his best lambs, and presented them to the Lord. (Genesis 4:4, TLB)

Every child who knows the Bible and every adult who has darkened the door of a church knows the name of this second son. He is the first innocent to suffer, the youth whose life was snuffed out by the jealous blow of his own brother.

Exactly why God favored Abel's offering is unknown to us but not to them. They knew. The pristine world was not cluttered with noise and distraction; God's will must have been crystal clear.

God's will for us today is clear enough, too. We know that loving service is the centerpiece, that greed and pride are spoilers. We know that "our way or no way" is offensive to God. We know that God wants our devotion, no matter what the cost.

Today give your best to God: your heart trusting in God's care, your mind devoted to knowing God deeply, your will eager to please the sovereign Creator.

Jealousy kills a relationship that God wants to nourish.

Abel's story is told in Genesis 4. He is also mentioned in Matthew 23:35; Luke 11:51; and Hebrews 11:4; 12:24.

Speaking without Words

ABEL

By faith he still speaks, even though he is dead. (Hebrews 11:4)

Odd that a person can "speak" so effectively through centuries and millennia, though the Bible does not record a single word from his mouth. Cain, the perpetrator, gets to talk rather at length in Abel's story (Genesis 4:1-14). Eve speaks, too. Adam had his say earlier. From Abel—nothing.

Except obedience. He brings the offering God desires.

Except eagerness. One cannot read of Abel without the sense that he enjoyed pleasing God.

Except innocent suffering. Abel follows brother Cain to the field and dies with a look of amazement and innocence in his eyes, as millions have since. Why the cancer? Why the accident? Why the war? Why *me?*

Abel's story reminds us of the evil that darkens our world, of lives lost to treachery and hatred. His death begs for moral judgment, for God to make things right again.

And that is exactly what God promises to do through the victory of Jesus Christ, our Savior. On Easter morning, Abel's life—and yours—was bought back, eternally, forever, by God's mighty power. Jesus said, "I am . . . the life," (John 14:6). Today, and each day of your life, trust Jesus Christ, God's Son, our Savior, for life eternal.

Jesus is God's answer to Abel's why.

Abel's story is told in Genesis 4. He is also mentioned in Matthew 23:35; Luke 11:51; and Hebrews 11:4; 12:24.

The Rapid Growth of Sin

LAMECH

If Cain is avenged sevenfold, truly Lamech seventy-sevenfold.
(Genesis 4:24, NRSV)

Lamech earns just a few brief verses in Scripture, but those words say much about the rapid advance of sin in the days after Adam and Eve. A descendant of Cain, Lamech was the father of the first musician and the first metalworker. But Lamech's contribution to the spiritual condition of humankind was a pitiful one.

First, we note that Lamech was the first polygamist, taking two wives, Adah and Zillah. This attempt to "improve" on God's design for marriage would bear sorrow and frustration for many who followed in his footsteps: Jacob, David, and Solomon are obvious examples.

Second, Lamech had a cavalier disregard for the value of human life. He tells his wives that he killed a young man (actually, "child" in the Hebrew) for striking him. Instead of showing remorse, he boasts of his deed and throws down a challenge: If anyone would dare settle the score for this murder, Lamech would be avenged seventy-sevenfold! Unlike Cain, who took God's protection gladly, Lamech seems to laugh off the need for any divine discipline or refuge.

Sin is like a weed. It can grow rapidly, even in adverse conditions. Are you ignoring the sprouts that are shooting up in your life? Ask God to help you pull up the weeds of selfishness and rebellion before the problem gets out of control.

It doesn't take long for sin to bear its poisonous fruit.

Lamech's story appears in Genesis 4:18-24.

Long-Term Faithfulness
ENOCH

It was attested before he was taken away that "he had pleased God." (Hebrews 11:5, NRSV)

When Jude was reviewing the history of human rebellion against God, he mentioned the warnings of Enoch the preacher, a man best known for being one of two Old Testament people who never died. (The other is Elijah.)

The book of Hebrews lists Enoch as the second figure inducted into the "Hall of Faith." By faith, Enoch pleased God. Enoch was a person who believed that God "exists and that he rewards those who earnestly seek him" (Hebrews 11:6). The book of Jude informs us that Enoch told others about the God in whom he believed. He warned them that God was to be worshiped and obeyed. But Genesis gives us the simplest description of Enoch's life—he "walked with God." God was as real, as immediate, as apparent in Enoch's life as taking a walk.

We who measure faithfulness to God in terms of weeks and days should be mindful of the example of Enoch's life. His faithfulness stretched out over three hundred years. He really spent some time with God! If your life were to be summarized at the close of this day, what three- or four-word description would fit best?

Faith lives one day at a time for a lifetime.

Enoch's life is recorded in Genesis 5:18-24, and he is mentioned in Hebrews 11:5 and Jude 14-15.

Living Life to the Fullest

METHUSELAH

Altogether, Methuselah lived 969 years, and then he died.
(Genesis 5:27)

If you asked most people if living a long life is a desirable goal, they would probably say yes. If you asked them why, they might tell you that they could travel to exotic places, experience the wonders of future technology, read book after book, and live life to the full. But how many have truly pondered what living life to the full means?

Methuselah's sole claim to biblical fame is his amazing life span—an incredible 969 years. But we really know little else about him. He is never mentioned in Scripture as a man of faith. We don't know if he even had a relationship with God, as did his father, Enoch. His long life certainly would have given him countless opportunities to draw close to God, but he may have ignored those chances just the same.

The length of our lives is not as important as is for whom we live them. A short life given in service to Christ brings more joy to God than a long life lived in selfishness and empty pursuits. Thank God today for the precious gift of life he's given you, and resolve with his help to dedicate each moment to obeying him and serving others.

A long life without God's presence is doomed to emptiness.

Methuselah is mentioned in Genesis 5:21-27 and in the genealogies of 1 Chronicles 1:3 and Luke 3:37.

A Righteous Reputation

NOAH

He was the only truly righteous man living on the earth at that time.
(Genesis 6:9, TLB)

Against the backdrop of a culture darkened by evil, Noah lived
a sparkling, exemplary life. He was the only follower of God left in
his generation, and thus his family was chosen by God to survive
the Flood. In a sense, he became the second father of the human
race.

In completing the giant boat that would bring him and his
family through God's watery judgment, Noah demonstrated faithfulness, obedience, and patience (the task took over a hundred
years!). Second Peter 2:5 also calls Noah "a preacher of righteousness," implying that he warned his friends and neighbors of the
wrath to come.

Noah wasn't perfect. He demonstrated a lack of self-control late
in life, when he got drunk on wine from his own vineyard. And
yet, when the Scripture summarizes his life, Noah is called a righteous man who walked with God—in sharp contrast to the others
of his day.

If someone today were to sum up your life in a sentence or two,
what would he or she say about you? What is your reputation?
What are you known for? If you are really serious about wanting
to live in a way that pleases God, you might wish to ask these questions of a trusted friend. The answers might surprise you or even
hurt your feelings, but they will give you some clear ideas on what
areas of your life need to change.

How you live determines how you will be remembered.

The story of Noah is found in Genesis 5:28–10:32.

Doing What God Commands

NOAH

And Noah did everything as God commanded him.
(Genesis 6:22, TLB)

Put yourself in Noah's sandals for a few moments. You see the world around you becoming more and more evil. God then announces to you his intention to judge the earth. You think, *It's about time something was done about all this ungodliness!* Then God tells you to begin building a ship large enough to house your entire family and representatives of each species of the animal kingdom!

As you reflect on these strange commands, you ponder the implications: *A giant boat miles from any water . . . what will the neighbors think? How do I explain this to my family? What do I, a man of the soil, know about shipbuilding?*

Noah's response to his newfound responsibilities was immediate. Genesis says, not once but twice, that Noah did everything as God commanded him. No rationalizing, no complaining, no stalling. Noah went right to work.

God has promised that we will never again need to practice the craft of ark-building. However, he still asks us to do certain things that our society will scorn. What does your lifestyle say to your non-Christian neighbors and friends? Are you living an obedient, Noah-like life? Pick one area of your life in which you have been resisting God, and take some steps toward obedience today. You'll definitely have a clear conscience, and your actions just might provide you an opportunity to share your faith with others.

The formula for pleasing God is simple: Trust and obey.

The story of Noah is found in Genesis 5:28–10:32.

The Risk of Faith

ABRAHAM

Do not be afraid, Abram. I am your shield, your very great reward.
(Genesis 15:1)

Travel plans today are surrounded with insurance policies. Anything of value has legal papers to assure passage of title to proper heirs. We have built layers of security around every important move we make.

In the ancient world, Abraham moved about by his wits, his strength, and—unusual for his time—his radical faith in the one God.

Faith gave Abraham his security. God would be Abraham's protector; God would prosper his life; God would take fear from Abraham's heart and give him courage. God, who sent this man into foreign territory, would show him truth that no one had yet uncovered. All this for Abraham, and all of it by faith.

Abraham could have said, "No way!" Not enough assurance; too much risk. Abraham, however, heard the Lord speak—alone, in visions, with unprecedented clarity—and believed.

Life today gains richness and meaning as we walk with God in faith, stretching resources, exhausting energies, pressing toward promises generously given to us throughout the Bible's amazing story. We need to experience Abraham's freedom, the liberty and joy of trusting in our *shield* and *reward*. We need to trust in God.

The living God is our security.

Abraham's story is told in Genesis 11–25. Abraham is also mentioned in Exodus 2:24; Acts 7:2-8; Romans 4; Galatians 3; Hebrews 2; 6; 7; 11; and James 2:21-24.

Taking God at His Word

ABRAHAM

We will worship and then we will come back to you. (Genesis 22:5)

What a twist! God promised a child to aged Abraham and Sarah; they waited. Finally the miracle birth came, and with it such a flood of joy in one home as the world had never before seen. Now the boy was to be given back to God in sacrifice by his father's own hand. It boggles the mind; it changes everything.

With stunning immediacy, Abraham set out on the journey. What feelings rumbled in his heart as he and the youngster hiked are left to our imagination. We only know that he obeyed, believing that God would provide a way to fulfill his promise. Hebrews says that he believed that God could raise the dead (Hebrews 11:19).

Just about everything that happens to us tests our faith. We seem to have too little money to give, though God says he will always meet our needs; will we believe? We want to take revenge, but God says he will avenge; will we believe? Christ died for our sins and says he will take them away if we will but trust in him; will we believe?

Accept God's promise and discover God's blessing.

Abraham's story is told in Genesis 11–25. Abraham is also mentioned in Exodus 2:24; Acts 7:2-8; Romans 4; Galatians 3; Hebrews 2; 6; 7; 11; and James 2:21-24.

No Problem Is Too Big

SARAH

Is anything too hard for the Lord? (Genesis 18:14)

After waiting so long (in vain) for a child, Sarah was skeptical, perhaps even cynical. Her ninety-year-old skin was wrinkled. Her eyesight was failing. Her bones were creaking. No doubt her thoughts were focused on issues of geriatrics—not pediatrics! Yet here was God telling her and Abraham that they were about to become parents.

The thought was outrageous, ridiculous, laughable. And so that's what Sarah did—she laughed to herself. Was it a sneering laugh? Was it a laugh due to embarrassment or shock? We're not told. But God heard her silent snickering and confronted her about it.

"You don't believe me," he seemed to be saying. "What's the big deal about me causing you to have a son late in life? Hey, I'm the God who created the universe out of nothing!"

Sarah tried to deny her disbelief, in much the same way we do. "I believe! I believe! Of course God is all-powerful! He can do anything!" we claim. But then we turn around in the next breath and focus on our problems. When we do, we become disillusioned, depressed, and despondent. "It's terrible!" we moan. "It's no use!" we yelp.

What "hopeless" situation are you facing today? Instead of looking at the size of your problem, why not meditate instead on the size of your God? Nothing—nothing at all—is too hard for him. Will you trust him to work in your life today?

God is all-powerful!

The life of Sarah is depicted in Genesis 11–25.

Waiting for the Promise

SARAH

Can Sarah, who is ninety years old, bear a child?
(Genesis 17:17, NRSV)

Think about how hard it is to wait—for a vacation or a tax refund check; in a long, slow line, especially when you're running late; to get your driver's license; for the results of a medical test; for an answer that could change your whole life.

Now imagine having to wait ninety years for something you want desperately. Would you have the patience to hang in there that long? That was the dilemma facing Sarah. She wanted children, but she was infertile. At age sixty-five she had long since given up her dream of being a mom, when God suddenly announced that she would indeed have a son. But then ten years dragged by, and nothing happened.

Eventually Sarah tired of waiting and tried to speed up the process. But God made it clear that Ishmael (the son of Sarah's servant Hagar) was not the child he had originally intended. Five more years ticked by, then another five. Finally, after fifteen more years (Sarah was then 90), God announced that the time was at last right. Abraham and Sarah got their bouncing baby, Isaac, and they learned—in the words of the old spiritual—that "God may make you wait, but he'll never be too late."

What are you waiting for today? Don't throw in the towel! God keeps every promise he makes. Resist the urge to rush things along. Hang in there. Too many times we get so caught up in our destination that we miss the wildness and wonder of the journey itself.

God's promises are always worth the wait.

The life of Sarah is depicted in Genesis 11–25.

The Drifter
LOT

Lot lived among the cities in the Jordan Valley, very near to Sodom.
(Genesis 13:12, NCV)

Perhaps you have heard this old saying: There are three kinds of people in life—those who make things happen, those who watch things happen, and those who say, "What happened?"

Lot seems to have been a member of the third category. As you read about him in Scripture, you get the impression of a guy who just floated through life, taking the path of least resistance. He never seemed to wrestle with difficult questions such as *What are the long-term consequences of this choice?* or *I wonder what God wants me to do?* Instead, he lived for the moment. He never anchored himself to the truth of God and so was swept along by a corrupt culture to places he probably never wanted to go. Lot and his family suffered death, incest, and disgrace because he allowed the world to shape his life and determine his direction.

Are you drifting? Do you have firm convictions about how God expects you to live? Have you anchored yourself to the truth of God? Do you have some definite goals in view? If you don't take specific steps to place yourself under God's direction, you will turn out like Lot, one of those poor souls who gets into one mess after another. Your life will be a tragic example of what might have been.

People who drift without God's direction usually end up where they don't want to be.

The story of Lot is found in Genesis 11–14; 19.

King of Righteousness

MELCHIZEDEK

He was priest of God Most High, and he blessed Abram. (Genesis 14:18-19)

Lot and his family had been taken prisoner in a war between several kings who lived in the region surrounding Sodom. Abram, with the help of 318 men, had rescued his imperiled nephew. In the aftermath of this victory, we are introduced to the mysterious character named Melchizedek. Coming out to congratulate Abram, this king/priest offered physical nourishment and spiritual encouragement. Then he disappeared, never to be heard from again. What are we to make of this unusual Bible personality?

The name *Melchizedek* means "king of righteousness." He was a priest not of a local deity (as was common among the Canaanite peoples) but of the one true God. Melchizedek blessed the Lord and also Abram.

Many scholars have speculated about the identity of Melchizedek. Some regard him as a king who was a "type" of Christ, meaning that aspects of his life prefigure or illustrate some later truth from the earthly life of Jesus. Other commentators suggest that Melchizedek was actually a preincarnate appearance of Christ. The most important thing about Melchizedek, however, is not so much who he was but what he did. He sought to know and worship the one true God. Furthermore, he honored the followers of the Lord.

We would do well to emulate Melchizedek's wholehearted commitment to God. Seek God today in the midst of a culture that is interested in lesser deities.

Melchizedek reminds us to live for Jesus!

The few details we have about the life of Melchizedek are found in Genesis 14:17-20; Psalm 110:4; and Hebrews 5–7.

Don't Look Back

LOT'S WIFE

But Lot's wife looked back, and she became a pillar of salt.
(Genesis 19:26)

She was one look away from reaching safe haven with her family. Gulping the gagging sulfurous air, she frantically followed her husband through the smoke. Perhaps she was startled to a sudden halt by the fiery orange bursts that ruptured the dim morning sky. Perhaps it was the thunderous crack of fire striking her neighbors' homes and the rooftops of familiar town buildings that whipped her around to see. Instantly, her eyes took in the dreadful scene, and her mortal frame disintegrated—her disobedience memorialized in grains of salt.

Why did Lot's wife so foolishly look back? Likely for the reason most familiar to us: She was thoroughly human. Like her, we often receive clear instruction from God yet still feel frightened and uncertain about where God is taking us.

When we are following God in new directions, the awareness of our former dreams and goals going up in flames behind us may be a sufficient temptation to distrust his leading. Are you looking back longingly at what you are leaving behind while trying to move forward into a deeper relationship with God? Jesus' clear warning to us is to "remember Lot's wife" (Luke 17:32). The only way out of this dilemma is to trust him in spite of your fears.

You cannot progress with God if you are longing for what might have been.

The full story of Lot's wife and her family's escape from Sodom is found in Genesis 18:1–19:29.

Running Away from Problems

HAGAR

Return to your mistress and act as you should, for I will make you into a great nation. (Genesis 16:9, TLB)

Escape is usually the most tempting solution to our problems. In fact, it can become a habit. Hagar, the servant-wife of Abraham, used that approach. When the going got tough, she usually got going—in the other direction.

Hagar's pregnancy caused her to look down on Sarah, who consequently punished her. Hagar ran away. When she returned to the family and gave birth to Ishmael, Sarah looked for any excuse to have Hagar and Ishmael sent away for good. In the desert, out of water and facing the death of her son, Hagar once again tried to escape. She walked away so she wouldn't have to watch her son die. Once again, God graciously intervened.

Have you noticed that God sometimes blocks our exits for our own good? He wants us to face our problems with his help. We see his provision most clearly in times of conflict and difficulty. Are there problems in your life for which you've been using the "Hagar solution"? Choose one of those problems, ask for God's help, and begin to face it today.

Run to God with your problems, not away from him.

Hagar's story is told in Genesis 16–21.

Discovering God's Faithfulness

ISHMAEL

Sarah noticed Ishmael—the son of Abraham and the Egyptian girl Hagar—teasing Isaac. (Genesis 21:9, TLB)

Have you ever wondered if you were born into the wrong family? That question must have haunted Ishmael at times. Sarah's pregnancy and Isaac's birth must have had a devastating impact on Ishmael. Until then he had been treated as a son and heir, but this late arrival made his future uncertain. During Isaac's weaning celebration, Sarah caught Ishmael teasing his half brother. As a result, Hagar and Ishmael were permanently expelled from Abraham's family.

Much of what happened to Ishmael was not his fault. He was caught in circumstances he had little power to control. Yet God saw to it that he was cared for. He provided refreshment when Hagar and Ishmael were in the desert. Later, God would make Ishmael's descendants into a great nation.

Ishmael's rescue testifies to God's faithfulness. Earlier Abraham had learned that Ishmael would inherit blessings. The fulfillment of that promise looked doubtful, however, after Hagar was abruptly sent packing. But in his timing, God unfolded his promise for Ishmael, which included a long life and many descendants.

Have you thought about God's faithfulness today? Even though we are unreliable and prone to sin, God welcomes us and sustains us as we are.

Even when family and friends let us down, God can be counted on to keep his promises.

Ishmael's story is told in Genesis 16–17; 21:8-21; 25:12-18.

The Importance of a Name

ISAAC

Sarah shall bear you a son; and you are to name him Isaac ("Laughter"), and I will sign my covenant with him forever. (Genesis 17:19, TLB)

Your name carries great significance. It sets you apart. It triggers memories. The sound of it calls you to attention anywhere.

Many Bible names accomplished even more. They often described important facts about one's past and hopes for the future. Abraham and Sarah's name for their son, Isaac—"he laughs"—must have created a variety of feelings each time it was spoken. It surely recalled Sarah's shocked laughter at God's announcement that they would be parents in their old age. At other times, Isaac must have reflected on the joyful laughter he brought his parents as their long-awaited answer to prayer.

Most important, Isaac's name testified to God's power. Perhaps Abraham and Sarah had assumed that God had forgotten his promise to give them a son of their own. But God overcame the barriers of old age and surprised the couple with a precious child. Isaac thus became a reminder of the holy laughter that God delights in giving to his children who obey him.

God is reaffirming his promises to us all the time.

Isaac's story is told in Genesis 17:15–35:29. He is also mentioned in Romans 9:7-10; Hebrews 11:17-20; and James 2:21-24.

Keeping the Peace
ISAAC

[Isaac] moved on from there and dug another well, and no one quarreled over it. (Genesis 26:22)

Isaac was generally a quiet man who kept to himself. But he was capable of resolute action when it was needed. His jealous neighbors, the Philistines, once crafted a malicious plot against him. In an area where water was as precious as gold, Isaac's hostile neighbors plugged up his wells two separate times and threatened to drive him away. Even though plugging another landowner's well was a serious crime, Isaac refused to let the incident provoke him to rash action. Instead, he and his men simply dug another well. Finally, there was enough room for everyone, and the dispute settled down. Isaac's willingness to compromise for the sake of peace headed off a bloody showdown.

Would you be willing to forsake an important position or valuable possession to keep the peace? In some situations, you may have a good reason to be angry. But are your rights the only issue at stake? You may face conflict with your friends, family, or coworkers this week. Ask God for the wisdom to know when to withdraw and when to stand your ground.

Keeping the peace sometimes means forfeiting your right to be angry.

Isaac's story is told in Genesis 17:15–35:29. He is also mentioned in Romans 9:7-10; Hebrews 11:17-20; and James 2:21-24.

The Honor of Service
ELIEZER

Whoever wants to be great among you must be your servant.
(Mark 10:43, TLB)

Eliezer was a friend and servant of Abraham. To describe him that way both tells all and tells too little, for he was perhaps the most exemplary servant in the Bible besides Jesus. Abraham was fortunate.

Here's his simple story. Abraham wanted to find a wife for Isaac. So Abraham called in his trusted servant Eliezer and gave him the outline.

Eliezer clarified what he was being asked to do. After considering and ruling out the alternatives with Abraham, he gave his word to do his best. He designed a careful plan, keeping in mind that he should leave room for God to work. As he traveled and searched, he practiced patience in his task and thankfully accepted God's guidance. And he respectfully followed his plan through to completion, bringing Rebekah to Isaac as Abraham had requested.

Eliezer's attitude and actions in carrying out his mission embody the honor and importance of service to others. He was what God wants us all to be first and above all: friend and servant.

Consider the variety of people you will rub shoulders with today. Will they receive service from you?

The greatest people are faithful servants.

Eliezer's story of service can be found in Genesis 24.

Family Favorites

REBEKAH

Isaac loved Esau, because he was fond of game; but Rebekah loved Jacob. (Genesis 25:28, NRSV)

The twin sons of Isaac and Rebekah were very different people. Esau is described as a skillful hunter, a man of the open country. He comes across as rough and tough, impulsive and spiteful. Jacob, on the other hand, is depicted as a quiet man, staying among the tents. We see him preparing stews and cooking up schemes to take advantage of others.

Perhaps these differences explain (at least in part) the parental favoritism that developed in Isaac's household. Isaac had a special bond with Esau, while Rebekah clearly favored Jacob. These preferences caused strife between Isaac and Rebekah and may have encouraged the poor choices and flawed personalities of each brother. Jacob became a trickster, while Esau became a rebel.

It is normal to feel drawn to certain individuals. We cannot help those feelings, nor should we feel guilty for having them. What is wrong is to accentuate the special feelings we may have for one family member over another. When we play favorites and give special treatment or extra attention to a mother, father, child, or sibling, we invite friction into our homes and cause emotional hurt in those we slight.

If family relations have turned sour, ask for an honest assessment from a Christian friend about how you are relating to each person in your family. Then ask God to supply the love that will heal the hurt.

Everyone suffers when family members play favorites.

The story of Rebekah is found in Genesis 24–27. She is also mentioned in Romans 9:10.

Deception's Price Tag

REBEKAH

My son, let the curse fall on me. Just do what I say; go and get them for me. (Genesis 27:13)

Rebekah remembered what the Lord had said: "The older [son] will serve the younger." *But how?* she probably wondered. *As the firstborn son, Esau is entitled to special privileges. He will be the recipient of Isaac's special blessings . . . unless we can somehow get Isaac to bless Jacob instead!*

Perhaps that is how Rebekah reasoned. Maybe that is how her scheme of deception came about. She planned and orchestrated the whole scam, and it worked. Isaac gave the blessing he had reserved for his elder son to his younger son, Jacob.

Rebekah got what she wanted, but she also got some additional unpleasant surprises: a rift between Esau and Jacob that took years to heal; a bitter Esau who threatened violence; a manipulative, demanding daughter-in-law in Rachel; and worst of all—a younger son who adopted her example of deceit.

Rebekah was exposed to a truth we need to wrestle with today: Sin doesn't pay—it costs! An immoral or unethical action may seem to offer a desirable payoff; but down the road, we will begin receiving notices of payment due!

Pragmatism is not the same as obedience. Don't do things on the basis of what will work. Make your decisions based on what is right.

Sin always has long-term consequences.

The story of Rebekah is found in Genesis 24–27. She is also mentioned in Romans 9:10.

Smoothing Over a Rough Situation

KETURAH

Abraham took another wife, whose name was Keturah.
(Genesis 25:1)

Keturah became Abraham's second wife after Sarah died. What a complicated family system she faced! Her husband was perhaps thrice her age. Although she gave birth to six sons, Abraham's entire estate was inherited by Isaac, his only son with Sarah. The memory of the "other woman," Hagar, and her son Ishmael no doubt lingered. We read that concubines lived in the household as well. These women had children. Keturah was a late arrival in the menagerie.

We don't know how Keturah handled the problems she faced. But her life bears witness to God's compassion for family messes. He honored Keturah with significant offspring. Among her descendants were the Midianites. Keturah was the ancestor of Moses' wife, Zipporah, and his wise father-in-law, Jethro.

God's biblical guidelines are intended to steer us around potential problems, including family difficulties. Like Keturah, we may not have ideal family circumstances. Parents divorce. Children rebel. Siblings quarrel. But if you obey God and show love even to those who are unloving, you may be surprised at the results. God is always working for our good, and he is eager to restore broken relationships. Invite him today to begin the healing process.

Even the rockiest family situations can be smoothed over by God's grace.

Keturah's place in Abraham's life is recorded in Genesis 25:1-8.

Ruined by an Impulse

ESAU

See that no one is . . . godless like Esau, who for a single meal sold his inheritance rights as the oldest son. (Hebrews 12:16)

Esau's life was filled with choices he must have regretted bitterly. He appears to have been a person who found it difficult to consider consequences, reacting to the need of the moment without realizing what he was giving up to meet that need. Trading his birthright for a bowl of stew is the clearest example of this weakness. He acted on impulse, satisfying his immediate desires without pausing to consider the long-range consequences.

We can fall into the same trap. When we see something we want, our first impulse is to get it. At first we feel intensely satisfied, and sometimes even powerful, because we have obtained what we set out to get. But immediate pleasure often clouds our sight of the future. We may feel so much pressure to indulge our appetites that nothing else seems to matter.

What are you willing to trade for the things you want? Do you find yourself, at times, willing to give up anything for what you feel you need now? Does your family, spouse, integrity, body, or soul get included in these deals? Ask God to help you clearly see the long-term effects of your choices this week.

Watch out for dangerously strong, impulsive desires.

Esau's story is told in Genesis 25–36. He is also mentioned in Malachi 1:2-3 and Hebrews 12:16-17.

28

Getting Rid of Anger and Jealousy

ESAU

So Esau hated Jacob because of what he had done to him.
(Genesis 27:41, TLB)

Common sense isn't all that common. In fact, the common thread in many decisions is that they don't make sense. Such was the case with Esau's resolution to kill his brother Jacob for receiving the blessings of Esau's birthright. In his bitter anger, Esau overlooked the fact that it was his foolish mistake to forfeit his birthright to his brother in the first place. His vengeful decision, girded by anger, sent Esau barreling toward the destruction of both brothers' lives. Fortunately, Esau eventually redirected his energy toward forgiving his brother, dispelling the bitterness between them.

Whenever we lose something of great value or when others conspire against us and succeed, anger may be the first and most natural reaction. In itself, that is not wrong as long as we direct the energy of that anger toward a solution and not toward ourselves or others as the cause of the problem. The alternative is to let anger critically impair your ability to make right decisions.

As Esau's life testifies, effectively dealing with anger increases the possibility of inheriting future blessings in troublesome relationships and situations. Think about some anger hot spots you may have concerning your past, your spouse, your workplace, or your friends. Where are you channeling your energy: toward yourself, the problem, or a solution?

Jealous anger pollutes clear thinking.

Esau's story is told in Genesis 25–36. He is also mentioned in Malachi 1:2-3 and Hebrews 12:16-17.

Uniquely Blessed

JACOB

*I am with you and will watch over you wherever you go. . . . I
will not leave you until I have done what I have promised you.*
(Genesis 28:15)

If there were a "most blessed" list in the Old Testament, Jacob
would be one of the top candidates. God named Jacob as the third
male in the Abrahamic line of promise. Wealth, many servants,
and an abundance of livestock were a sign of God's favor upon
Jacob. He was granted the woman he loved in marriage, and she
bore him two sons. His other wives bore him several other sons,
and God bestowed on Jacob the fatherhood of the twelve tribes of
Israel.

It is important to realize that God gave his blessings with full
knowledge of Jacob's shortcomings. Although Jacob was uniquely
blessed by God, he also proved to be not so unique in his ability to
lie, deceive, and assert his independent nature. He was not the perfect hero. Instead, he was just like us: trying to please God, yet
often falling short.

The Christian life is often an awkward dance of two steps forward and three steps back; the key is that God honors our efforts
in spite of our errors. As you pray, put into words your desire to be
available to God. You will discover that his willingness to use you
is even greater than your desire to be used.

God makes allowances for human mistakes in his perfect plan.

Read about Jacob's life in Genesis 25–50.

Clinging to God

JACOB

[Your name] is Israel—one who has power with God. (Genesis 32:28, TLB)

During the early years of Jacob's life, he lived up to his name, which means "grabber." He stormed through life, grabbing every desire that lured his greedy heart. He grabbed Esau's heel at birth, and by the time he fled from home, he had also grabbed his brother's birthright and blessing.

When we see Jacob again, as a young man returning to his homeland in the prime of his life, he had accumulated not one wife but two and a stockpile of wealth, servants, and animals. Soon, however, Jacob was grabbing again. This time, by the Jordan River, he grabbed on to God and would not let go. He realized his dependence was on the God who had continued to bless him. No longer known as Jacob, who ambitiously adhered to his possessions, he became Israel—the one who clings to God.

Contrary to contemporary wisdom, the one who grabs the most toys in this life does not come out a winner. All of a person's assets become liabilities if he or she has not gained the single most important possession: a relationship with the living God. Which personality characterizes your life right now: Jacob, grabbing all he can in life, or Israel, claiming God as his greatest gain?

Security is not found in the ownership of goods, but in a relationship with God.

Jacob's story is told in Genesis 25–50.

Riding a Coattail of Blessings

LABAN

I have learned by divination that the Lord has blessed me because of you. (Genesis 30:27)

What do the Scriptures tell us about Laban? We know that he was the brother of Rebekah, the brother-in-law of Isaac, and the uncle of Jacob. We read that he had two daughters, Leah and Rachel. We discover that Laban was a wealthy shepherd with a history of deception in his dealings with others. (That may explain how he became wealthy!)

Nowhere in Genesis do we find any evidence that Laban ever had much interest in the God of Abraham, Isaac, and Jacob. In fact, he seemed much more devoted to his pagan idols. And yet, Laban was no dummy. He recognized the unmistakable overflow of benefits that surrounded Jacob. "Stay here!" Laban pleaded. "As long as you're around, it seems that the God of your fathers keeps blessing my business."

It is easy to fall into a routine where we ride the spiritual coattails of others. We discover that we can taste a little bit of the goodness of God even from a distance, even without a life of commitment. And yet, if we're selfish and worldly like Laban, we don't really belong. We're just along for the ride. We're on the outside looking in. We're close to God . . . but not really.

Don't settle for that kind of long-distance, secondhand relationship with God. Tell God today that you want to know him intimately. Then hold on to your hat!

It's a blessing to know the people of God; it is a far greater blessing to know God.

Laban's life story is found in Genesis 27:43–31:55.

Prisoner of Insecurity

LEAH

This time my husband will treat me with honor, because I have borne him six sons. (Genesis 30:20)

Leah lived in a world where women were considered property. Daughters were tokens used by fathers to finish deals. Leah's father, Laban, gave her to Jacob, who did not love her as much as he loved her younger sister, Rachel. But God loved her completely.

Leah desperately wanted her husband to cherish her. The names she chose for her sons expressed her longing to be noticed. She also competed fiercely with Rachel. The sisters began to measure their worth by the number of children they could bear. Leah won the fertility contest, but the victory did not capture Jacob's affection.

When we fail to live at peace with the important people in our lives, we create problems that may last for years. Although God loved Leah, we are not told that she acknowledged that fact. Her refusal to appreciate God's love also made her unable to love others completely.

When we struggle to love others, we need to remember the simple fact that God loves us.

Leah's story appears in Genesis 29–35.

Turbulent Character

REUBEN

Turbulent as the waters, you will no longer excel. (Genesis 49:4)

Jacob summed up the life of Reuben best when he said that he was "turbulent as the waters." He meant that Reuben could be dependable one moment and treacherous the next. Consider the highlights (and lowlights) of his life:

Reuben displayed a lack of backbone when his brothers concocted a plot to kill Joseph. Reuben gave tacit approval while scheming to save Joseph, a hope that was later dashed when the brothers sold him to some Ishmaelites. Reuben also demonstrated a severe lack of self-control when he slept with his father's concubine Bilhah.

Later in life Reuben offered to take responsibility for the safety of young Benjamin on a proposed trip to Egypt. "You may put both of my sons to death if I do not bring him back to you," Reuben told Jacob. Some see this offer as courageous. Others view it as still another example of Reuben's weakness, since he was willing to sacrifice his boys but not himself.

All in all, Reuben's life is unremarkable. He is not the most evil character we find in Scripture. And yet, nothing about him is outstanding or worthy of emulation.

Spend some time today evaluating your own life. Would those who know you well describe you as "turbulent as the waters"? Or are you reliable and committed to your beliefs? Do you stand out as someone who compromises or someone with deep-seated convictions?

Unreliable people live unremarkable lives.

The story of Reuben is told in Genesis 29–50.

The Difference God Has Made

JUDAH

Do not let me see the misery that would come upon my father.
(Genesis 44:34)

When we first meet Judah in Scripture, he is successfully urging his brothers to sell Joseph into slavery. All agree that it seems like a good plan. Joseph is the favorite son with the colorful jacket and the big head. "Might as well make a little money off this cocky troublemaker!" the brothers agree.

Yet at the end of the book of Genesis, we notice that Judah's callousness is gone. When it appears that young Benjamin (the new favorite son of Jacob) will be arrested for theft, Judah appeals for the release of his baby brother. "It would kill my father to lose another son!" Judah pleads to his yet unrecognized brother, Joseph. "Take me instead."

Judah's transformation is a marvelous example of how God can change a life. The young Judah was opportunistic, selfish, dishonest, and indifferent to the feelings of others. The older Judah was thoughtful, unselfish, responsible, and compassionate.

In what areas have you seen God change you? What would your close friends or family members say is the biggest difference Christ has made in your life? Spend a few minutes thanking God for the way he has worked in your life. Then ask him to show you new ways in which you need to change.

The same Christ who laid down his life for you can make you a person who lays down your life for others.

Details about the life of Judah can be found in Genesis 29:35–50:26.

Shamed and Forgotten

DINAH

Some time later she gave birth to a daughter and named her Dinah.
(Genesis 30:21)

As far as we know, Dinah was an only daughter. She had ten older brothers and two younger ones. When Dinah was probably a teenager, she and her family moved to Shechem.

Apparently no one really paid much attention to Dinah until she went out for a walk one day in the city of Shechem. During her visit to town she was raped by Shechem, the son of the city's ruler. Violated and shamed, Dinah found herself in the center of a family crisis. Shechem asked his father to arrange a marriage with Dinah. But in Jacob's and his sons' eyes, Dinah had been damaged and their family had been insulted. Jacob failed to provide any fatherly leadership in this situation, and his sons proceeded to slaughter the men of Shechem.

In all of this the victim was overlooked. Dinah was neither comforted nor consulted. Instead, her family treated her with almost as much disrespect as Shechem had. Dinah's brothers profited from the massacre of Shechem. Meanwhile, Dinah slipped back into oblivion and is never mentioned again. Her story reminds us of the tragedies that occur when family members are careless with each other. Someone ends up paying a high price.

Family honor is not as important as honoring each member of our family in a Christlike manner.

Dinah's sad moment in the spotlight is recounted in Genesis 34.

The Trap of Envy

RACHEL

"Give me children or I'll die," she exclaimed to Jacob.
(Genesis 30:1, TLB)

Why did godly men like Abraham, Jacob, King David, and Solomon have multiple wives? It may have been that God allowed this practice to ensure the continuation of family lines, or to provide for women who might have otherwise remained single in a warlike culture where men were frequently killed in battle. Whatever the reason, polygamy always created tension and bitterness in families.

Rachel and Leah, the wives of Jacob, are a good case in point. Leah was less loved by Jacob but extremely fertile. Rachel was favored by Jacob but barren. Rachel became jealous of her sister and fearful of losing her husband's love. This, in turn, caused her to become obsessed with motherhood. "I must have children!" she panicked. "Do something, Jacob, or I'm going to die!"

When we struggle (with infertility, financial reversal, family troubles, or any setback), we are prone to notice others who are doing well. We become envious. In time we become bitter, falling into the trap of thinking that life itself hinges on our problems being fixed or solved.

A better response in the midst of difficulty is to look to God. He is all we really need. His presence is far more valuable than anything else. Remember the words of the psalmist: "Whom have I in heaven but you? And earth has nothing I desire besides you" (Psalm 73:25).

Jealousy keeps us from remembering what really matters.

The complete story of Rachel is found in Genesis 29:1–35:20.

Beauty Secrets

RACHEL

Rachel was lovely in form, and beautiful. (Genesis 29:17)

Rachel was, in today's parlance, a head turner, a beauty queen. She quickly caught the eye of Jacob, who found her so desirable that he agreed to work seven years for her father in order to marry her.

And yet, if we look beyond Rachel's figure and face to her underlying character, we see some very unattractive qualities. First, she is portrayed as jealous and demanding. When she learned she was unable to bear children, her complaining and accusing sent Jacob into a rage.

Second, she is pictured as desperate and conniving. Rather than trusting God to provide her with children in his timing, she tried to "help God out" by sending her servant girl to bed with Jacob. She is seen stealing religious artifacts from her father and then lying about her involvement in the theft. All in all, the Scriptures do not paint a pretty picture of this pretty woman!

The lesson of Rachel is especially relevant to people who live in a culture obsessed by youth and glamour. Keep in mind that outer loveliness quickly fades. Inner beauty is far more critical to God, and he makes that character available to anyone who is filled with the Spirit of God. The longer and closer we walk with God, the more attractive we become.

It's possible to be good looking and not very attractive at the same time.

The complete story of Rachel is found in Genesis 29:1–35:20.

A Family Man

BENJAMIN

She named him "Ben-oni" ("Son of my sorrow"); but his father called him "Benjamin" ("Son of my right hand"). (Genesis 35:18, TLB)

Jacob had twelve sons by four different women. Benjamin was born last, the second son of Rachel. His older brother was Joseph. Benjamin grew up with the problems and privileges of a youngest child. He also lived with the knowledge that his mother died giving birth to him.

Benjamin was still young when a second tragedy shattered his life. His brother Joseph disappeared and was presumed dead. His ten half brothers returned home sheepishly with Joseph's blood-soaked coat. Jacob concluded that his favorite son had been killed by wild animals. From then on, Benjamin became his father's main concern.

Meanwhile, in Egypt, Joseph was riding a roller coaster of success and failure. A widespread famine eventually brought the family back together, but not before Benjamin was once again thrust into the center of a family crisis.

Perhaps because of all these events, Benjamin was a family man. The only word or action of Benjamin's recorded in the Scriptures occurs in Genesis 45:14, "Benjamin embraced [Joseph], weeping." He was the most prolific of all of Jacob's sons, fathering at least ten male children himself.

Tragedies often help us realize what's important in life. Benjamin's losses made him deeply appreciate his loved ones. Take time each day to show that appreciation to your own loved ones.

God even knows about tomorrow; can you trust him today?

Benjamin's story is told in Genesis 35:16–49:28.

Holding Your Tongue

JOSEPH

So they hated him even more because of his dreams and his words.
(Genesis 37:8, NRSV)

Joseph couldn't help the dreams he kept having. They were visions from God about the future. But Joseph was perhaps a little too eager to share these dreams with his brothers, who were already jealous of the great affection their father, Jacob, had for the boy.

In one dream, the brothers were binding sheaves of grain when suddenly Joseph's sheaf stood up, and the others hurried to bow down to it. In the second vision, Joseph observed the sun, moon, and eleven stars bowing down to him. These were obvious glimpses into the future—divine peeks at what lay ahead for Jacob's family down in Egypt.

Common sense would seem to say, "I'd better keep such dreams to myself. The situation with my siblings is volatile enough." But Joseph, obviously youthful and immature, blabbed it all. And the results were what we might expect.

While self-assurance and confidence are admirable qualities, we need to be careful that we don't become cocky and boastful. Nobody likes a braggart. Remember the wisdom of Proverbs 27:2: "Let another praise you, and not your own mouth; someone else, and not your own lips." Resist the urge to make yourself look better than others. Those who exalt themselves, the Scriptures say, will be humbled.

Your confidence in God should be quiet and humble.

Joseph's story is found in Genesis 37–50. He is also mentioned in Hebrews 11:22.

40

No Excuses for Sin

JOSEPH

How then could I do this great wickedness, and sin against God?
(Genesis 39:9, NRSV)

Mistreated by his brothers, torn away from his family, sold into slavery, transported to a foreign country, made to be a household servant . . . no question about it, Joseph knew all about raw deals. It's true that Joseph had boasted to his brothers. But a little bragging hardly deserved this kind of treatment!

The average Joe, no doubt, would have become bitter in Joseph's situation—angry at the ones directly responsible and angry at God for sitting back and letting it all happen. With that resentment at full boil, how do you think most folks would have responded when offered the opportunity for some secret sexual pleasure? The rationalization would no doubt sound like this: "I'm miles from home. No one will ever know. I deserve some happiness. Besides, I didn't initiate this thing."

But look closely at Joseph's response. He recognized that sin is still sin—no matter what the circumstances. And so he fled from Potiphar's wife like a scalded dog! Joseph was a man of impeccable character and integrity. The opportunity for indulgence merely brought out what was inside him.

What about you? Do you rationalize and compromise when situations become unpleasant? What is revealed about you when life deals you a losing hand?

The real fruits of character will show in our private lives.

Joseph's story is found in Genesis 37–50. He is also mentioned in Hebrews 11:22.

The Sovereign Hand of God

JOSEPH

God turned into good what you meant for evil. (Genesis 50:20, TLB)

When Joseph finally revealed himself to his brothers, they were terrified . . . and rightly so. After all, years ago they had nearly killed him before deciding to sell him into slavery. Somehow, however, much to their amazement, Joseph had become the second most powerful man in Egypt. The brothers recognized that their lives were in Joseph's hand. They cowered before him, trembling, and waited for him to pronounce judgment.

Instead, they heard their long-lost brother speak words of consolation. Joseph told them not to be angry with themselves, for God had sent him to Egypt so that he could preserve his family from the famine that had engulfed the land. Joseph encouraged the brothers to make the reunion complete by bringing their father, Jacob, to Egypt.

Rather than being vengeful, Joseph was thrilled. "Isn't it amazing?" he seemed to be saying, "God orchestrated this whole episode!" By standing back and looking at the big picture, Joseph saw the sovereign hand of God. He realized that God can master terrible situations to benefit his children.

What a marvelous, comforting truth! God is in control of your life today. Trusting in that fact today can be the difference between joy and despair.

Few truths can change our lives like the knowledge that God is in control.

Joseph's story is found in Genesis 37–50. He is also mentioned in Hebrews 11:22.

Being a Judge of Character

POTIPHAR

The blessing of the Lord was on everything Potiphar had, both in the house and in the field. (Genesis 39:5)

Potiphar was the captain of Pharaoh's royal guard. One day he purchased Joseph from some Midianite slave traders and put him to work in his home. This was the best decision Potiphar ever made. Joseph was not only talented, but God was with him. He was a man of integrity. Because of Joseph, Potiphar began to prosper greatly.

However, while Potiphar was noticing Joseph's amazing work ethic, Potiphar's wife was noticing Joseph's handsome face and strong biceps! She tried to seduce her Hebrew servant, but Joseph continually resisted her advances. One day after Potiphar's wife had been scorned again, she accused Joseph of attempted rape. Potiphar had Joseph thrown into prison. Because he listened to an evil woman, Potiphar got rid of the best overseer in all of Egypt.

What lesson can we learn from the life of Potiphar? Mainly, the importance of judging character as well as ability. Had Potiphar been more observant, he would have seen that Joseph was not merely an administrative whiz, he was also a young man of integrity. We, too, need to be careful that we are not guilty of over-emphasizing talent and underemphasizing character. Both qualities are important, but character matters far more in the long run.

Anyone can be a judge of talent, but it takes insight to be a judge of character.

The story of Potiphar is found in Genesis 37:36; 39.

Satisfying Selfish Desires

POTIPHAR'S WIFE

And though she spoke to Joseph day after day, he refused to go to bed with her or even be with her. (Genesis 39:10)

Potiphar's wife knew what she wanted, and she knew his name, too! He was Joseph, the handsome young Hebrew servant her Egyptian husband had purchased from a caravan of Midianite traders. She tried to seduce Joseph day after day after day. He repeatedly spurned her tempting offers, until finally she literally grabbed him. He did what any godly person would do—he fled like a scared rabbit. But she—feeling scorned and embarrassed—cried, "Rape!"

Never mind that Joseph had done nothing wrong. Never mind that he had done everything right. All Potiphar's wife could see was that she didn't get what she wanted. Denied the thrill of chasing and capturing her prey, of feeling a few moments of illicit pleasure, Potiphar's wife became angry and hurt. Consumed with selfish feelings, she wanted Joseph to pay. Because Joseph had rejected Potiphar's wife, he would spend several years in jail.

Are you thinking only of what you want and scheming only to satisfy your own desires? Not only does such behavior dishonor God, it also leads to sin and disappointment. Instead of using others, ask God today to help you encourage and serve them. Joseph is a perfect example of one who lived out such a commitment. His life wasn't easy, but he was blessed at every turn.

***Sin is spelled** S-e-l-f-I-s-h-N-e-s-s.*

The story of Potiphar's wife is found in Genesis 39.

Fearing God More than Men

SHIPHRAH AND PUAH

But the midwives feared God and didn't obey the king.
(Exodus 1:17, TLB)

Shiphrah and Puah, two Hebrew midwives, were undoubtedly
tense and a little confused when they were summoned to appear
before the ruler of all Egypt. Yet that confusion must have given
way to shock, fear, and even anger when they found out why they
had been called. Pharaoh ordered them to kill all the boys born to
Hebrew women from that moment forward. But even though they
were placing their lives in jeopardy, the women refused to comply.
They engineered a strategy of passive resistance that undermined
Pharaoh's zero-population-growth plan. The births continued,
and Israel grew to a mighty nation.

Shiphrah and Puah never hesitated when faced with the choice
of serving God or obeying the sinful demands of a human ruler.
They were confident that God would sustain them if they stepped
out in faith. Christians today may not be ordered to participate in
murder, but we may be encouraged to join in causes or activities
that clearly violate God's commands. Like the courageous midwives, we may face risks when obeying God—ridicule, isolation,
and even physical harm. But we can act knowing that God will
honor our efforts as he did the efforts of Shiphrah and Puah.

Obedience to God brings his protection and blessings.

Shiphrah and Puah's story is found in Exodus 1:15-21.

Entrusting Children to God's Care

JOCHEBED

When she saw that he was a fine child, she hid him for three months.
(Exodus 2:2)

During Jochebed's lifetime, conditions for the Israelites were harsh
and hopeless. They were oppressed without mercy. They had even
become slaves. Jochebed already had two young children when an
edict was passed ordering male babies to be killed at birth. The
people resisted, and babies continued to survive. Jochebed's third
child turned out to be a handsome boy whom she determined to
keep alive.

For three months, all went well. But when the baby became
impossible to hide, Jochebed chose in desperation to put his life in
God's hands. She did what every parent eventually must do: She
let go of her child.

So Moses was set afloat in the Nile's gentle waves. And God
performed the first of several miracles that would unfold over the
years. Moses' rescuer turned out to be a princess, who unwittingly
placed the child back in his own mother's arms for raising. God
literally gave Jochebed's child back to her.

It is always difficult for a parent to let go of a child. But if you
are a parent, learn from Jochebed and realize that entrusting our
children to God's care is the best security we can have. Pray for
their safety and spiritual well-being, and trust in God's promises.

**When confronted with an impossible situation, is there really a
better choice than trusting God?**

Jochebed is mentioned in Exodus 2; 6; Numbers 26; and
Hebrews 11:23.

Running ahead of God
MOSES

He supposed that his kinsfolk would understand that God through him was rescuing them, but they did not understand.
(Acts 7:25, NRSV)

Even though Moses had been reared as an Egyptian in Pharaoh's household, he was unable to forget his heritage or turn a deaf ear to the plight of his enslaved countrymen. Somewhere along the line he sensed that he might be the one chosen by God to bring freedom to his people.

And so he finally acted, coming to the aid of a slave who was being mistreated, killing the man's tormentor. The next day he tried to mediate a dispute between two Hebrews. From a human perspective, Moses' actions were gutsy, risky, and praiseworthy. From a divine perspective, Moses' behavior was all wrong. God had a better way and a better time planned for bringing about the deliverance of his people. Moses still had some lessons to learn—lessons in humility and patience—before he would be ready for the great task of leading the children of Israel out of Egyptian bondage and into the Promised Land.

It is admirable to want to serve God. It is not admirable, however, to "run ahead of God." We must wait until he clearly leads. Before you begin any new venture for God, seek the counsel of older, wiser Christians. Spend a great deal of time in prayer. Make sure your motives are pure and that God has obviously directed you. Then serve with all your heart!

We must do things in God's way and in God's timing.

The story of Moses is recorded in the books of Exodus, Leviticus, Numbers, and Deuteronomy.

Living with an Eternal Perspective
MOSES

He chose to be mistreated along with the people of God rather than to enjoy the pleasures of sin for a short time. (Hebrews 11:25)

There came a time in Moses' life when he had to make a big decision: Would he enjoy the good life as an adopted Egyptian, or would he cast his lot with his poor, enslaved Jewish brethren? The contrast between the two options could not have been more stark: a life of sensual ease versus a life of hardship, uncertainty, and pain.

Moses chose what most people would consider the less attractive option. He had caught sight of the vast reality of God, so he looked beyond the temporary glitter of Egypt to the eternal truths that had been revealed to his Jewish forefathers.

In slightly different ways we each must make the same decision: Will we remember the life-changing truth that one day we must stand before God and give an accounting for the way we have spent our time on earth? Will we side with a corrupt culture that makes choices on the basis of feelings, hormones, majority rule, and statistics—or will we embrace the eternal truths of Scripture and let them be our sole rule for life and practice?

Look back over the last month of your life. Evaluate your attitudes, motives, and actions. Have you been living with heaven in view? If not, ask God to help you develop an eternal perspective.

An eternal perspective helps us live as we should during our brief stay on earth.

The story of Moses is recorded in the books of Exodus, Leviticus, Numbers, and Deuteronomy.

No Excuse Will Suffice

MOSES

Moses said to the Lord, " . . . I am slow of speech and slow of tongue." (Exodus 4:10, NRSV)

The more Moses listened to the voice emanating from the burning bush, the more fearful he became. God was in the bush, telling Moses he had been selected to lead the Israelites out of Egyptian bondage.

There must be some mistake, Moses thought. He had a long list of excuses for why he couldn't be God's man. He was eighty years old, having spent the previous forty years tending sheep in the desert. He wasn't theologically trained and therefore wouldn't be able to adequately explain which god (among the many the Egyptians acknowledged) had sent him. To top things off, Moses was not an eloquent speaker.

One by one, God shot these excuses down. Then he provided the surprised and scared Moses with the ultimate audiovisual lesson. Before his very eyes, God transformed an ordinary shepherd's staff into an extraordinary tool for deliverance. It was as if God was saying, "Moses, I can do the same thing with your life. But first you have to quit making excuses. And then you have to trust me."

God says essentially the same thing to us. He has an exciting purpose for your life. He has amazing plans he wants you to accomplish. But if you focus on your weaknesses and cling to your doubt, you'll never know anything beyond mediocrity. Let him work in you and through you, and the world will marvel at the results.

If God has selected you for a task, no excuse will suffice.

The story of Moses is recorded in the books of Exodus, Leviticus, Numbers, and Deuteronomy.

A Moment to Regret
MOSES

You will not bring this community into the land I give them.
(Numbers 20:12)

The nation of Israel has had many grim moments in its history, but for sheer misery, few eras can match the period of wandering recorded in the book of Numbers.

Instead of enjoying a new life of blessing in the Promised Land, the twelve tribes had been sentenced to stumble around in the desert because of their unwillingness to trust God. If the children of Israel weren't complaining about the lack of water, they were moaning about the food. In between they were grumbling against the leadership of Moses and attending about twenty funerals per day!

We can hardly blame Moses for getting fed up with this bunch of bellyachers. But he let anger and pride consume him. Instead of speaking to the rock from which God intended to provide water for his people, Moses struck it. And he whacked it not once but twice!

God's judgment was immediate. For failing to obey, Moses and Aaron would not be permitted to enter Canaan. Should we regard this decree as harsh and extreme? No. We should see it as a sobering reminder of the holiness of God and the ugliness of sin.

There is no question that Moses was forgiven for his impulsive act. However, that one incident changed the course of his life. As Moses found out, it is possible to do something in an instant that you will regret for the rest of your life.

Though God can blot out any sin, he does not always take away its consequences.

The story of Moses is recorded in the books of Exodus, Leviticus, Numbers, and Deuteronomy.

A Team Player

AARON

Tell Aaron everything I say to you, and he will announce it to Pharaoh. (Exodus 7:2, TLB)

Older than Moses by three years, Aaron was chosen by God to be Moses' spokesman to Pharaoh and high priest for the Israelites. Together they would lead the people to a Land of Promise, far away from Egyptian whips and chain gangs. Aaron did not have Moses' strength of will or visionary leadership, but he could speak with clarity and (usually) followed loyally. He stood at Moses' side through many confrontations with Pharaoh and his magicians.

Capable lieutenants turn good leaders into great ones. Few worthy projects are accomplished by individuals acting alone. Teamwork is the key, and a staff of trusted helpers is a leader's greatest resource. God increased the strength of each one, Moses and Aaron, by their joint appointment to lead the Exodus.

We play at the top of our game when, as part of a motivated team of people, our personalities and talents are stretched to reach important goals for God's kingdom. Your role may be spokesperson, gofer, or crew chief. Whatever the assignment, God deserves your best.

Great leaders know whom to follow.

Aaron's story is told from Exodus 1—Deuteronomy 10. He is also mentioned in Hebrews 5.

A Crowd Pleaser

AARON

They gave me the gold. (Exodus 32:24)

Aaron was senior pastor in a congregation of nearly a half million people, but he still made mistakes, and one of them was colossal. One day the people wanted an idol—something physical and visible—around which to rally, and Aaron gave in. He supervised construction of the golden calf. He did not even raise a protest or urge an alternative.

Had Aaron lost his marbles? Confronted by Moses, he certainly tried to play the part of an innocent bystander caught in the middle of a movement bigger than he could stop. It was as if the people had thrown him their gold, and *presto!* here's this calf-thing.

"Due to circumstances beyond my control" may be a reasonable excuse for losing an umbrella in a hurricane, but there's no good reason to entertain pagan worship. Aaron, spiritual leader of Israel, should have been a stronger advocate for God's truth. The lesson he learned carried a high price.

Here is an example of what can happen when we let the popular wind blow us away—far away—from God's ideal for us. Aaron should have held on. He could have. God would have seen to the rebels. When "isms" or ideologies make their appeal, keep your loyalty rooted in the one true God.

The most popular movement is weaker than God's truth.

Aaron's story is told from Exodus 1—Deuteronomy 10. He is also mentioned in Hebrews 5.

Wanting Back in the Spotlight

MIRIAM

Miriam and Aaron spoke against Moses because of the Cushite woman whom he had married. (Numbers 12:1, NRSV)

It is sometimes difficult to watch others succeed. It can be especially hard to celebrate the success of a sibling. Such was the case of Miriam, the older sister of Moses.

Miriam had stood by as Moses was raised in the luxury of Pharaoh's palace. She had watched as God used her kid brother to lead the Israelites out of Egyptian bondage. She had remained at the foot of Mount Sinai with the people of Israel, while Moses got to go up on the mountain and enjoy a face-to-face discussion with God. Moses always enjoyed the spotlight. Her role was subordinate and less visible.

Rather than accepting her place in God's plan and serving with gladness, Miriam allowed herself to be overcome by feelings of resentment. She and Aaron attacked Moses' choice of a wife. Then they got around to their real complaint: "We're God's servants, too. Don't forget all the contributions we've made!" It was a clear case of rebellion against the leadership of Moses, and God quickly ended it by inflicting Miriam with leprosy.

We need to serve in the place where God has put us, with the abilities he has given us. Instead of worrying about others, we need to "worry" about our own faithfulness. When we regularly thank God for the gifts he has given us, we find that we don't have the time to be envious of others—not even our siblings!

Gratitude can help prevent ungodly actions.

The story of Miriam is found in Exodus 2; 15 and Numbers 12; 20.

Watching the Evidence

JETHRO

Then Jethro, Moses' father-in-law, brought a burnt offering and other sacrifices to God. (Exodus 18:12)

Seeing is believing, the old saying goes, and sometimes it is the only avenue to belief. Jethro's quiet observation of the faith of his son-in-law Moses was crucial to his own salvation.

Jethro did not grow up as a Hebrew. He belonged to a community that worshiped many gods. But God revealed himself to Jethro over the course of forty years. Jethro was able to watch God at work, molding Moses into a leader. So when Jethro saw and heard from Moses what God had done for the Israelites, he needed no further evidence for the supremacy of Moses' God over all other gods.

Jethro's conversion is a critical reminder that unbelievers may watch for evidence of God's power in our lives much more carefully than they listen to our words. The quality and genuineness of our relationship with unbelievers critically influences the effectiveness of our witness. Over forty years passed before Jethro was ready to commit to God. Are you willing to be patient as you daily live out your witness in front of those you love?

Our lives are the most widely circulated and studied evidence for belief in God.

Jethro's story is told in Exodus 2:15–3:2; 18:1-27.

Prescription for Spiritual Health

JETHRO

Moses listened to his father-in-law and did everything he said.
(Exodus 18:24)

Jethro had a good eye for seeing problems. During a visit to Moses' encampment, Jethro realized that the magnitude of his son-in-law's responsibilities was grinding him down. The people were constantly taking their disputes to Moses, who would graciously listen from sunrise to sundown and hand down the verdicts. Jethro observed that this task detained Moses from more important work and suggested that Moses delegate his arbitration to others. Jethro proposed guidelines for selecting the replacements and a list of job responsibilities for the new appointees. This formula, he believed, would relieve Moses' stress while keeping the people happy.

Sometimes life's pressures blind us to the more important duties we should be carrying out. At such times, we need to heed the advice of godly friends who can restore our perspective. Likewise, we need to be alert to our Christian brothers and sisters who may be so overwhelmed with church or career responsibilities that they may be neglecting time with God. Every believer can use a Jethro to lessen the likelihood of spiritual burnout.

Mentors can give us sound advice for spiritual health.

Read about the details of Jethro's visit to Moses in Exodus 18:1-27. Other details about his life are recorded in Exodus 2:15–3:2.

Searching Out Unconfessed Sin

ZIPPORAH

"Surely you are a bridegroom of blood to me," [Zipporah] said.
(Exodus 4:25)

In the days after he had killed the Egyptian, Moses lived in the desert, tending flocks. Here he married Zipporah and fathered two sons. Some time later, God told Moses to return to Egypt to lead the Hebrews out of slavery.

On the journey there, Moses was reminded of some unfinished business. He had forgotten or ignored God's command to circumcise his second son. Now God was angry with him, and his life was in danger. Zipporah quickly performed the operation on her son. After she finished, Moses recovered rapidly.

When we suffer physically or emotionally, we should examine our lives to see if we are harboring any deliberate sin. God could be using the ailment to focus our attention on our unconfessed thoughts and deeds. If our suffering results from disobeying God's commands, James 5:14-16 promises that we can find the same quick relief that Moses found by decisive confession and obedience in faith.

If your well-being has been affected by sin, take to heart Zipporah's cure.

Zipporah's story is told in Exodus 2:21-22; 4:18-26.

Attention to Small Details

ITHAMAR

These are the records of the tabernacle, . . . the work of the Levites being under the direction of Ithamar son of the priest Aaron.
(Exodus 38:21, NRSV)

God chose Aaron's sons to be responsible for the care of the tabernacle—the huge worship tent that Israel used during its years in the wilderness. God gave careful instructions for the orderly dismantling, moving, and setting up of the tabernacle each time Israel moved. Ithamar, the youngest of Aaron's four sons, got the detail work. He had to make sure everything was in its proper place.

Ithamar's older brothers Nadab and Abihu apparently decided that details could be overlooked. They treated God's directions in a disrespectful way and were killed for their insolence. But Ithamar took pains in doing "all the things that the Lord commanded." Considering the many detailed lists found in the Law, Ithamar performed a remarkable feat. He knew what God wanted and how he wanted it done. He served God with a proper attitude.

Ithamar reminds us how carefully we ought to obey God. God wants us to be thoroughly holy people, not a rough approximation of the way his followers should be. This week, assess your life and see where you have failed to heed God's instructions. Then resolve to let the Holy Spirit bring those areas into alignment with God's will.

The greatest acts of obedience sometimes involve attention to the smallest details.

The life and ministry of Ithamar are recorded in the following passages: Exodus 6:23; 28:1; 38:21.

God's Craftsman

BEZALEL

I have chosen Bezalel son of Uri, . . . and I have filled him with the Spirit of God. (Exodus 31:2-3)

What happens when God's Spirit fills a person? That man or woman receives special preparation to do God's work. But what God actually asks someone to do with his or her gifts varies greatly from person to person.

In Bezalel's case, God filled an artist with his Spirit in order to produce works of uncommon beauty and usefulness. Bezalel was given "skill, ability and knowledge in all kinds of crafts—to make artistic designs for work in gold, silver and bronze, to cut and set stones, to work in wood, and to engage in all kinds of craftsmanship" (Exodus 31:3-5). Elsewhere (Exodus 35:34) we are told that Bezalel and Oholiab were also effective instructors in artwork. Every object used in worshiping God, from the large movable tabernacle to the smallest utensil, was created by a person equipped by God for fine work.

When God's Spirit fills us, plain work takes on holy character. The medium may not be "spiritual" in the strictest sense (preaching, ministering, healing, praying) but may actually be necessary, practical work (like the acacia wood frames for the curtains in the tabernacle), done in such a way that the Mover behind the craftsman fingerprints the product. See your tasks today as God's uniquely prepared jobs for you to perform to his glory.

God, the Creator of beauty, receives honor through faithful craftsmanship.

Bezalel's story is told in Exodus 31:1-11; 35:30–36:3.

Doing What We Know

NADAB AND ABIHU

They offered unauthorized fire before the Lord, contrary to his command. (Leviticus 10:1)

Nadab and Abihu had quite a spiritual pedigree. They were sons of the high priest Aaron—and in line to take his place. They were nephews of Moses, the great leader who spoke face-to-face with God. They were part of God's covenant people Israel, recipients of a miraculous redemption from Egypt. They had seen God's power and holiness demonstrated in the plagues on Egypt and in the giving of the Law on Mount Sinai. They had been consecrated for ministry in a solemn ceremony in front of the tabernacle and all the people. They had a firsthand knowledge of the Jewish sacrificial system and the ugliness of sin that necessitated it.

And yet, despite such exposure to the truth about God and what it takes to relate to him, Nadab and Abihu disobeyed God in a very public way. Their sin cost them their lives. It is believed that the sons of Aaron brought unconsecrated coals from elsewhere to burn on the altar of God. Whatever the particulars, their behavior was brazen enough to warrant immediate, deadly discipline from God.

The deaths of Nadab and Abihu remind us of this truth: It is not enough to know what to do; we must also do what we know! Are you ignoring certain commands of God? Is your obedience selective? If so, be assured that your actions may have serious consequences!

Familiarity with the truth does not equal faithfulness to the truth.

The story of Nadab and Abihu is found in Leviticus 8–10.

The Value of Godly Role Models

ELEAZAR

The Lord said to Moses and Aaron, ". . . Get Aaron and his son Eleazar and take them up Mount Hor. Remove Aaron's garments and put them on his son Eleazar." (Numbers 20:23-26)

Eleazar, son of Aaron, was an excellent understudy, well trained for his eventual leading role as the high priest of Israel. In order to assume such a responsible and potentially stressful undertaking, Eleazar had to be thoroughly prepared. An understudy benefits from having both the script and a human model of the role. Since childhood, Eleazar had been able to observe Moses and Aaron. Now he could learn from watching Joshua, with whom he was paired to lead the people into the Promised Land. Eleazar served as a trusted adviser to Joshua and supervised everything in the tabernacle.

An understudy must know the lead role completely and be willing to step into it at a moment's notice. What life lessons are you learning from those around you? God may have put certain people in your life in order to prepare you for future positions of leadership and responsibility. If you are single, take notice from married couples you respect. If you are planning to have children one day, observe the model of godly parents. Learning from those around us is an effective way to prepare for what God has planned for our future.

At every stage in life, there are lessons to learn from those who walk beside us.

Eleazar is mentioned in Leviticus 10:16-20; Numbers 3:1-4; 4:16; 20:25-29; 26:1-3; 27:15-23; and Joshua 14:1; 24:33.

A Trustworthy Guide

HOBAB

Do not leave us, for you know where we should camp in the wilderness, and you will serve as eyes for us. (Numbers 10:31, NRSV)

Moses married into a family that gave him several priceless relationships: his wife, Zipporah; his wise father-in-law, Jethro (also called Reuel); and a brother-in-law named Hobab, who knew the Sinai desert like the back of his hand. Hobab guided the people of Israel as they traveled in the wilderness.

Hobab grew up with Moses during those forty years the future leader spent away from Egypt. Shepherds who didn't learn their way around the Sinai peninsula didn't survive. A seasoned guide with thirty years' experience, Hobab was an ideal choice to lead the people as they traveled.

By complimenting Hobab's skills, Moses let him know that he was needed. People cannot know you appreciate them if you do not tell them they are important to you. Complimenting those who deserve it builds lasting relationships and helps people know they are valued. Think about those who have helped you this month. What can you do to let them know how much you need and appreciate them?

Recognize the value of every person in the body of Christ.

Hobab's quiet but necessary role is recorded in Numbers 10:29-32.

Boundless Faith

CALEB

We should go up and take possession of the land, for we can certainly do it. (Numbers 13:30)

Intelligence experts are like masters at jigsaw puzzles. They piece together information until it makes a coherent picture. Rarely, however, do the pieces fit together so neatly. More often huge gaps remain. Most intelligence reports, then, depend on the grid on which the pieces of information are laid. For Caleb that grid was faith in God; for the other spies, it was fear of the Canaanites.

Caleb was the Israelites' "can-do" person. Sure, he saw the fortified cities and militia and sheer numbers of opposing forces. But doesn't faith mean we step out and see what God can do?

That was Caleb's secret: not his strength, but God's. Few people in Bible history get the divine affirmation Caleb received in Numbers 14:24: a different spirit, a wholehearted follower. We can almost see God bursting with pride over this man.

Do you have a mission? does your church? Is it big enough to stretch your faith? Do your planners and fund-raisers and strategists agree that human will alone cannot make it happen? Take Caleb's "can-do" attitude to your church, to your home, to your job. Be prepared for "realists" who have no faith. Be prepared, too, for setbacks, delays, and moments of discouragement. Trust God for the miracles you're aiming at. Help others grow in faith along the way.

God makes big promises to those who follow him in faith.

Caleb's story is told in Numbers 13–14 and Joshua 14–15. He is also mentioned in Judges 1 and 1 Chronicles 4:15.

Ready and Hopeful

CALEB

I am still as strong today as the day Moses sent me out; I'm just as vigorous to go out to battle now as I was then. (Joshua 14:11)

Caleb had good reason to be depressed. He was at the prime of life during the spy mission, but forty-five years had passed because of others' failure of faith. At forty he had counseled the people toward Canaan; but now he was eighty-five.

Were these words mere boasting, as men of all ages are inclined to do? Maybe not. Perhaps Caleb had set a path for his life as different from the mainstream as his faith had been a generation earlier. Knowing his mission, frustrated at delay, he determined to keep himself in shape—and in full faith—for the day the Lord would say, "Go!"

Thus Caleb, courageous at forty, was ready for the most important work of his life at eighty-five, brimming with faith and high expectation. Far from diminished or beaten, Caleb's confident attitude had survived the wilderness wanderings. He was ready to lead Judah into Hebron.

Does your life march along with dreams frustrated and goals unmet? Take a cue from Caleb—each day ready, each day hopeful. Take heart and keep strong!

Your life's journey is in God's hands. Be ready for surprises and always keep faith.

Caleb's story is told in Numbers 13–14 and Joshua 14–15. He is also mentioned in Judges 1 and 1 Chronicles 4:15.

Cultivating Bitterness

KORAH

Korah son of Izhar . . . became insolent and rose up against Moses.
(Numbers 16:1-2)

Korah was a whiner, a complainer, a grumbler. To him the glass was always half empty. Rather than concentrating on all his blessings (and they were many!), he focused on what he didn't have. His discontentment turned into jealousy and then resentment. Overcome with bitterness, he challenged Moses, God's appointed leader. His rebellion resulted in his death and that of many other Israelites.

Imagine how differently things might have turned out. Suppose Korah had spent his time, energy, and emotion thanking God for delivering him and his family from Egyptian bondage. Imagine if Korah had regularly expressed appreciation to God for the privilege of being a Levite and for the opportunity to work in and around the tabernacle. Consider the difference if Korah had prayed daily for Moses and Aaron, the leaders of Israel. There's no doubt that if Korah had cultivated contentment, his witness would have brought glory to God.

How can we guard against grumbling? Practice the art of appreciation. Thank God often for the many blessings he has given you. Focus on what God has called you to do. Serve faithfully, and leave issues like prestige, prominence, and position in God's hands.

If you're trying to grab the spotlight, or if you're mad that someone else is enjoying the limelight, beware!

Grumbling is a denial of God's work in our lives.

The sad story of Korah is found in Numbers 16:1-40. He is also mentioned in Numbers 26:9-11 and Jude 11.

Prophet for Hire

BALAAM

Balaam . . . fell in love with the money he could make by doing wrong. (2 Peter 2:15, TLB)

Some craftsmen in the ancient world made tents; others forged tools; some built homes; but Balaam practiced sorcery. For a fee, you could hire Balaam to cast spells that would help your cause and hurt your opponents. That's how he made his living, and he made it quite well.

One day, in the middle of his successful career, Balaam hit upon a problem. Asked by the Moabite king Balak to curse the Israelites, Balaam discovered the true God. He had invoked gods and spirits every working day, but this day he hit a wall. God did not want him to curse the chosen people. To his credit, Balaam suppressed his greed and complied with God's instruction. (Choices were limited in this regard, since Balaam saw God's avenging angel, poised to strike him if he chose to disobey.) Balaam even confessed admiration for "the Lord" and taught the pagan Moabites about God's character (Numbers 23:18-24).

But in the end, Balaam's encounter with the true God made no dent in his greed. He went back to Moab during the Israelite attack and there met his end.

Guard yourself against greed. Give sacrificially, and let God worry about your career.

Love of money will confuse your life, blur right and wrong, and muddle your sense of purpose.

Balaam's story is told in Numbers 22:1–24:25. He is also mentioned in Numbers 31:7-8, 16; Deuteronomy 23:4-5; Joshua 24:9-10; Nehemiah 13:2; Micah 6:5; 2 Peter 2:15-16; Jude 11; and Revelation 2:14.

A Necessary Zeal

PHINEHAS

He was zealous for his God, and made atonement for the Israelites.
(Numbers 25:13, NRSV)

Phinehas grew up during the forty years of Jewish wandering in the wilderness. He was born into a priestly family. Aaron was his grandfather; Eleazar, his father. He was convinced that it was time to obey God and enter the Promised Land. He hoped the lessons from the wilderness had been learned.

How dismayed Phinehas and other godly people must have been when the Israelites left the wastelands and almost immediately plunged into the worship of pagan gods and sexual sin. God demanded that the ringleaders be put to death, along with those who indulged in blatant immorality.

As if to aggravate the crisis, one Israelite flouted God's directive by taking a Midianite woman into his tent for sex in the sight of Moses and the nation. Phinehas resolutely carried out God's punishment, killing them both with a spear. God confirmed the justice of his action by stopping a plague that had taken thousands of lives.

A zeal like that of Phinehas takes obedience to God with utmost seriousness. It recognizes that sin is death and that obedience is life. Those who understand the holiness and awesomeness of God become zealous. In what areas of your life have you developed zeal for God's causes? How could you bolster your passion for him in other ways?

Zeal for anything other than God is the greatest folly.

Phinehas appears in the following Old Testament passages:
Numbers 25:1-13; Joshua 22:13, 30-33; Judges 20:26-28; and
1 Chronicles 9:20.

God Can Change Anyone

RAHAB

By faith Rahab the prostitute did not perish with those who were disobedient, because she had received the spies in peace. (Hebrews 11:31, NRSV)

From a human perspective, it's difficult to understand why the Bible should speak favorably of Rahab. She was a prostitute. She belonged to the Canaanites, a heathen people who indulged in idolatry. She was a liar who deceived her own leaders and helped "the enemy" escape. She was a traitor who helped orchestrate the overthrow of Jericho.

Yet look at Rahab from a divine perspective. She had developed a healthy fear of the God of Israel. She was willing to become a part of God's covenant nation. The writer of Hebrews explicitly tells us that Rahab's welcoming of the Jewish spies was a visible demonstration of faith.

In her post-Jericho life, Rahab married Salmon and ultimately became the great-great-grandmother of King David! Imagine that—a Canaanite prostitute becoming part of the ancestral line of Israel's kings, including the nation's greatest king, Jesus Christ. Rahab epitomizes the kind of transformation that is possible when a person puts his or her faith in God.

The issue for us today is not what we are doing for God, but what he is willing to do for us. Our efforts at right living cannot make us right with God. Have you recognized God as the true King of your life? Have you trusted in his power alone to save you and change you? If God can transform a heathen prostitute, he can certainly change you!

Faith paves the way to a right relationship with God.

The complete story of Rahab is found in Joshua 2; 6.

The Cost of Selfishness

ACHAN

Why have you brought calamity upon us? (Joshua 7:25, TLB)

Achan stood openmouthed with the other Israelites and watched God crush the fortified city of Jericho. He had heard Joshua say not to take anything for themselves, or the entire nation would suffer. But he chose to act on his desires rather than God's directions. He thought the robe he took was too beautiful to burn. And the gold and silver he hid? Surely God wouldn't miss a few bars, right? Wrong!

Achan missed the reason for God's command. Because his perspective was self-centered, he couldn't see what was at stake. God was building a nation of people who understood that private actions lead to public consequences. Achan believed in the rule many live by today: "As long as no one else gets hurt or sees what I'm doing, I can do it." But his actions led to suffering and humiliation for the nation, and death for his own family.

We don't always know how our actions will affect other people. But if we assume that our actions won't affect others at all, we will be making a terrible mistake. How many of your plans and actions today would be changed if someone were right beside you every moment? Remember, others are *always* involved. God doesn't miss anything.

Our desires do not override God's directions.

Achan's story is told in Joshua 7:1-26; 22:20; and 1 Chronicles 2:7.

Training a Leader

JOSHUA

Then [Moses] laid his hands on him and commissioned him, as the Lord instructed. (Numbers 27:23)

Regardless of what some people claim, leaders are made, not born. Gifted individuals must have training, hands-on experience, and good role models if they are ever going to realize their leadership potential. Joshua got it all.

He had led the attack on the Amalekites. He had accompanied Moses (at least halfway up the mountain) when God issued the Law on Mount Sinai. He had been at the tent of meeting when God spoke to Moses face-to-face. He had been one of the twelve men sent to spy out the land of Canaan. All in all, his was an impressive resume.

But perhaps the most valuable aspect of Joshua's leadership preparation was the privilege he had of observing Moses in action. As his personal aide, he got to watch him deal with jealous and rebellious and stubborn people. He saw how Moses handled national crises and smaller administrative nightmares. Most important of all, Joshua got an insider's look at Moses' intimate relationship with God.

In fact, the Bible frequently features this kind of leadership mentoring program. Elisha had Elijah. The disciples had Jesus. Timothy had Paul. Do you have an older, wiser role model to whom you can look? Ask God to provide you with a Moses. Then ask God to help you become a Joshua.

Spiritual leadership is God-given skill.

In addition to the book that bears his name, details about the life of Joshua can be found throughout Exodus, Numbers, and Deuteronomy.

Being Strong and Courageous

JOSHUA

Do not be frightened or dismayed, for the Lord your God is with you wherever you go. (Joshua 1:9, NRSV)

It's easy to understand Joshua's fear and anxiety. One, he was following in the footsteps of the legendary Moses. Two, his "army" was as awe-inspiring as a ragtag band of schoolchildren. Three, the land before them was filled with fierce tribes of people who were not exactly going to lie down and play dead.

God recognized these concerns in Joshua. How else do we explain the repeated attempts by the Lord to comfort Israel's new leader? Four times in the very first chapter of the book of Joshua we hear the words "Be strong and courageous." But these weren't just empty exhortations. God gave Joshua solid reasons why he didn't need to fear. "I'm going to give you the land," God promised. "I'll never leave you," God declared. "You have my law to guide you," God reminded.

In short, Joshua faced the same decision we all face every single day of our lives. "Am I going to trust what God has said, and am I going to obey what God has said?" That was, and is, the bottom-line issue for the people of God.

Are you feeling anxious or afraid today? The solution lies in doing what Joshua did: Remember the promises of God, and respond in faith.

If God is with us and we're with him, we have nothing to fear.

In addition to the book that bears his name, details about the life of Joshua can be found throughout Exodus, Numbers, and Deuteronomy.

Forgetting to Ask God

JOSHUA

The men of Israel sampled [the Gibeonites'] provisions but did not inquire of the Lord. (Joshua 9:14)

Before the Israelites entered the Promised Land, God warned his people not to get chummy with their new neighbors. Inspired (but perhaps a little fearful), the Israelites conquered Jericho, and, with some difficulty, Ai. Then they encountered the Gibeonites.

The people of Gibeon were aware of the fate of Jericho and Ai. It was obvious to them that the Israelites (and their God) were invincible in battle. And so the Gibeonites concocted an elaborate trick. They pretended to be people from a faraway nation. They came humbly, asking for a peace treaty, offering to become slaves.

The ploy worked. Rather than checking out the Gibeonites' story carefully, Joshua and his people dispensed with the need to seek wisdom and guidance from God. Days after signing an agreement with this supposedly distant enemy, the Israelites discovered that the Gibeonites practically lived next door!

In a similar way we need discernment as we attempt to sort out the various deals and offers that come our way daily. How often we make detrimental—if not devastating—decisions, all because we forget to ask God what he thinks. Today, rather than making your own plans and then asking God to bless them, ask God to show you his will.

The more discerning we are, the less deceived we'll be.

In addition to the book that bears his name, details about the life of Joshua can be found throughout Exodus, Numbers, and Deuteronomy.

Faith and Preparation

EHUD

The Lord . . . gave them a deliverer—Ehud, a left-handed man, the son of Gera the Benjamite. (Judges 3:15)

Ehud's career as a judge in Israel was highlighted by a violent deed that freed his people from the oppressive Moabites. His story reads much like a modern adventure-movie script. The hero carefully plots an attack and fashions the weapon to accomplish his task. A bold and shocking murder of a king is carried out in an isolated upstairs room, followed by a fast getaway. In the ensuing war with Moab, Ehud leads God's people to a swift and decisive victory.

You may feel that Ehud's life is difficult to relate to. However, we must not ignore the life lesson of this leader. Ehud demonstrates intentional and resourceful obedience. He invested much energy in designing a plan to obey God *and* relied on God's help to carry through with that plan. How often do we tell God of our intentions to honor him but falter when we attempt to follow through on our promises? Ehud demonstrated unwavering determination to not only listen to God, but also to obey him, whatever the cost. To follow his example, you can begin by asking God to show you how he can use some unique quality or ability (like Ehud's left-handedness) for his purposes.

God is ready to use our unique qualities to accomplish his work.

Ehud's adventure is told in Judges 3:12-31.

A Song for God's People

DEBORAH

May all your enemies perish, O Lord! But may they who love you be like the sun when it rises in its strength. (Judges 5:31)

What song do you sing? This verse is the last stanza in the famous song of Deborah, fourth, and only female, leader of Israel during the long and difficult period following Joshua's death. She organized a military response to the aggression of Jabin, a Canaanite kingpin, whose army included a fearsome nine hundred iron chariots. Foot soldiers facing this armada would be like modern infantry advancing against tanks and artillery.

In Israel's army, the determining factor was never the order of battle, but always the faith of its leaders. In an ugly, evil era, Deborah called the nation to its mission. For forty years the people prospered under her leadership. In one decisive moment, she did not flinch at Sisera's overwhelming military advantage but pressed her countrymen to victory—by prayer, by words of encouragement, by her presence. In the end, her bully adversary lost his army, his life, and his honor.

What song do you sing? Deborah took the noonday sun as her symbol of God's strength—too bright for direct view, but its heat and light everywhere evident. She found a song that encouraged her faith and gave that song to the nation.

When God fills your heart, your song becomes a chorus everyone wants to sing.

Deborah's story is told in Judges 4–5.

Reluctant Warrior

BARAK

If you go with me, I will go; but if you don't go with me, I won't go.
(Judges 4:8)

Barak stood before a once-in-a-lifetime opportunity and stepped forward—tentatively. He was summoned by Deborah, the current judge (leader) of Israel and given a mission. Deborah informed Barak that God had chosen him to lead in the defeat of Sisera and his Canaanite forces. Although he had God's assurance about the outcome of his mission, Barak insisted on Deborah's presence throughout the operation. Chosen to be a general, he settled for being a lieutenant. Deborah made all the command decisions. Sisera himself was killed by Jael, a Kenite woman.

The New Testament lists Barak among the faithful of the past (Hebrews 11:32). But the flaws in his faith also remind us that we seldom fully allow God to work through us. What might have happened if Barak had not insisisted on altering the original plan? We will not always have the luxury of others' company when we are carrying out God's plans.

How many times today will you have to choose between doing "what everyone else is doing" and what God's Word instructs you to do? Our obedience must not depend on our companions of the moment. Trusting God will inevitably bring us to places where we have to stand alone. However, like Barak, we can rest assured that God will make sure our obedience results in a positive outcome. What will be your response if you find yourself in Barak's sandals today?

Obeying God may require acting alone.

Barak's story is found in Judges 4–5. He is also mentioned in Hebrews 11:32.

Ready to Obey

JAEL

The Lord will hand Sisera over to a woman. (Judges 4:9)

Sometimes people in the same family choose to support opposite sides of a war. Israel declared war with Canaan. Heber the Kenite, a descendant of Moses' father-in-law, was on "friendly terms" (Judges 4:17) with the Canaanites. But his wife, Jael, decided to ally herself with the cause of Israel.

During the decisive battle of the war, Sisera, the Canaanite commander, sought refuge in Heber's camp, and Jael invited him into her tent. He let down his guard and went to sleep, trusting Jael to keep watch. Instead, she drove a tent peg through his temple and killed him. When Barak, the leader of Israel's forces, came looking for Sisera, Jael presented him with the body.

Jael's rather gruesome act is an important illustration of the decisiveness needed in a believer. Not only did her obedience cause Jael to break from her husband's values, but she also willingly put herself in danger. Although we may never be brought to such a precarious position, there will be many occasions that call for the same resolute determination exhibited by Jael in order to demonstrate our allegiance to God. Make it your resolve to obey.

Are you prepared to obey immediately in any situation?

Jael's actions are recorded in Judges 4:11–5:31.

Preparing for God's Work

GIDEON

When the angel of the Lord appeared to Gideon, he said, "The Lord is with you, mighty warrior." (Judges 6:12)

Gideon had a limited vision, but he was committed to it. His challenge was to obtain food for his family even though hostile invaders were making it almost impossible. But Gideon was resourceful. He put a winepress to double duty by using it to hide the grain he was threshing from the enemy. An angel appeared one day to give him a different challenge: God wanted Gideon to lead Israel against the Midianites.

Most of us want to know God's plan for our lives. And many falsely assume that God's guidance has nothing to do with what we're currently involved in. Between deadlines at work, hectic car-pool schedules, and a marathon of phone calls, we often think God's call will have to come "when all of this is over." However, God's call to Gideon came when he was completely immersed in the task at hand. Looking back, he must have realized that many of the qualities he developed during the threshing-floor days served to prepare him for the next step in God's plan. Remember Gideon as a man who obeyed God by giving his attention to the task at hand. Then trust God to use each of today's tasks to prepare you for tomorrow.

Even menial tasks can prepare you for God's future plans.

Gideon's story is told in Judges 6–8. He is also mentioned in Hebrews 11:32.

His Strength, Not Our Weakness

GIDEON

The Lord turned to him and said, "Go in the strength you have. . . . Am I not sending you?" (Judges 6:14)

When we first encounter Gideon in the Bible, he appears as the type who tends to see a glass as half empty rather than half full. His response to God's call to lead the Israelites into battle was a barrage of excuses. First, he hinted that God could save the Israelites himself if he wished. Second, he reminded God of the lowly status of his extended family, whom he claimed to be the poorest of the poor. Third, he pointed to himself and his own potential inadequacies. Blinded by his limitations, Gideon didn't believe God could use him at all. But God could, and he did.

Like Gideon, we are sometimes our own worst critic, especially as we try to discern God's plan for our lives. Every phobia, excuse, and failure immediately comes to mind! However, reminding God of our limitations implies that he does not know everything about us or that he has failed to evaluate our character. In response to our excuses, God says, as he said to Gideon, "Go in the strength you have" (Judges 6:14). His grace and provision are more than enough to make up for what you may lack. Don't spend time making excuses. Instead, spend it doing what God wants.

Your potential in God's plan is limited only by your excuses.

Read more about Gideon and his excuses in Judges 6–8.

Waiting for Another Sign

GIDEON

Then Gideon said to God, "If you are really going to use me to save Israel as you promised, prove it to me in this way." (Judges 6:36-37, TLB)

"Prove it!" is a cherished phrase in the evolving language of a child. And to us, Gideon's request that God fulfill a series of experiments with a wool fleece may seem to resemble the same childish desire for hard evidence. Was Gideon really testing God, or was he simply seeking assurance?

In either case, it is clear that Gideon's motive was right (to obey God and defeat the enemy), but his particular method was flawed. After asking for a miracle and receiving it, he still did not believe. He delayed his obedience because he wanted another miracle to confirm his calling. Gideon's demand for extra signs was an indication of unbelief.

Today the greatest source of God's guidance is his Word. Unlike Gideon, we have God's complete revealed message to humankind. Unfortunately, we share Gideon's tendency to wait for more confirmation when we should be obedient. If you want to have more of God's guidance, don't ask for signs—study God's Word.

Don't let a fleece substitute for the wisdom of God's Word.

Gideon's story is recorded in Judges 6–8.

A Cold-Blooded Killer

ABIMELECH

On one stone [he] murdered his seventy brothers. (Judges 9:5)

Abimelech was a cold-blooded man. To secure his own future, he ended the lives of sixty-nine half brothers, Gideon's children (Abimelech was Gideon's son by a Shechemite prostitute). Killing so many is not easy. It takes planning, teamwork, and a certain heartless poise. One must be deaf to cries for mercy, one victim after another. One must regard the murders as a job, a task, a career step. The messiness of the killing field must not deter one from his purpose—to secure political control.

Abimelech could handle genocide, but he couldn't count. By God's mercy, one half brother escaped, Jotham. Didn't Abimelech count the corpses? Didn't he know one was still alive? Only three years after the holocaust at Ophrah, a speech by Jotham and a rebellious spirit among the people of Shechem toppled Abimelech, who died dishonorably, the victim of a dropped millstone. In more ways than one, Abimelech had never learned to look up.

Viciousness still claims its victims. Peace is still a fragile truce with evil. The day is coming, however, when a just God will judge brutality and vindicate the suffering of the innocent.

Injustice, evil, and bloodshed should compel us to pray for the Day of the Lord.

God will not forget the victims of injustice.

Abimelech's story is told in Judges 8:31–9:57. He is also mentioned in 2 Samuel 11:21.

The Way of Reconciliation

JEPHTHAH

Then Jephthah sent messengers to the king of Ammon, demanding to know why Israel was being attacked. (Judges 11:12, TLB)

For some people, talking is not avoiding action; it is the beginning of action. They approach a conflict with the full intention of settling issues verbally, but they do not hesitate to use other means if words fail. Jephthah was this kind of person.

Jephthah's first approach to conflict was to talk it out. He tried this strategy of negotiation with the Ammonites. He clarified the issues so that everyone knew the cause of the conflict. He used firm but conciliatory language to state Israel's position. But the king of Ammon ignored his message and prepared his troops for battle anyway.

How do you handle conflict? Do you lean toward reconciliation or quick retaliation? Even if you are inclined to talk it out first, choose your words carefully. Jephthah's message to the Ammonite king avoided personal insult but refused to give in to threats. Remember his strategy the next time you encounter conflict. Make it your first aim to peaceably talk through the problem if possible.

When managing conflict, words are a powerful asset if they support the cause of resolution, not retaliation.

Read more about Jephthah's style of conflict management in Judges 11:1–12:7.

Promises That Shouldn't Be Made

JEPHTHAH

So Jephthah led his army against the Ammonites, and the Lord gave him the victory. (Judges 11:32, TLB)

A promise is a promise. But some promises, like Jephthah's promise to sacrifice as a burnt offering whatever came out to greet him on his return, should never be made. In biblical times, a promise made to God carried as much force as a written contract between two parties. Jephthah, a brave warrior, made a weighty vow to God in return for his help in conquering the Ammonites. It is not clear why Jephthah felt compelled to make this promise; in any case, it was unnecessary.

We do not know what actually happened to his daughter—the one who came to meet him—whether she was burned as an offering or set apart as a virgin, thus denying Jephthah any hope of descendants, since she was his only child. What we do know is that his rash vow brought him unspeakable grief.

In the midst of personal turmoil, it is easy to make foolish promises to God. How many times have you found yourself beginning a prayer: "God, if you'll get me out of this one, I *promise* I'll . . ."? These promises may sound very spiritual when we make them, but they often produce only guilt and frustration when we are forced to fulfill them. Jephthah reminds us of the cost of making spiritual "deals"—they only bring disappointment. Instead of pouring out promises to God for the future, commit to obey him today.

God does not want promises for the future, but obedience for today.

Jephthah's tragic story is told in Judges 11:1–12:7.

Awestruck by God's Goodness

MANOAH

The angel of the Lord ascended in the flame of the altar while Manoah and his wife looked on; and they fell on their faces to the ground. (Judges 13:20, NRSV)

Dark and painful episodes marked the Old Testament time of the judges. The people had occupied the land of Israel, but they had not conquered it completely. Instead of trusting the God who had been so faithful to them, the Israelites traveled in a confused circle of sin, judgment, repentance, and rescue. God sent judges to clean up the mess: women like Deborah and men like Gideon. And one of the most famous judges was born to a humble man named Manoah.

Like most honest fathers, Manoah was overwhelmed by parenthood. Anxious to do what was right, Manoah asked God to send the messenger with further counsel. The angel repeated instructions he had already given Manoah's wife.

Apparently Manoah thought it might be a good idea to stay in touch with this mysterious being. He offered the angel a meal and tried to learn his name. The angel insisted instead that an offering to the Lord would be more appropriate, and then the angel ascended in the smoke of their offering fire. Manoah and his wife realized that they had received a divine messenger. Hearing from God scared Manoah even more than having a child!

Manoah's experience teaches us that God's help may come in many forms, but we should never forget its true source. Nor should we forget to be grateful!

God will bless those who seek his counsel.

Manoah and his wife are introduced in Judges 13.

Staying Too Close to Temptation

SAMSON

Finally, after [Delilah] had nagged him with her words day after day, and pestered him, he was tired to death. (Judges 16:16, NRSV)

Samson, as everyone knows, possessed unearthly strength. However, many people mistakenly identify Samson's famous long hair as the source of his great strength. Not so. The real reason for Samson's power was that God was with him and had chosen him to deliver the Israelite people from the Philistines.

So why the long hair? As an infant, Samson had been set apart as a servant of God known as a Nazirite. To symbolize their devotion to God, Nazirites vowed not to cut their hair. Cutting one's hair meant breaking the Nazirite vow and losing the sense of God's presence as disobedience always does.

Knowing that background helps us better understand the episode involving Samson and Delilah. Delilah was a temptress hired by the Philistines to find out the reason for Samson's strength. She did her job well, whining and nagging until Samson caved in. The secrets Samson revealed ultimately cost him his life.

When we stay in situations where our convictions are being challenged, we are likely to compromise. Don't allow anyone, no matter how convincing or attractive, to entice you into doing something that you know is wrong. The consequences of disobedience are devastating!

The longer we remain in tempting situations, the more likely we are to succumb.

The story of Samson is found in Judges 13–16.

One Last Chance

SAMSON

O God, please strengthen me just once more, and let me with one blow get revenge on the Philistines for my two eyes. (Judges 16:28)

Samson had blown it. Chosen by God to deliver his people Israel from the Philistines, Samson had allowed lust to consume his life. Though married, he visited prostitutes, and then he met Delilah. Chasing after this infamous temptress, Samson was like an ox going to the slaughter. Delilah trapped him and turned him over to the Philistine leaders. They humiliated Samson, gouging out his eyes and turning him into a circus sideshow freak.

In spite of his disobedience, Samson at least had the sense to look to God one last time. He prayed for the strength to do what he had been chosen to do. And God heard his prayer. In pushing down the pillars of the temple of Dagon, Samson killed several thousand prominent Philistines and their leaders.

What can we learn from this sad story? Simply that God never stops loving his children. When we cry out to him in humility, no matter what we have done, God hears and answers.

Are you feeling guilty because of sinful choices? Are you reluctant to pray because of unwise decisions you have made? No matter how far you may feel you are from God, no matter how low you have sunk, God stands ready to hear from you and answer you. If God could still work in Samson's situation, he can still work in yours!

We are never in a place where God can't hear our prayers.

The story of Samson is found in Judges 13–16.

How to Lose Friends the Fast Way

DELILAH

She prodded [Samson] day after day until he was tired to death. So he told her everything. (Judges 16:16-17)

Delilah's name is synonymous with treachery and beauty. We know the first quality because of her infamous treatment of Samson. We infer the second because this world-class strongman could not resist her. In one important way, she was the stronger of the two.

To her it seemed like such a game. This physical behemoth, so much stronger than she, would be putty in her hands. When the deed was done, she taunted him, "Samson, the Philistines are upon you!" Wasn't she surprised to discover that with his hair clipped, she was his equal in physical strength, too?

Delilah is a study in how not to treat people, how not to develop friendships, how not to nurture intimacy. Do the opposite of Delilah, and you're probably on the right track.

Are you the listener people need? Are you the steady friend few people have? Delilah treated people like sport. We need always to relate as ambassadors of God's love.

If you have trouble forming friendships, try concentrating less on your troubles and more on the potential of each day to reveal God's blessing to you. When that spirit defines you, the phone will start ringing.

Deceive people and they will abandon you. Encourage people and God will bless you with a crowd of friends.

Delilah's story is told in Judges 16.

Introducing Others to God
RUTH AND NAOMI

Your people shall be my people, and your God shall be my God. (Ruth 1:16, TLB)

Logic tells us that Ruth and Naomi should not have been close. Ruth was young; Naomi was old. Ruth was from Moab; Naomi was from Israel. Most likely there were religious and language barriers. Throw in the customary potential for in-law friction, and it's a wonder that Ruth and Naomi could even be civil, much less close.

What enabled these women to forge such a close relationship? As Naomi prepared to leave Moab and return to her homeland, Ruth voiced her strong commitment to her mother-in-law. Her final statement is compelling. "Your God [will be] my God." Apparently Naomi was instrumental in introducing Ruth to the one true God! Naomi's testimony and walk with God had been so real and so vibrant that Ruth was motivated to know him and follow him—even if that meant leaving Moab.

We can find similar success in relationships if we will let the love of Christ flow through us. When our lives are yielded to God, we exhibit the fruit of the Spirit: love, joy, peace, patience, kindness, goodness, faithfulness, gentleness, and self-control. These are the qualities that make for incredible relationships—even between people who have little in common.

When God is honored, improbable relationships become incredible ones.

The story of Ruth and Naomi is found in the book of Ruth. Matthew 1:5 also mentions Ruth.

Worthy of Trust

RUTH AND NAOMI

"I will do whatever you say," Ruth answered. (Ruth 3:5)

Imagine being in a foreign culture. Imagine being there with the mother of your deceased spouse. Suddenly your mother-in-law is trying to play matchmaker. She is describing for you a plan to get you engaged to a distant relative of hers. And she is urging you to trust her. Would you do so?

That was the dilemma facing Ruth as Naomi tried to get her and Boaz together. When we look behind and beyond all the ancient, obscure Jewish customs in this story, what we really have is a relationship marked by the highest levels of trust. Ruth followed her mother-in-law's instructions to the letter. And just as Naomi said, Boaz ended up taking Ruth as his wife.

Trust like this develops only over time and only in relationships where the parties prove to be trustworthy, kind, and unselfish.

What about you? Do friends and family members sense that you are always looking out for their best interests? Do you keep your word? Have you proven to be consistently reliable so that your spouse or children would willingly follow your advice (even when it seems a little scary or offbeat)?

Ask God to make you more and more trustworthy. Then make a concentrated effort today to demonstrate your unselfish concern for those you love.

Healthy relationships place a premium on trust.

The story of Ruth and Naomi is found in the book of Ruth. Matthew 1:5 also mentions Ruth.

Giver of Refuge

BOAZ

May you be richly rewarded by the Lord, . . . under whose wings you have come to take refuge. (Ruth 2:12)

The words spoken by Boaz to Ruth were her welcome to Israel. She was foreign, a young widow, without work, and vulnerable. Boaz owned a lot of land and was related to Ruth's deceased husband. He understood the need to provide care. He also had a strong sense of God's providence and mercy. His estate would be the tangible expression of God's protection to Ruth.

What if Christians today understood their homes as God's pavilion for needy people? "Come," we might say, "take refuge under the wings of the Almighty." That very old way of talking would have to be modernized: "Here's the fridge, there's the shower—clean up, let's eat, and praise the Lord!"—or something like that.

We catch the tone and depth of Boaz's welcome only if we truly see that all we have is part of God's wonderful kingdom. When people enter our homes, they come under God's big umbrella.

Ruth would still spend days gleaning grain in the dirt and heat of Boaz's vast farm, but provision was now *assured.* Boaz did not hesitate to share with the foreigner a portion of all God had given to him.

Generously provide for strangers and newcomers so that the goodness of God, overflowing toward you, will flow on to them.

Your home is a place of God's refuge.

Boaz's story is told in the book of Ruth. He is also mentioned in Matthew 1:5.

A Holy Reason for Hard Work
BOAZ

The man will not rest until the matter is settled today. (Ruth 3:18)

Naomi assured Ruth that when Boaz put his mind to a task, things happened. Ruth could wait with high expectation; by evening her future would be clear.

We could use Boaz's skill at getting things done. Work transforms the world. The architect shapes buildings from crude materials. The merchant matches customer needs with sensible prices and durable products. Good work brings order from chaos. It sorts priorities and establishes routes to meeting needs. It negotiates agreeable settlements. But why work hard?

Most people would say, "To enrich yourself." People work to achieve wealth and power. Is that all?

The Bible affirms that good work is motivated by love. God exerts himself because he loves us. Our work is first a loving response to God and then a loving hand to others. No, not every transaction of every day is a gushy experience in hand-holding friendship. But the Bible's point is clear: The work you do counts for greatness only when it's done because you really care for others. And only God can give you that care. Boaz had it and kept to the task until it was done.

Whatever your trade or profession, ask God to give you a new sense of love for the people you serve.

The proper motive for work is love.

Boaz's story is told in the book of Ruth. He is also mentioned in Matthew 1:5.

Reason to Obey
ELKANAH

Am I not more to you than ten sons? (1 Samuel 1:8, NRSV)

Some husbands are insensitive by nature; others are insensitive out of ignorance. Elkanah loved his wife Hannah. She was deeply troubled about being childless, but Elkanah didn't hold her barrenness against her. After all, he had another wife who was fertile. Why didn't Hannah understand that he loved her just as she was? Elkanah didn't know that the more he expressed his love to her, the more she was taunted by Peninnah (the other wife) for her inability to bear children.

When God honored Hannah's prayer by giving them a child, Samuel, Elkanah seems to have realized he was only a small part of a much larger plan. He demonstrated his love for his wife by allowing her to follow through on her vow to dedicate Samuel to the Lord. He may not have understood his wife's deed, but he knew enough to support her actions. Besides his consistent love for Hannah, Elkanah made a steady effort to respond reverently to God. Their later fruitfulness in having five other children bears witness to the way in which their relationship was strengthened by their obedience.

God requires our obedience even when we don't understand all the reasons for doing something.

The record of Elkanah's life can be found in 1 Samuel 1–2.

Protecting Ourselves from the Hurt

PENINNAH

[Hannah's] rival kept provoking her in order to irritate her.
(1 Samuel 1:6)

Elkanah's household was a cauldron of simmering emotions. Like many of his contemporaries, he had two wives. Hannah, whom he dearly loved, had no children; Peninnah, his other wife, had many. Hannah was despondent over her infertility. Peninnah used her ability to conceive to taunt Hannah. But at long last, God heard Hannah's prayers and gave her a son, Samuel, who would grow up to become a great judge and prophet.

Most people know Peninnah's feelings. Sometimes, like Peninnah, we keep people at a safe distance by lashing out at them, but the cost is isolation and loneliness.

Have you been deeply hurt by others in your family? Do you feel jealous or angry or bitter toward someone else? Are you tempted to get back at that person? Christ wants to meet you in your pain, show you his compassion, and give you the courage to reach out in love to others—even to those who have hurt you most. Will you let the Lord show you a better way to approach relationships in your family?

Tense family relationships are often those most in need of Christ's healing.

Peninnah's story is found in 1 Samuel 1.

On Loan from God

HANNAH

I asked him to give me this child, and he has given me my request; and now I am giving him to the Lord for as long as he lives.
(1 Samuel 1:27-28, TLB)

Hannah might have had many excuses for being a possessive mother. After all, she had spent many years yearning for the children she could not bear. And now she was given a gift from God—a son. But when God answered her prayer, she followed through on her promise to dedicate Samuel to God's service.

Her prayer of thanks shows us that all we have and receive is on loan from God. She discovered that the greatest joy in having a child is to give that child fully and freely back to God. She entered motherhood prepared to do what all mothers must eventually do—let go of their children.

When children are born, they are completely dependent upon their parents for all their basic necessities. This causes some parents to forget that those same children will grow toward independence within the span of a few short years. Being sensitive to the different stages of that healthy process will greatly strengthen family relationships; resisting or denying that process will cause great pain. We must gradually let go of our children in order to allow them to become mature, independent adults.

All we have and receive is on loan from God.

Hannah's story is told in 1 Samuel 1–2.

Raising Godly Children

SAMUEL

And the boy Samuel continued to grow in stature and in favor with the Lord and with men. (1 Samuel 2:26)

Samuel, the last judge and first great prophet of Israel, had a rich spiritual heritage. His mother, Hannah, was a devout woman who dedicated him to God from birth. Consequently, Samuel grew up in and around the tabernacle, watching the high priest offer sacrifices to God and helping him in his daily tasks.

Samuel became a godly leader. He anointed the first two kings of Israel. He stood up to King Saul when the monarch acted foolishly. And he is listed in God's great "Hall of Faith" (Hebrews 11).

What does the life of Samuel show us? Children (even at a very young age) are able to make significant spiritual commitments and substantial contributions to the work of God.

Are you making an effort to create a positive spiritual environment for your children to grow up in? Do you give your kids opportunities to serve alongside you when you are doing the Lord's work? Granted, we don't want to be pushy parents who cram our faith down the throats of our kids. But we also can't afford to wait until they are teenagers to try to instill spiritual values in them. Begin today. Teach your children about God's character and the importance of serving him. Perhaps one of them will become a modern-day Samuel!

Don't underestimate the spiritual depth of children!

The story of Samuel is found in 1 Samuel 1–28. He is also mentioned in Psalm 99:6; Jeremiah 15:1; Acts 3:24; 13:20; and Hebrews 11:32.

Living a Life of Integrity

SAMUEL

Here I stand. Testify against me in the presence of the Lord and his anointed. (1 Samuel 12:3)

As Samuel prepared to relinquish leadership to Saul, the new king of Israel, he gave a farewell speech. Samuel asked the assembled masses to judge his life. In so many words, he threw down this challenge: "Examine my record. If I have done any wrong, tell me now!"

The crowd unanimously affirmed that Samuel's life was one of integrity. "You have not cheated or oppressed us," they replied. "You have not taken anything from anyone's hand." In other words, Samuel's reputation was spotless. God may have intended this testimony to challenge Saul, but it also honored Samuel's life of faithfulness.

Would you have the courage to stand up in front of your classmates, neighbors, family members, colleagues, and church body and ask the same set of questions? Why or why not? Or, put another way, imagine yourself nominated to a high government position. Suddenly the media is digging through your personal history looking for dirt. Would they find anything?

If you haven't lived a sterling life, claim the forgiveness and cleansing offered by Christ. Then think of one specific activity you need to stop doing and one you need to begin doing so that your behavior matches what you say you believe.

A good name is worth more than all the riches in the world.

The story of Samuel is found in 1 Samuel 1–28. He is also mentioned in Psalm 99:6; Jeremiah 15:1; Acts 3:24; 13:20; and Hebrews 11:32.

Pointing Our Children to Christ

SAMUEL

When Samuel became old, he made his sons judges over Israel.
(1 Samuel 8:1, NRSV)

At least two facts are clear from the life of the prophet Samuel: (1) He was a faithful servant of God, and (2) his sons were wicked men who used their power for selfish purposes. How can we reconcile these two facts? How is it possible for godly parents to have rebellious children?

Occasionally we hear stories about people with a public reputation for godliness who are tyrants at home. Such hypocrisy was not present in Samuel's life—the Scriptures speak of him as a man of integrity. It's possible that Samuel was guilty of spiritual workaholism, though, again, the Scriptures never state that fact. Ultimately, whether a parent is good or bad, each and every child has a will and the freedom to make choices. Samuel's boys chose to reject the ways of their father.

Our children must grow up and decide for themselves whether they will believe and obey what we have taught them about God. We can pray diligently and model our faith. We can instruct and encourage. We can try to mold and shape and point our kids in the right way. But ultimately, they will each decide for themselves to embrace or reject Christ. No one else can make that decision for them.

If your kids are walking with the Lord, thank God with a heart full of joy. If your children are not following God's ways, don't punish yourself. Take comfort in the fact that God can change even the most stubborn heart.

There are no guarantees for raising godly children.

The story of Samuel is found in 1 Samuel 1–28. He is also mentioned in Psalm 99:6; Jeremiah 15:1; Acts 3:24; 13:20; and Hebrews 11:32.

Backing Down from Confrontation

ELI

The guilt of Eli's house will never be atoned for by sacrifice or offering. (1 Samuel 3:14)

Eli was an Old Testament person with a very modern problem. Eli ignored difficult situations rather than resolving them. His sons, both priests, brought Eli grief and ruin with their disrespectful behavior. God had pointed out his sons' errors, but Eli's attempts to reprove them were halfhearted at best.

Because he was the high priest, Eli's reluctance to discipline his sons brought disastrous consequences. Eli's sons were making a mockery of their solemn priestly responsibilities. Eli invited God's judgment by refusing to put an end to the sin that was poisoning the worship of Israel. The consequences of his failure as priest and parent affected every succeeding generation in his family.

Like Eli, we may want to avoid becoming involved in situations where confrontation is unavoidable. It isn't always easy to "play the heavy." Is there something in your life, family, or work that you allow to continue even though you know it is wrong? When faced with a moral issue that requires decisive action, do you react hesitantly or with resolve?

Effective confrontation involves decisive action.

Eli's story is told in 1 Samuel 1–4. He is also mentioned in 1 Kings 2:26-27.

The Source of Our Power
ELI

When the messenger mentioned what had happened to the Ark, Eli fell backward from his seat. (1 Samuel 4:18, TLB)

The Israelites, under Eli's leadership, thought of the ark of the covenant as their lucky charm. They carried it into battle with them, believing that the ark itself—the wood and metal box—was their source of power. Consequently, Eli was devastated when he was told the ark had been captured by the Philistines during a battle.

Eli had become more concerned with the symbols of his religion than with the God they represented. The ark of the covenant had become a relic to be protected rather than a reminder of the Protector. His faith shifted from the Creator to the created.

It may be easier to worship things we can see, whether buildings, people, or Scripture itself, but such tangible things have no power in themselves. The Bible can be merely a respectable religious relic, or it can be the sharp and effective Word of God. Your attitude toward it is largely shaped by your relationship to the God from whom it comes. A relic or antique has to be carefully stored away; God's Word has to be used and obeyed. Which attitude accurately describes your approach to the Word of God?

God maintains an active relationship with us through his Word.

You can read about Eli's priestly reign in 1 Samuel 1–4. He is also mentioned in 1 Kings 2:26-27.

Shaping Our Children's Character

JOEL, SON OF SAMUEL

His sons did not walk in his ways. They turned aside after dishonest gain and accepted bribes and perverted justice. (1 Samuel 8:3)

As an old man, Samuel appointed his sons Joel and Abijah to be judges over Israel in his place. But they turned out to be corrupt, much like Eli's sons (1 Samuel 2:12). We don't know why Samuel's sons went wrong. Perhaps Samuel's mistake came when he appointed new judges instead of waiting for God to choose a successor to his office.

Was Samuel a bad parent? We may never know. We aren't even sure if he was unaware or simply ashamed of his sons' behavior. When the people demanded a king because of Samuel's age and the unreliable character of his sons, the prophet objected only to their wanting a king. Apparently he couldn't argue with their other observations. Joel is not mentioned in 1 Samuel again.

Joel was certainly not the first child unable to handle the position and prestige that his parents possessed. We must be careful not to blame ourselves for the sins of our children. Yet we also must not excuse ourselves from the responsibility for shaping our children's character.

If your grown children are not following God, don't blame yourself for something that is no longer your responsibility. But if your children are still in your care, know that what you do and teach can profoundly affect your children for a lifetime.

Bring your children up in the training and instruction of the Lord.

Joel and his brother are mentioned in 1 Samuel 8:1-9.

Passing On Family Values

KISH

There was a man of Benjamin whose name was Kish.
(1 Samuel 9:1, NRSV)

In ancient Israel a person could be identified in three ways: by family lineage, by tribal ancestry, and by social status. The Bible introduces Kish in all three ways, but he is chiefly remembered as the father of Saul, the first king of Israel.

Kish lived in a time of change. The people of Israel had failed to conquer Canaan. They were led by judges who responded to crises but who could not restore spiritual health to Israel. The nation clamored for a king.

One day Kish sent Saul to find several donkeys that had wandered off. Saul never found the donkeys, but he did meet Samuel the judge during his search. Though the events appeared to be coincidental, God had arranged a divine appointment between Samuel and Saul. Kish's son returned home as the newly appointed king of Israel.

When Kish sent Saul after the donkeys, he was preparing his son for the responsibilities he would inherit one day. He trained Saul to be his heir without knowing his son would be king. Like Kish, we seldom know what paths our children will follow. We can't even be sure they will absorb the best we can offer them. But a stable family provides the best way to transmit important values. How do you help your children develop skills they will need every day? Ask God to help you develop the wisdom and discernment you need to be the best parent you can be.

Your child's best inheritance is a godly upbringing.

Kish is mentioned briefly in Scripture: 1 Samuel 9:1-3; 14:51; and Acts 13:21.

99

Looks Can Be Deceiving

SAUL

Saul [was] an impressive young man without equal among the Israelites—a head taller than any of the others. (1 Samuel 9:2)

If you were looking for a king in 1050 B.C. (and the Israelites were), Saul definitely would have caught your eye. He was physically imposing, and he was from a prominent, wealthy family. Some scholars even speculate that Saul was exceptionally handsome.

Saul's appearance, however, could not make up for some severe personal liabilities. As king, Saul repeatedly disobeyed God. He made unwise, impulsive decisions. Saul also lacked self-confidence, which led to extreme bouts of jealousy. He became a murderous, unstable, paranoid ruler. Who could have foreseen that such a nice-looking guy would have become such a terrible king?

If ever there was a culture that was hung up on appearance and on externals, it is ours. We spend billions of dollars every year on clothes and cosmetics and health equipment designed to make us look better on the outside. But how much time and money are we willing to invest to improve our inside?

Make the commitment today to spend time developing character. Memorize the Beatitudes. Read a good book on some aspect of the Christian life in which you need help. Spend half a day in prayer. Ask God for the strength to eliminate bad habits and begin good ones.

Inner character is far more important than outer credentials.

The story of Saul is found in 1 Samuel 9–31. He is also mentioned in Acts 13:21.

Submitting to God

SAUL

Surely, to obey is better than sacrifice, and to heed than the fat of rams. (1 Samuel 15:22, NRSV)

It wasn't that King Saul couldn't get things right; it was that he wouldn't do the right things. His entire career was marked by rebellious attitudes and disobedient actions.

Early in his reign, Saul was faced with a crisis. The Philistines were gearing for an attack on Israel. The Jewish troops were losing heart and beginning to go AWOL. The prophet Samuel had told Saul that he was coming to offer the necessary sacrifices so that Israel could enjoy the blessing and presence of God as they went into battle. But Saul waited, and Samuel didn't come. Impatient and under increasing pressure, Saul brazenly assumed the role of the priest and offered the sacrifices himself. It was a serious offense that cost his descendants the throne.

Later, in another infamous act of disobedience, God gave Saul clear instructions to defeat the evil nation of Amalek and destroy it completely. Saul carried out only part of the Lord's command. He defeated Amalek, but he kept some of the plunder. Samuel rebuked Saul again. Saul's response was to offer rationalizations and excuses.

God doesn't want our justifications and explanations. God doesn't want us doing "good" and "godly" things in the wrong way, at the wrong time, or for the wrong reasons. God wants our complete submission. Are you obeying God fully today?

Obedience is essential to a thriving Christian life.

The story of Saul is found in 1 Samuel 9–31. He is also mentioned in Acts 13:21.

An Unrepentant Heart

SAUL

Saul was afraid of him and jealous because the Lord had left him and was now with David. (1 Samuel 18:12, TLB)

The life of Saul is a sad illustration of the consequences of sin and an unwillingness to turn to God for help. When we first meet Saul, he is a young, handsome, physically impressive man. He initially enjoys the filling of the Holy Spirit and seems to have a bright future as king.

But then he begins making selfish decisions. He inappropriately offers a sacrifice. He makes a rash vow that almost causes him to murder his son Jonathan. He keeps forbidden plunder from the defeat of Amalek. He is filled with jealousy and fear at the success and popularity of David. Paranoid, Saul orders the murder of eighty-five priests whom he suspects are loyal to David. His last spiritual consultation is with a medium. In the end, Saul commits suicide. Not a very impressive resume, is it?

Someone has said that every life is worth examining, even the bad ones, for at least they serve as examples of how *not* to live. Certainly that is the case with Saul. He expressed regret and sorrow for his deeds, but he never really repented of his sin. He allowed himself to be overcome by sinful attitudes that drove him away from God, to the very brink of insanity, and finally over the edge.

Don't let sin get a foothold in your life! If you are constantly angry, jealous, or fearful, talk to a mature Christian leader. Get help before you drift into real danger.

The path to ruin often begins with unconfessed sin.

The story of Saul is found in 1 Samuel 9–31. He is also mentioned in Acts 13:21.

The Covenant of Friendship

JONATHAN

And Jonathan made a covenant with David because he loved him as himself. (1 Samuel 18:3)

The deep friendship between Jonathan and David is surprising for a number of reasons. First, God selected David instead of Jonathan (son of Saul and prince of Israel) to become the second king of Israel. Second, Jonathan's father, Saul, was intensely jealous of David and tried repeatedly to kill him. Third, David was a multi-talented individual who was much more popular with the masses than either Saul or Jonathan.

Jonathan and David should have been at least wary of each other, if not outright enemies. Yet they were able to overcome these potential obstacles and forge a model friendship. Perhaps the outstanding quality of their relationship was loyalty. That loyalty was grounded in a profound devotion to God. This higher commitment is what enabled their friendship not just to survive but to thrive in times of confusion and conflict.

Are you a fair-weather friend? Do you walk away from relationships when difficulties arise? Do you defend a friend under attack? Can you rejoice when friends succeed, or are you secretly jealous and bitter? If your human relationships are weak, examine the depth of your loyalty to God. You may be surprised at what you find.

Terrific friendships are sustained by loyalty.

The life of Jonathan appears in 1 Samuel 13–31. He is also mentioned in 2 Samuel 1; 9.

Defying the Odds
JONATHAN

Nothing can hinder the Lord from saving, whether by many or by few. (1 Samuel 14:6)

When Saul was chosen king, God had guaranteed Israel rescue from the predatory Philistines. No doubt Jonathan was aware of this promise. And so, when Jonathan and his armor bearer encountered a Philistine outpost at Micmash, they decided to launch a two-man invasion.

After this dynamic duo had killed about twenty of the enemy soldiers, God shook the earth, causing the Philistines to panic even further. The ones who weren't killed by Jonathan or his sidekick or their own confused countrymen were killed by the other Israelites who joined the battle. The victory was decisive because Jonathan decided to believe God and step out in faith.

Logic tells us that Jonathan was foolish to attempt such a feat in the face of overwhelming odds. At least he should have notified his father of his plans! But faith by its very nature includes risk taking. And occasionally faith requires us to do illogical things on a grand scale.

In what area of your life today do you need to take a step of faith and believe God for the impossible? Do you have a relationship that needs mending? a friend who needs to know Christ? a habit that needs to be broken? Realize this—the God we serve is the same God who proved faithful to Jonathan.

Success comes not from great faith, but faith in a great God.

The life of Jonathan is depicted in 1 Samuel 13–31. He is also mentioned in 2 Samuel 1; 9.

Consumed by Jealousy

MICHAL

When she saw King David leaping and dancing before the Lord, she despised him in her heart. (2 Samuel 6:16)

Michal had seen firsthand how jealousy had turned her father, King Saul, into a bitter, suspicious, paranoid man. His inordinate fear of potential rivals ruined most of his relationships, robbed him of joy in life, and eventually rendered him insane.

Michal unwisely followed in her father's footsteps. Her immature love for David was possessive and selfish. She craved his affection and became envious of the devotion and passion he reserved for God. Eventually she voiced her feelings, chiding David for his extravagant display of emotion in worshiping before the returning ark of God. David explained to his jealous wife that he didn't care how silly his celebrating looked—his highest allegiance was to God. To one right with God, such a statement would be cause for joy. But to a soul consumed by jealousy and bitterness, David's words cut like a knife.

How do you rank on the jealousy scale? Do you demand that your spouse or best friends or children put you first? Do you feel glad or sad when those you love most love God most? As believers we need to be careful that we don't look to other people to fill the deep needs of our souls. That approach to relationships can only lead to jealousy and disappointment. Let God meet the deep emotional needs of your heart. Embrace his will for your life. Then you will be able to rejoice when those closest to you put him first.

Jealousy can lead to devastating bitterness.

The story of Michal is found in 1 Samuel 14—2 Samuel 6. She is also mentioned in 1 Chronicles 15:29.

The Need for Decisiveness

ABNER

Abner said to him, "Go back home!" So he went back. (2 Samuel 3:16)

Abner was a practical man. First and only commander of the army of his cousin Saul, Abner could make decisions, issue orders, and force compliance. Abner was a "can-do" general.

Contrast Abner with poor Paltiel, who had become second husband to Michal, Saul's daughter. When David finally had the power to demand that Michal be returned to him, Paltiel was brokenhearted. Abner, escorting Michal to David as part of a plea bargain, had to deal with this emotionally distraught man. His words carried no sympathy. He simply gave Paltiel an order. And that order saved Paltiel's life.

Making decisions that affect other people is stressful. We hem and haw over options; we calculate risks; we stew over how they'll take it. Some people just can't decide, trapped by all the possible outcomes.

But there are times when we have to be like Abner—decisive. We may wish his hard exterior were softer and gentler. But Abner could assess a situation and move clearly to a decision that achieved important goals. The next time you're faced with a decision that affects others, pray with intensity; then act in faith with bravery and resolve.

Making decisions takes faith in God's care for our circumstances.

Abner's story is told in 1 Samuel 14:50—2 Samuel 4:12. Abner is also mentioned in 1 Kings 2:5, 32; and 1 Chronicles 26:28; 27:16-22.

Learning from Mistakes

ABNER

Abner replied, "Who are you who calls to the king?" (1 Samuel 26:14)

Abner was the man who made Saul's kingship a political reality. He organized and commanded a large army and did so with a general's instincts. Against the Philistine Goliath, Abner played a strategic waiting game that paid off when David stepped forward. Years later, outwitted by the renegade David (1 Samuel 26), Abner conceded his mistake, but not before crashing David's ego with a stunning verbal comeback. Here's the setting:

Under cover of night, David stole past Abner's sentries, taking Saul's own spear and canteen, glorious souvenirs that would surely embarrass the entire Israelite high command. At dawn David climbed upon a rock on a hill opposite Saul and began to taunt, in effect saying, "Look what I've got!" Abner, who knew very well who was boasting, answered David with aplomb, covering his own astonishment and at the same time minimizing David's feat.

Abner survived the episode, while lesser leaders would have found themselves demoted or jailed. He could take a hit without falling apart. He was a cat who always landed on his feet.

The next time you're caught in an embarrassing bind, own up to the situation—face the music head-on, without falling apart, and God will see you through.

God will help you learn from your mistakes.

Abner's story is told in 1 Samuel 14:50—2 Samuel 4:12. Abner is also mentioned in 1 Kings 2:5, 32; and 1 Chronicles 26:28; 27:16-22.

Challenging Our Expectations

JESSE

I am sending you to Jesse of Bethlehem. I have chosen one of his sons to be king. (1 Samuel 16:1)

Jesse is most frequently mentioned in the Bible in connection with two of his descendants: King David and Jesus, the King of kings. Though never royalty himself, Jesse was chosen by God to father an eternal dynasty.

One day Samuel the judge showed up in Bethlehem with a flask of oil. He asked to see Jesse's sons. Jesse dutifully had his boys appear in their order of birth. But for some reason he failed to call his youngest, David. Samuel had to ask, "Is there another?" Apparently Jesse's older sons *looked* good enough to pass for kings. But God told his judge, "The Lord does not look at the things man looks at. Man looks at the outward appearance, but the Lord looks at the heart" (1 Samuel 16:7). Jesse may have overlooked his youngest son, but God saw in the lad the makings of an outstanding leader.

Jesse's story reminds us that much of what God does in and through us comes from his choosing, not our expectations. It was logical, Jesse thought, that Samuel would choose one of his mature sons to be king. But God defied conventional wisdom in choosing David. We should not always presume that God wants the same things we want. We need to constantly seek his guidance and study his Word if we are to please him.

Have you asked God about his plans for your life today?

Jesse's part in the grand story of God's plan is found in 1 Samuel 16:1-13; 17:12-58.

Putting on God's Armor

GOLIATH

Who is this uncircumcised Philistine that he should defy the armies of the living God? (1 Samuel 17:26, NRSV)

Goliath was a giant with an attitude. In modern times, this Old Testament character might have been called "The Intimidator." He immobilized an entire army of Israelites by challenging one of them to duel with him. He made them forget they had a champion mightier than any human. It took a bold shepherd boy to remind them all that they were the army of the living God.

Goliath's strengths were so obvious (size, armor, self-confidence) that others missed his vulnerability. For Goliath had a glaring weakness that never occurred to him until David's stone struck him down. When David was given Goliath's kind of weapons, he quickly concluded he couldn't even function, much less fight, with those tools. Goliath's strengths would have been David's handicaps. David instead chose the two weapons he knew he could rely on: his trust in God and his shepherd's sling.

David had armor to match Goliath's, but it was invisible. Ephesians 6:10-18 describes in detail the resources that God places at our disposal. How unfortunate that we face our world each day on its terms and too often try to match its weapons. God's weapons are not as obvious, but they never fail us! How much of your spiritual armor are you wearing today?

Put on the spiritual armor God provides for you.

Goliath's rise and fall are recorded in 1 Samuel 17.

Training for Our Mission
DAVID

You come against me with sword and spear and javelin, but I come against you in the name of the Lord Almighty. (1 Samuel 17:45)

In history's most famous fight, David makes his mission plain. This is to be a showdown between secular and spiritual power, winner take all.

Everything changes if David misunderstands his mission. "Golly, Goliath, my scaredy-cat brothers put me up to this!" or "We're filming an ad for this new sling," or "It's national stardom if I hit the first shot" all miss the mark.

To understand his mission, David needed a personal history of prayer, worship, and faith. He needed prayer for the courage to challenge the giant. He needed worship to know it was a spiritual battle. And he needed a well-practiced faith to believe he could succeed. Then, and only then, he stepped out of the trenches onto the plain.

All of us carry on David's fight, righteousness against evil. Our adversary is the lie that will increase sales, the kiss that will violate vows, the compromise that makes all claims of truth one jumbled stew. David knew perhaps better than anyone else that a decisive spiritual battle must be engaged that day, that it must be his, and that it must be now. He was ready.

Are you?

By prayer, worship, and the practice of faith, we train for the mission God puts before us.

David's story is told in 1 Samuel 16—1 Kings 2. David is also mentioned in Amos 6:5; Matthew 1:1, 6; 22:42-45; Luke 1:32; Acts 13:22; Romans 1:3; and Hebrews 11:32.

A Cherished Friendship

DAVID

Go in peace, for we have sworn friendship with each other in the name of the Lord. (1 Samuel 20:42)

David and Jonathan had a friendship that made each a stronger person. They trusted each other completely and were loyal above all other human ties.

How does such friendship develop? Surely from attractions that are deeply personal, as hard to explain as a preference for red over blue. But "chemistry" does not sustain these bonds. They come from a common faith, a singular and shared mission, and from the practice of *agape*, the New Testament word for other-minded love, which harbors no jealousies and seeks the good of the other above all.

We have few such friends. Sadly, many people have no one like this.

Among the many descriptions of God throughout the Bible, his friendship with us is presented as steady and strong, the *agape* kind. God seeks our best; God loves us deeply.

One of God's great gifts to us is the gift of friendship. We should make good friends and stay loyal and true to them. We should also know God as a friend. He stays with us when all others leave.

Develop, protect, and nurture your friendships each day, every day, and especially today.

A personal relationship with God through Jesus Christ is an intimate friendship characterized by loyalty, love, and trust.

David's story is told in 1 Samuel 16—1 Kings 2. David is also mentioned in Amos 6:5; Matthew 1:1, 6; 22:42-45; Luke 1:32; Acts 13:22; Romans 1:3; and Hebrews 11:32.

One Sin Leads to Another

DAVID

David invited [Uriah] to eat and drink in his presence and made him drunk. (2 Samuel 11:13, NRSV)

In committing adultery with Bathsheba, David put pressure on himself to make a few more decisions than just the one to have sex with someone else's wife. David did not need to entice Uriah, her husband, into coming home to sleep with Bathsheba to cover up what he had done. He did not need to deceive Uriah, his court officials, and his army commanders about what was really going on. He did not need to dispose of Uriah, one of his best soldiers. Yet David's first moral compromise put great pressure on him to make others, and that is exactly what he did. Had he turned from his sin right away, he and others would have been spared the pain of further compromising.

It is crucial to stop and confess our sin instead of trying to cover it up. David's start down the road of adultery led him (and others) to pay heavy tolls. He was wrong to think, *I've already done* this, *so I may as well do* that. He thought he had no choice, but he was wrong.

Whenever you sin, don't think, *I may as well go even further and make matters worse.* God prefers that you turn back before things really get out of hand—and he'll enable you to do so, if you're willing.

Admitting your sin early and confessing it is better than making matters worse with more sin.

David's story is told in 1 Samuel 16—1 Kings 2.

The (Temporary) Triumph of Evil

DOEG

Why do you boast of evil, you mighty man? (Psalm 52:1)

At first sight, being the inspiration for one of David's psalms would seem to be an honor, but in Doeg's case, it was a harsh judgment. Even though David was familiar with the violence and bloodshed of war, he was horrified by the news that Doeg had slaughtered innocent men, women, and children. David felt responsible because a lie he told (see 1 Samuel 21:1-3) made it possible for Doeg to betray the entire town of Nob.

Doeg fits the description of a ruthless killer. His false testimony about the priests of Nob conspiring with David against Saul made the king furious. Doeg ordered his own guards to kill eighty-five priests in spite of their claim of innocence. When the guards refused, Doeg readily stepped in to commit the atrocities himself. Then he attacked the priests' families without mercy. Only one person from Nob lived to tell David the sad news.

Doeg reminds us that people can become committed to evil. Their actions may hurt and even kill others. Even though it may seem like godly people have been unfairly treated, God has promised that evil people and their plans are only temporarily successful. God remains in control.

Our challenge to follow God's guidance remains even in the face of evil opposition.

Doeg's story is told in 1 Samuel 21–22.

A Man of Worship

ASAPH

David arranged for Asaph and his fellow Levites to minister regularly at the Tabernacle. (1 Chronicles 16:37, TLB)

Next to David, Asaph wrote more psalms than any other author. Eleven of Asaph's compositions appear in what is known as the third book of Psalms. We do not know much about his background or personality. We do know that Asaph was the father of several generations of worship leaders in the days of the tabernacle and temple. He and his fellow Levites were responsible for writing and performing music that would "invoke, thank, and praise the Lord." Asaph was also the first to direct choirs. He led his fellow priests in songs of thanksgiving.

A glance at Asaph's compositions tells us how seriously he took the task of worshiping God. His powerful psalms remind his readers of God's majesty and faithfulness, of his mercy and patience. They remind us, too, of our utter dependence on God. Asaph proclaims that God can be counted on to rescue and uphold his people.

Studying the works of Asaph and the other psalmists takes us into the heart of worship. We need the daily refreshment of these words to bring perspective to our hurried lives, to remind us that we are meant to worship and love God with our whole being. Meditate on these words as often as you can.

The Lord makes us strong! Sing praises!

Asaph is mentioned in the following passages: 1 Chronicles 15:19; 16:5, 7, 37; 25:1, 6; and 2 Chronicles 5:12; 20:14. In addition, he wrote Psalms 50; 73–83.

Failing to Meet His Potential

JOAB

Now you yourself know what Joab son of Zeruiah did. . . . He killed them, shedding their blood in peacetime as if in battle. (1 Kings 2:5)

Joab had the stuff of a great leader. He knew what he wanted. He was brilliant at planning and goal setting. He invariably implemented his plans without a hitch. He possessed boundless energy. He was confident and courageous. He was shrewd.

And yet, despite a few military successes, Joab never lived up to his potential. Why? Because even with his many talents and abilities, Joab lacked a moral compass. A true pragmatist, he concerned himself with what worked rather than with what was right. We find no evidence that Joab ever sought God's guidance or strove to live according to God's laws. Instead, the record reveals a man who generally reacted out of anger, resorted to treachery, and did whatever it took to reach his goals.

Because Joab's life was ruled by vengeance, it is not surprising to discover that he died a violent death. But the lesson from Joab's life is broader than that. Ambition that ignores God's direction always leads to pain and sorrow.

Are you seeking to do God's will today—in every area of your life? Or are you ignoring his standards in the ambitious pursuit of your own desires?

In the end, our success is measured by our obedience.

Joab's story is told in 2 Samuel 2—1 Kings 2. He is also mentioned in 1 Chronicles 2:16; 11:4-39; 19:8-15; 20:1; 21:2-6; 26:28; and in the title of Psalm 60.

All for One and One for All

DAVID'S MIGHTY MEN

All those who were in distress or in debt or discontented gathered around [David], and he became their leader. (1 Samuel 22:2)

David's brigade of fugitives, mercenaries, and renegades must have enjoyed a fearsome reputation during Saul's reign, for the king could not capture them, and neighboring Philistine rulers tolerated them. They are usually described as intensely loyal to David. Actually, like most people, their loyalty depended on David's success. After the sacking of their city, Ziklag, they talked openly of mutiny (1 Samuel 30:6), but David's leadership prevailed.

They certainly performed with valor and were known for their ferocity and fearlessness. The elite units, known as the Thirty and the Three, were probably generals in charge of local militia. The final name on the list in 2 Samuel 23 is of one who refused to betray his leader even while his leader betrayed him. These men were not mere military robots who did David's bidding.

We could learn from the loyalty and camaraderie these men enjoyed, given our American penchant for individualism and our tendency to disappear from a church if things don't go our way. The mighty men stuck together, followed good leadership, and pulled their weight. They had no sluggards.

We would do well to imitate this example. With God's help, consider how you might be like them today.

Might is not in force of arms, but in fellowship with the Spirit of God and in boldness to obey the Lord.

The mighty men are mentioned in 1 Samuel 22—2 Samuel 23:39 and 1 Chronicles 11–12.

Telling the Truth When It Hurts

GAD

Thus says the Lord: "Three things I offer you; choose one of them, so that I may do it to you." (1 Chronicles 21:9-10, NRSV)

The prophet Gad faithfully gave King David wise counsel on three separate occasions.

First, the prophet tracked down David when he was hiding from Saul and instructed him to return to Judah. Second, after David disobeyed God's long-standing order against taking a census, Gad arrived to deliver the consequences. The king had to choose between a three-year famine, a three-month military defeat, or a three-day plague. Gad must have been grimly pleased that his king placed himself only at God's mercy by choosing the third alternative.

When David expressed overwhelming remorse over the suffering caused by his sin, Gad stepped in a third time with direction for the king. He immediately instructed David to buy a certain piece of land and erect an altar there so that he might ask for relief from the plague.

Our best friends save their influence for times that really matter. Gad wasn't interested in controlling David but in serving him for God's sake. A friend who will tell us the truth we don't want to hear will be of greater value than a dozen friends who fill our ears with false comfort. Do others know you as a friend who speaks the truth?

Good counsel begins with honesty.

Gad's ministry to David is recorded in 1 Samuel 22:5; 2 Samuel 24:10-25; 1 Chronicles 21; 29:26-30; and 2 Chronicles 29:25.

The Gift of Mercy

ABIATHAR

To Abiathar the priest the king said . . . "You deserve to die, but I will not put you to death now." (1 Kings 2:26)

God mercifully allowed Abiathar to avoid certain death twice during his lifetime. The first time, he escaped with nothing but the ephod on his back—a special robe identifying him as a priest. A vengeful King Saul had all the other priests and their families in the city of Nob killed for helping David, but David welcomed Abiathar into his protection.

David trusted Abiathar for many years. But instead of a lifetime of gratefulness to God and loyalty to David, Abiathar eventually conspired against David and Solomon, God's choice for the next king. But he was again shown tremendous mercy and lost only his priestly position as punishment for his disloyalty.

There are many times in our lives when we are given second chances and experience great mercy. Perhaps you have been given another chance in a damaged relationship or an important opportunity you thought you'd blown. Some people would call it good luck. We know it to be a gift from the merciful hand of God. Like Abiathar, we may be tempted to neglect our gratefulness to God and to others for their graciousness. Make it a point this week to remember the many "second chances" you have recently received, and express your thanks.

Thank God for the many ways you experience his mercy.

Abiathar's story is found in 1 Samuel 22:6–23:13 and 1 Kings 1:1–2:27.

Single-Minded Selfishness

NABAL

Why should I take my bread and water . . . and give it to men coming from who knows where? (1 Samuel 25:11)

Nabal lived during David's rise to power. In fact, Nabal benefited from David because his men offered a region of security for Nabal's herds to graze. But when David sent men to Nabal's house with a courteous request for supplies, they were rudely turned away. His own men were shocked at Nabal's harshness. They hurried to warn Nabal's wife, Abigail, who clearly possessed the level head in the family.

Meanwhile, David set out with four hundred angry men to confront Nabal. Abigail met him, armed with gifts and apologies. David accepted Abigail's excuse and spared Nabal's household. While his wife was pleading for his life, Nabal was home, hosting a party. When he was sober the next morning, Abigail explained his close call with David. Nabal's shock and fear were such that he died within days.

Single-minded selfishness often produces success. People who refuse to be distracted by the needs of others can bring all their energies to bear on their goals. But if we allow anyone or anything to become the center of our lives other than the God who made and loves us, our world will become as fragile and fearful as Nabal's. The lesson is clear: Everything we have comes from God. Dare we be selfish when God has given to us so freely?

Generosity is a hallmark of God's saints.

Nabal's folly is recorded in 1 Samuel 25:1-39.

Stepping into the Line of Fire

ABIGAIL

I accept all blame in this matter. (1 Samuel 25:24, TLB)

The beautiful wife of pugnacious Nabal had nothing to apologize for. She was putting out her husband's fire. Nabal had refused to supply provisions for David's troops, though they had protected his plantation. Stunned at Nabal's discourtesy, David was en route to avenge the insult. Abigail stood between them, sensibly handling the tension, negotiating a settlement.

Her speech to David is a brilliant example of strength, cleverness, and dignity. First and foremost, she deflected blame from Nabal to herself, which put David in a most awkward position. He could hardly take revenge on a beautiful and defenseless woman. Then she reminded David of God's sure justice; David wouldn't need to take revenge because God would do it for him. Finally, she reminded David of his coming greatness. Why clutter his good conscience with a hasty act of violence against a fool? Fire out.

Abigail did not have to answer for her husband's actions. Yet she did because she saw a greater evil coming if David followed through on his emotional venting: inappropriate vengeance and the deaths of innocent people.

It takes practice to learn the difference between meddling in business not your own (bad—Proverbs 26:17) and wounding a friend (good—Proverbs 27:6). When someone smart is about to do something dumb, consider stepping into the line of fire. Even better, when you see a fight coming, ask God to show you a smart way to end it.

Some fights just aren't worth it.

Abigail's story is told in 1 Samuel 25—2 Samuel 2.

Expecting a Rescue

ABIGAIL

David and his men wept aloud until they had no strength left to weep. (1 Samuel 30:4)

What turmoil racked David's life! He had abandoned his home-land, become a warrior for the countrymen of Goliath, intended to march against Saul and battle fellow Israelites, was rejected by Philistine generals, and now the Amalekites had ravaged Ziklag. It was so bad that David's own men were close to mutiny.

To make matters worse, Abigail was a hostage. The beautiful voice of reason and faith who had at once cooled David's blood lust (1 Samuel 25) and warmed his heart—this winsome woman whose look could tame a lion, whose grace under fire had stopped David flat in his tracks—was a captive of the Amalekites.

David prayed and sought the counsel of godly advisers. Then he led his men to the recovery of all the captives and stolen property.

At some point in the melee that wrecked the Amalekites' party, David approached his precious bride, grateful beyond words to see her alive and well, eager to celebrate God's deliverance with her. We can imagine that a bedraggled but confident Abigail whispered to him, with a twinkle in her eye, "Nice work, Dave. What took you so long?"

Solve problems; don't despair of them. Pray, gather advice, and act.

Abigail's story is told in 1 Samuel 25—2 Samuel 2.

Dabbling with the Demonic
WITCH OF ENDOR

There is a medium at Endor. (1 Samuel 28:7, NRSV)

King Saul, who had made a lifetime of foolish decisions, was about to make one of his worst. Afraid because a large Philistine army was poised to attack, he sought guidance from the Lord. He received no answer. When he ran out of patience, he consulted a medium for answers.

He found a woman in Endor willing to do the dirty work. This woman feared Saul, but she did not fear God. She knew that God had commanded the Jews to have nothing to do with mediums, divination, sorcery, spirits, or witchcraft, but she practiced these black arts anyway. After receiving assurances that she would not be harmed, she called up Samuel's spirit.

Samuel was no consolation to the troubled king. He reminded Saul that God had turned away from him because of his sin. Worse still, Samuel revealed that Saul would die the next day. Indeed, the Philistines routed Israel's army, and Saul and his sons died as the prophet had predicted.

Most Christians know that dabbling in tarot cards, palmistry, and other occult practices can seriously harm their spiritual lives. And, as Saul discovered, knowing the future is pointless if it is a future without God's guidance and blessing. What about you? Are you trifling with sin in a vain attempt to control your own destiny? Remember that dependence on God is the only hope we have for a secure future.

Choose this day whom you will serve.

The witch of Endor's story is told in 1 Samuel 28:1-25.

Willing but Unable

ISH-BOSHETH

When Ish-Bosheth son of Saul heard that Abner had died in Hebron, he lost courage, and all Israel became alarmed. (2 Samuel 4:1)

Ish-Bosheth probably never planned to be king. His older brother Jonathan was the obvious choice to replace their father, King Saul. Then, in a single day, Saul, Jonathan, and two other brothers were killed in battle. We can infer that Ish-Bosheth's absence from the battle indicated a lack of heart for fighting or leading.

Much like his father, Saul, Ish-Bosheth was a hesitant and ineffective king. Though he was a surviving son of the king, Ish-Bosheth owed his position to Abner, Saul's commander, who had put him on the throne. Yet Ish-Bosheth was also afraid of Abner's own power. His reign barely lasted two years. When Abner was killed, Ish-Bosheth must have realized the weakness of his position. The king was soon murdered by two of his own officers.

Ish-Bosheth confused an opportunity with a responsibility. Like him, we often allow ourselves to be compelled to fill a need, regardless of its incompatibility with our gifts and strengths. Abner offered the throne to him, but he could have declined. He certainly did not ask for God's counsel. Even when the door before us seems wide open, we are wise to pray before we go in.

We are sometimes strongest when we recognize our weakness.

Ish-Bosheth's short reign is discussed in 2 Samuel 2:8–4:13.

Marveling at Grace

MEPHIBOSHETH

He did obeisance and said, "What is your servant, that you should look upon a dead dog such as I?" (2 Samuel 9:8, NRSV)

Mephibosheth was the son of David's best friend, Jonathan. At the age of five, Mephibosheth had been crippled in an accident—this tragedy right on the heels of the deaths of his father and grandfather Saul.

Because of a covenant he had made with Jonathan, David located Mephibosheth and treated him with extreme generosity and kindness. He restored his family property to him and invited Mephibosheth to be a regular guest at the king's dinner table.

As we read the story of Mephibosheth, we are struck by his attitude of gratefulness. He never quite seemed to understand the reason for David's graciousness. Yet he never took the king's generosity for granted. He just enjoyed and marveled at the goodness that was constantly poured out on him.

Is this your response as you consider all that God has done for you? Stop what you are doing and take a few minutes to review the blessings that God has lavished on you. Let his grace bowl you over. Then express your gratitude through prayer, through song, and through a life that is devoted to him.

The right response to grace is extreme gratefulness.

The story of Mephibosheth is told in 2 Samuel 4; 9; 16; 19; 21.

A Reliable Master

MEPHIBOSHETH

Let him take it all, since my lord the king has arrived home safely.
(2 Samuel 19:30, NRSV)

David faced an unusual test of his generosity when he was forced by Absalom, his own son, to flee Jerusalem. Mephibosheth stayed behind. Mephibosheth's servant Ziba betrayed his master by reporting to David that Mephibosheth hoped to gain the throne himself as a result of Absalom's revolt against the king. Circumstances seemed to verify Ziba's account, but David allowed Mephibosheth to defend himself. He claimed to have been left behind by Ziba.

After Ziba's accusation, David had turned all of Mephibosheth's lands over to him. Following Mephibosheth's plausible defense, David ordered the two to divide the estate. But the crippled son of Jonathan quietly gave up his claim to any property. He considered both his life and the lands to have been David's unexpected gifts to him, and he did not take them for granted. He was simply grateful to see David back on the throne and his own relationship with the king renewed.

There may well be times in which we identify with Mephibosheth: alone, hurt, betrayed, unworthy. But God will keep his word to us. We can trust him. Mephibosheth had a dependable king; we have an absolutely reliable and faithful sovereign, the Lord Jesus Christ. How have you recognized his rule in your life?

Even if sin has left us crippled in some way, God's grace will eventually restore us.

Mephibosheth's moments in David's life are recorded in 2 Samuel 9:1-13; 16:1-4; 19:24-30.

Selfish Motives

ZIBA

Ziba my servant betrayed me. (2 Samuel 19:26)

Ziba's job was to take care of Saul's crippled grandson, Mephibosheth. But Ziba spent most of his time taking care of himself. He turned his responsibility to feed Mephibosheth into a meal ticket for himself.

When Absalom's rebellion against David was underway, Ziba put himself in the king's path and misrepresented the intentions of Mephibosheth in order to gain David's gratitude. He hoped that his revelations would lead to a privileged position once David was restored. He transformed himself from protector to predator.

What are your motives when you work for someone else? Are you dedicated to serving their best interests or your own? Don't be a phony, pretending to be a faithful employee while scheming to prosper personally. Giving in to selfish motivations always undercuts your character as an employee and a person.

Time flushed out Ziba and his true motives. It will do the same to you. Examine yourself to see whose best interest you have in mind.

There is more joy in serving than in personal gain.

Ziba's story is told in 2 Samuel 9:1-13; 16:1-4; 19:24-30.

A Chain Reaction of Sin

AMNON

And as for you, you would be as one of the scoundrels in Israel.
(2 Samuel 13:13, NRSV)

Amnon was king David's firstborn son. He set in motion one of the most shameful and destructive series of actions in the royal family. He allowed himself to become obsessed with sexual desire for his half sister Tamar. When his attempt to seduce Tamar failed, he raped her. Then, his "desire" for her became loathing, and he humiliated her. He even made it look like the incest was his sister's fault. Tamar's brother Absalom later avenged her shame by killing Amnon.

David was an ineffective father. He failed to train or discipline his children. Although he found out and was furious about Amnon's actions, he did nothing. Amnon, like most of the rest of his siblings, was a child out of control. He was frustrated when he couldn't have his way and disgusted when he got his way. Without discretion, he acted upon the impulse of his own desires, and his actions brought tragedy to the lives of others. The Bible records not even a hint of remorse for what he had done to his own sister. The end result was self-destruction.

Family relationships can be sources of strength or systems of dysfunction. Each individual act of selfishness or selflessness we do is part of a chain reaction within the system. As in Amnon's case, the choice we make is laden with potential to positively or negatively affect those we love. We may be creating in our own children one or the other of these histories. In what specific ways have you been settling the painful issues of the past in your own life? In what ways are you contributing to a better past for your children? Look for ways to begin a positive chain reaction of love and peace in your family.

Families can be havens of trust or cauldrons of jealousy and hatred.

Amnon's story is told in 2 Samuel 3:2; 13:1-39.

Victim of Lust

TAMAR

Don't force me. Such a thing should not be done in Israel!
(2 Samuel 13:12)

Tamar was a victim. As the daughter of King David by his third wife, Maacah, her life changed forever when her half brother Amnon felt attracted to her and devised a plan to seduce her. When she refused Amnon's advances, he overpowered and raped her.

Her problems multiplied after this tragic incident. Amnon's intense lust changed to hatred. Absalom, her full brother, became angry when David did not punish Amnon. He took matters into his own hands and killed Amnon, starting a feud with David that would eventually lead to Absalom's attempted rebellion and ultimately his death.

Tamar's life was torn apart by sexual abuse. What Amnon did to her was not motivated by love but rather by lust. Our society is polluted by films, videos, magazines, and other media that glorify lust. It is marketed as adult stimulation, but it is the same selfish abuse of others that motivated Amnon when he attacked his half sister.

Are you harboring lustful thoughts? Do you excuse it because you think no one knows and no one will get hurt? Polluting your thoughts and desires *will* eventually hurt the people in your life whom you say you love. If you are ensnared in a habit of lust or suffer from abuse, God can heal you and give you a new life. Seek help from a caring church.

Impure thoughts are not harmless thoughts.

Tamar's story is told in 2 Samuel 13:1-34.

The Long Shadows of the Past

TAMAR

What about me? Where could I get rid of my disgrace? (2 Samuel 13:13)

Tamar voices our heart's deep concern when we are overcome with guilt and shame. Whether it is a result of our own doing or, like Tamar, through no fault of our own, we desperately seek to somehow get rid of our disgrace. We do not find the strength within ourselves. And even those closest to us may dismiss or downplay our situation, much as Absalom and David did. Phrases like "Everything will be fine" or "Try to forget it" don't console. Only God knows the depth of human shame, and only he can heal life's pain.

Sometimes we do not have a choice about what happens to us. But the choices we make concerning the disgraceful incidents in our lives are crucial to our well-being during the rest of our lives. We don't know if Tamar turned to God in answer to her question. Her choice may have been to continue living in desolation. How will you choose to let your past influence your future?

When our past seems to have ruined our future, we can come to God for hope.

Tamar's tragedy is described in 2 Samuel 13:1-22.

Deadly Advice

JONADAB

Jonadab was a very shrewd man. (2 Samuel 13:3)

David's son Amnon had a close friend and a big problem. He had an attraction to his half sister Tamar that bordered on obsession. Amnon's friend and cousin Jonadab eventually noticed something was wrong.

Amnon trusted Jonadab and told his friend about the problem. Jonadab proposed a "solution" that ignored the obvious moral questions, one that was virtually guaranteed to make Amnon's situation worse. Perhaps it didn't occur to Jonadab that Amnon would actually rape his half sister if given a chance. But his scheme to get Amnon and Tamar together put both in danger. Jonadab's off-the-cuff suggestion began a spiral of evil that climaxed with Amnon's murder at the hands of Absalom, Tamar's brother.

Careless advice can be deadly if given without thought for the consequences. We may tell ourselves that we are not responsible for what others do, but we should never give advice flippantly. Consider what would happen if someone did just what you suggest *before* you suggest it.

Good advice always flows from God's precepts.

Jonadab's friendship with Amnon is recorded in 2 Samuel 13:1-38.

Fallen Youth

ABSALOM

If only I were appointed judge in the land! (2 Samuel 15:4)

Absalom was the consummate politician. His smile and appearance were charming; his ability at "working the crowd," without equal; his speeches, simple self-advertisements that modern spin doctors would love; and he had the right family connections. Absalom promised the people all that King David (his father) was apparently not delivering.

In retrospect, we see Absalom as a failed leader whose shallow character and outright treacheries spoiled his grand campaign promises. After Absalom died, people throughout Israel were saying, "We knew all along. . . ." But many people had been fooled.

Who will win your allegiance and respect today? We need people of integrity and vision to accept leadership roles, but too often all we get are people of ambition, greed, and hot air. The blame is ours. If we want leaders who exhibit virtue and a strong sense of servanthood, we must nurture them. We must pray for them as youngsters and work with them as protégés.

Support youth ministries in your church. Befriend neighborhood kids. Give kids responsibilities, especially in church, wherever you can. Be honest with them and expect them to be honest with you.

Building virtue, stamina, and compassion into young people takes an immense investment of resources and time. Are you involved?

Absalom's story is told in 2 Samuel 3:3; 13–19.

A Rebel Is Restored

AMASA

May God deal with me, be it ever so severely, if from now on you are not the commander of my army in place of Joab. (2 Samuel 19:13)

When we first meet Amasa, he has been chosen to replace Joab as the leader of Israel's army, then under the sway of the rebel Absalom. Amasa was no dark-horse candidate; he was a blood relative of both David and Absalom. Amasa chose poorly—his army was defeated by troops loyal to David. But instead of being executed, Amasa was named the commander in chief of the reunited army of Israel.

Some see Amasa's appointment as a shrewd political move on David's part to win over the rebellious faction of Israel's army, and perhaps this is so. But taken from Amasa's perspective, David's gesture must have seemed astounding and unbelievably kind. For here was a rebel, a trusted family member who had deserted his king in the hour of need, being welcomed back with all forgiven. Amasa and his troops responded gratefully; they were "as one man," according to Scripture.

In the same way, God astounds us daily with his marvelous grace. We are forgiven for all of our past rebellions and called "friends of God" (John 15:14). How do you respond to the grace God shows you every day? Thank him today for his tremendous mercy and kindness.

Forgiveness is God's means of healing and restoration.

Amasa's story can be found in 2 Samuel 17:25-26; 19:13-15; 20:4-13.

Making Friendships That Count

HIRAM, KING OF TYRE

He had always been on friendly terms with David. (1 Kings 5:1)

Among the gifts we leave our children are the friends we make along the way. King David of Israel and King Hiram of Tyre in Lebanon became allies and partners. When Solomon became king of Israel, he knew he could count on Hiram for help. Their relationship was formal but trusting. As Hiram had supplied David with building materials for his palace, so now he provided the cedar logs and craftsmen to assist in the building of God's temple. Apparently Hiram was a believer in the God of Israel.

Does your family know your friends, or are they strangers to each other? If this were your last day on earth, would you leave behind a source of personal support for those you love? An inheritance means more than money.

Making friends with those outside your family will show your children how to choose their friends and may well supply them with a much-needed source of help in the future.

A wise parent makes friends for his or her family.

Hiram's story is told in 2 Samuel 5:11; 1 Kings 5; 9; and 2 Chronicles 2.

Struck Down by Carelessness

UZZAH

The Lord's anger burned against Uzzah because of his irreverent act.
(2 Samuel 6:7)

Uzzah was struck dead by the Lord when he ignored God's longstanding command against touching the ark of the covenant. The ark had been housed in Uzzah's house for many years while David was seeking a permanent home for it. When the time came to move the ark, the Lord's commands for how to move it were ignored, and it started to fall to the ground. Uzzah reached out to stop the fall of the ark and was immediately struck dead for touching the sacred box.

Perhaps housing the ark for so many years had reduced Uzzah's awe and respect for it. God's clear instructions were ignored; the people who were moving this sacred object treated it with little regard for its significance.

Likewise, becoming involved in the inner workings of a church or ministry can reduce your sense of awe and wonder about its services and events. Watching the human efforts required to operate a church can diminish reliance on God's supernatural power.

Anyone involved in ministry leadership must keep the focus on God by maintaining an active prayer life and study of God's Word. Keep God's commands fresh in your mind, respect what is holy, and focus your efforts on God's supernatural power, not human efforts.

It is wise to respect God and his Word.

Uzzah's story is told in 2 Samuel 6:1-8 and 1 Chronicles 13:1-11.

Confronting Sin

NATHAN

The Lord sent Nathan to David. (2 Samuel 12:1)

It's appropriate that Nathan means "gift," for in Nathan, God had given King David a very great gift. Nathan was a prophet, an adviser, and a chronicler of Israel's history. He was the man who brought David the good news of God's blessing. He was also the man who brought David the bad news of God's discipline for committing adultery with Bathsheba and sending Uriah to his death in battle.

The twelfth chapter of 2 Samuel recounts how Nathan confronted David about his sin. Nathan told David a moving parable about a wicked rich man (with plenty of sheep) who took the only lamb of a poor man to serve to his guest. When Nathan finished his story, David was livid. "The man who did this deserves to die!" he snapped.

Nathan had the courage to look the king in the eye and say, "You are the man!" Then Nathan outlined for David the consequences of his sin. God used this bold prophet to bring David to his senses and to repentance.

Do you have someone in your life who holds you accountable, who asks you the tough questions, who loves you enough to tell you the truth—even when it hurts? If you do, thank God for the wonderful gift he has given you. If not, ask the Lord to bring such a person into your life. We all need a Nathan!

We need people in our lives who will boldly yet lovingly tell us the truth.

The story of Nathan is found in 2 Samuel 7—1 Kings 1. He is also mentioned in 1 Chronicles 17:15 and 2 Chronicles 9:29; 29:25-26.

A Trustworthy Follower

BENAIAH

A valiant warrior from Kabzeel, a doer of great deeds. (2 Samuel 23:20, NRSV)

David surrounded himself with powerful warriors, whose accounts of personal accomplishments are remarkable. Besides their physical prowess, their most notable characteristic was their loyalty. Benaiah was an exceptional officer in David's army. The king demonstrated his trust by putting Benaiah in charge of his personal bodyguard. Benaiah never betrayed that confidence.

The roots of David and Benaiah's relationship probably began during the hectic days in the wilderness when David was trying to avoid Saul's attempts to kill him. He was part of a ragtag band of those who were in trouble or discontented for one reason or another (1 Samuel 22:2). David turned them into an effective fighting force. Benaiah watched his leader remain true to God, and he determined to be true to David. As a result, the Bible records the amazing, wholehearted efforts of Benaiah in his service to David.

Loyalty must rest on the way our leaders demonstrate their faithfulness to God. When we determine an authority to be a faithful follower of Christ, we need to show our allegiance and support. How much effort have you put forth in supporting faithful Christians in positions of leadership?

We owe our loyalty to Christ and to those who truly serve him.

The actions of Benaiah are recorded in 2 Samuel 8:18; 20:23; 23:20-23; 1 Kings 1–2; and 1 Chronicles 11:22-25; 27:5-6.

Defending a Mistake

HANUN

I will deal loyally with Hanun son of Nahash, for his father dealt loyally with me. (1 Chronicles 19:2, NRSV)

David's relationship with Hanun began with the best intentions. Hanun's father, king of Ammon, had been on cordial terms with David. When Hanun succeeded to the throne, David sent a welcoming party to the new king. But Hanun was led to believe the worst about David. Instead of being received with diplomatic courtesy, David's envoys were treated as spies and humiliated. Hanun shaved their beards, cut their robes, and sent them home.

Hanun and his counselors belatedly realized that they had provoked David's anger. But instead of humbly admitting their mistake, they compounded their problems by hiring allies to defend themselves against David. David's gesture of peace had unexpectedly become a prelude to a war in which Hanun was soundly defeated. Former neighbors became enemies.

Defending what we know to be wrong is a costly and futile effort. Jumping to wrong conclusions, responding to others with prejudice, and misunderstanding other people's intentions are all familiar mistakes we make. God wants us to put aside our pride and seek reconciliation, even if we feel like we are the offended party. Is there a conflict in your life right now because of misunderstood intentions?

Don't let pride keep you from repairing broken relationships.

David's dealings with Hanun are recounted twice in the Old Testament: 2 Samuel 10:1-19 and 1 Chronicles 19:1–20:3.

It Takes Two

BATHSHEBA

She came to him. (2 Samuel 11:4)

The guilt was shared. David, who should have been with his army, was lounging in Jerusalem when sexual desire overcame his better judgment.

When the invitation came to spend a night in the palace, did Bathsheba hesitate, consider excuses, or otherwise resist? What motivated her to say yes? Was it the flattery of a king's invitation?

Two intelligent adults denied their separate responsibilities and made illicit love. Dishonoring God, they suffered for it. Their child died, but in the end Bathsheba knew something more about her Lord.

Nothing escapes God's eyes. You cannot steal away at night as if God were dozing and morality were on break.

Sin has consequences. She became pregnant and lost the child. She also lost her husband.

God can forgive and restore. A union where nothing was done right produced an heir to the throne and a forefather of the Messiah.

No matter how much you've sinned, never lose hope.

God can bring hope from despair, order from chaos.

Bathsheba's story is told in 2 Samuel 11–12 and 1 Kings 1–2. A related passage is Psalm 51.

A Promise Remembered

BATHSHEBA

Bathsheba bowed low and knelt before the king. (1 Kings 1:16)

Many years earlier, Bathsheba and King David had enjoyed a night of sex in one of the most infamous liaisons of all time. And following their sorrow and guilt, loss of their baby, and shame at David's plot against Uriah—after all that—David and Bathsheba had become proud parents of a child they named Solomon.

Now Bathsheba, whose feelings are never revealed in Scripture, walks into David's room. With him is another beautiful young woman, and in her presence Bathsheba says, "Our son, O king, the one you promised would sit on the throne."

David recalls. He's had lots of children, none of them successful, one a traitor.

"It's time, David," she said. Then Nathan appears to support her with his news. And David rouses himself for one last kingly duty, the transfer of power.

We know little about Bathsheba the person, but at least we know this: She never stopped believing, and she wasn't afraid to confront the most powerful man in her world.

Faith means action based on your best sense of God's will, before it's too late. Let confidence in God drive you to do what must be done today.

Faith overcomes fear.

Bathsheba's story is told in 2 Samuel 11–12 and 1 Kings 1–2. A related passage is Psalm 51.

A Principled Man

URIAH

As surely as you live, I will not do such a thing! (2 Samuel 11:11)

On this night Uriah was a better man drunk than King David was sober. David had impregnated Uriah's wife, Bathsheba, while Uriah was away, serving in the war. David brought him home to cover his adultery. If he could get him to sleep with his wife, no one would suspect anything unusual.

But Uriah would not sleep with his wife, even after David got him drunk. His thoughts were on the men whom he commanded on the battlefield. Uriah would not grant himself privileges his men could not also enjoy, even with the king's permission.

Uriah's strict adherence to his principles cost him his life. When King David purposely put him in harm's way, not even the mighty Uriah could single-handedly hold off the enemy forever. Rightly so, he is remembered as one of the great men of Israel (see 2 Samuel 23:39).

True leaders have personal integrity and commitment to the shared cause. Leading others means leading by example. You can't tell someone else what they should do for a business or a ministry if you are not willing to operate by the same standards.

Leaders quickly learn that there are many times when it is appropriate to postpone pleasure and comfort for the greater cause. Are you consistent in your moral principles even when no one is watching, willing to forgo pleasure to do what would please God?

Talk is cheap; example is everything.

Uriah's story is told in 2 Samuel 11:3-24.

A Wise and Discerning Heart

SOLOMON

I will give you a wise and discerning heart, so that there will never have been anyone like you, nor will there ever be. (1 Kings 3:12)

With the death of King David, the mantle of leadership passed to his son Solomon. Early in his reign as Israel's third king, Solomon had a dream in which the Lord spoke to him. Essentially, he told the new monarch, "Ask for whatever you want, and I will give it to you." Imagine such an offer. The options were staggering!

But Solomon didn't hesitate. He immediately requested wisdom. "Give your servant a discerning heart to govern your people and to distinguish between right and wrong" (1 Kings 3:9). This humble response thrilled the heart of God. He granted it and added, "Moreover, I will give you what you have not asked for—both riches and honor—so that in your lifetime you will have no equal among kings" (1 Kings 3:13).

Wisdom differs from knowledge in that wisdom is "skill in living." It is knowing not just facts, but what to do in the various situations of life. According to the Bible, someone with an IQ of 180 can be a fool, while a high school dropout can be extremely wise. The difference lies in the ability to understand and live out God's truth.

Ask God to make you a wise person. Then spend some time today reading the wise sayings of Solomon in the book of Proverbs.

A lack of knowledge is not a problem; a lack of wisdom is.

The life of Solomon is told in 2 Samuel 12:24—1 Kings 11:43.

Happiness Is Knowing God

SOLOMON

Fear God, and keep his commandments; for that is the whole duty of everyone. (Ecclesiastes 12:13, NRSV)

Everyone has ideas about where to find lasting happiness. Some people search for satisfaction in wealth. Some believe meaning and purpose are found in acquiring power or prestige. Some are convinced that the way to find fulfillment is through pleasure. Some put their faith in the acquisition of knowledge. Others believe that if they can accomplish certain goals or feats, they will achieve a sense of wholeness.

Solomon has a unique message to those who are traveling all these avenues in the quest for ultimate meaning. During his life, he searched exhaustively for something to give his life purpose. He tried it all (and had it all), and after sampling in abundance everything this world has to offer, he concluded that the way to escape a dull, meaningless existence is to enter into a relationship with God.

Whatever you are looking to for happiness and purpose in life, realize this: You will never amass more money, more fame, more accomplishments, or more wisdom than Solomon did. And if he was unable to find fulfillment in those things, what makes you think you will be different?

If you have never opened yourself to Christ, do so today. Invite him to invade your life and infuse you with peace and purpose. Remember the words of St. Augustine: "You have made us for yourself, O God, and our hearts are restless until they find their rest in you."

Ultimate fulfillment is found only in knowing God.

The life of Solomon unfolds in 2 Samuel 12:24—1 Kings 11:43.

Close Encounters of the Wrong Kind

SOLOMON

As Solomon grew old, his wives turned his heart after other gods, and his heart was not fully devoted to the Lord his God. (1 Kings 11:4)

Solomon was a mediocre king. He didn't blow it as badly as Saul, but on the other hand, he never lived up to the promise of his father, David. Solomon was a guy who began well but faded fast. He inherited a prosperous, thriving kingdom. He reigned during a time of great peace. He enjoyed wealth and wisdom. He had a chance to really leave a mark. Instead, he left behind a kingdom that divided soon after his death, never to reunite. What happened?

Solomon's marriages to foreign wives was a big part of the problem. When Solomon brought these women into his palace, they invariably brought with them their unhealthy religious beliefs and practices. Before long, Solomon was making concessions and compromising his own faith in order to please the numerous women in his life.

Solomon's sad end reminds us of the importance of not entering intimate relationships with unbelievers. We can and should befriend them (how else can we share the love of Christ with them?). However, we must not risk an emotional bond that jeopardizes our devotion to God.

Are you too close to someone who doesn't share your belief in Christ? Ask God for the strength to make whatever changes are needed in that relationship.

A close relationship with the wrong person can devastate your relationship with God.

The life of Solomon is found in 2 Samuel 12:24—1 Kings 11:43.

Good Advice and Godly Advice

AHITHOPHEL

O Lord, I pray you, turn the counsel of Ahithophel into foolishness.
(2 Samuel 15:31, NRSV)

Ahithophel was a trusted adviser of King David for many years.
The qualities of his counsel, however, do not become apparent
until the Bible records the details of Ahithophel's betrayal of
David. Ahithophel's counsel always answered the question "What's
the shortest distance between two points?" He was a straight-line
thinker whose suggestions were practical, efficient, and direct.
Once he switched loyalties from David to Absalom, his only concern was to guide his new king to success.

What mattered most to Ahithophel were his plans. He was used
to being followed without question. Even his betrayal of David
gives no evidence of personal conflict between them. Ahithophel
simply decided David was no longer fit to be king and it was time
to back Absalom. But when his counsel was rejected by Absalom in
favor of Hushai's, Ahithophel could not handle the devastating
loss of face. He calmly returned home, ordered his affairs, and
hung himself. Ahithophel's straight-line thinking took him right to
the end of his rope.

The most practical plans and effective efforts are pointless if
they serve the wrong purpose. Unfortunately, we are capable of
successful schemes while disobeying God. Target some areas concerning your family, vocation, or ministry in which you may have
settled into a compromising pattern of "what works." How can
you invest the time and prayerful energy into God's plans of what
could work? Straight-line thinking must be balanced by compassion and God's direction. Too often we want to take shortcuts;
Jesus said, "Go the second mile!" (Matthew 5:41).

Good plans are not necessarily God's plans.

Ahithophel's story is told in 2 Samuel 15–17.

Loyal in All Circumstances

HUSHAI

Ahithophel was the king's counselor, and Hushai the Archite was the king's friend. (1 Chronicles 27:33, NRSV)

Ahithophel's counsel could be trusted, but his loyalty was suspect. Hushai proved himself loyal to the point of death. When Absalom usurped the throne of David, Hushai was willing to follow his king into exile. Ahithophel followed Absalom. Hushai must have been well up in years, for David frankly told him he would slow down the escape if he insisted on going along. Instead, David sent Hushai back to the palace to do what he could to confound Absalom's plans.

Hushai was able to convince Absalom that he had switched loyalties. He was then able to challenge Ahithophel's counsel in such a way that he allowed time for David to accomplish his escape and organize his forces. He didn't try to stop Absalom, only delay him. His advice was reasonable and acceptable. Absalom didn't realize, however, that Hushai's advice helped David more than it helped him.

Hushai's service reminds us of the importance of loyalty. Ahithophel's loyalty was fickle; it was determined solely by who held power. Hushai's loyalty was to David, and changing circumstances did not weaken it. To what degree can others depend on you? How many people would trust you with their lives?

Could your friends trust you with their lives?

Hushai's loyal actions are recorded in 2 Samuel 15:32–17:22 and 1 Chronicles 27:33.

Loyal to a Fault

ABISHAI

Abishai son of Zeruiah came to David's rescue. (2 Samuel 21:17)

Fearless Abishai saved the king's life by jumping in front of a screaming Philistine ready to kill and able to do it. We have no details except that David was exhausted, escape routes were blocked, and only Abishai could stop the sword.

Fearless Abishai was a general's ideal soldier and worst nightmare. He was loyal to his king to a fault. Anything David wanted, he would do—and more. Abishai was reckless about his own safety, the Israelite equivalent of a Special Forces soldier who stopped at no obstacle and calculated no risk. Those qualities were also his weakness, for Abishai would act without thinking. His loyalty to David would have driven him to kill even more than he did, in the name of serving the king, if David had not stopped him on three separate occasions.

Great leaders need Abishai's courage, but also something more: moral judgment. His stark raving loyalty to David was too much. God urges that we learn restraint, wisdom, insight, discretion. Responsible leaders need to discern the times, to know when to back off and when to pursue, to press toward a goal and yet to show mercy along the way. Serve your king, spouse, friend, but do not worship him or her.

The best kind of loyalty to others is guided by loyalty to God.

Abishai's story is told in 2 Samuel 18:1–23:19. He is also mentioned in 1 Samuel 26:1-13; and 1 Chronicles 2:16; 11:20; 18:12; 19:11, 15.

Practicing Prejudice

SHEBA

Now a troublemaker named Sheba . . . shouted, "We have no share in David! . . . Every man to his tent, O Israel!" (2 Samuel 20:1)

Sheba led a rebellion against King David by inflaming tribal jealousy. He shouted that since David wasn't from the tribe of Benjamin, he wasn't one of them and would not give them fair treatment. The rebellion ended quickly when David's army besieged the city where Sheba was hiding and demanded his head be cut off and thrown over the city wall.

Sheba led his rebellion by appealing to prejudice. Racial and ethnic identity may make us proud, but they also can make us divisive. Sheba counted on that.

Some political leaders today still use the divide-and-conquer strategy. Like Sheba, they exalt themselves by emphasizing racial differences and charging that any leader from a different background cannot fairly represent or lead any people from another group. They talk about unity and equality, but they practice division and prejudice.

What's more important to you—the differences between you and another person or the similarities you share? Is your opinion of a leader influenced by his or her racial or ethnic background? An effective leader is much more than superficial qualities. A community and a nation can only be unified if we judge leaders (and all people) on the basis of their character and not the color of their skin.

When looking for a leader, it's what's inside that counts.

Read Sheba's story in 2 Samuel 20:1-22.

We Matter to God

ABISHAG

She took care of the king and waited on him. (1 Kings 1:4)

Chosen for her youth and beauty, Abishag found herself one day the live-in nurse of the great but old King David. Her job was to keep the king warm. Within months her patient died. We know little about their relationship except that they never had sexual intercourse.

Almost immediately after David's death, Abishag became the bargaining chip in a power struggle between his sons Solomon and Adonijah, and his widow Bathsheba. For Adonijah, Abishag was probably little more than a possible angle to renew his claim on the throne of David. Bathsheba, herself acquainted with being treated as an object, may have been trying to do Abishag a favor as well as to pacify Adonijah. Solomon gave his half brother no room for doubt. He assumed Adonijah was planning to use Abishag to fight for the throne. These maneuvers make one fact clear: No one cared what Abishag thought. She might as well have been listed with the furniture.

Home and work are both settings in which persons are sometimes treated as objects. You may be hurt today by such treatment. Family members may withhold appreciation. Fellow workers may treat you like just another office machine. Resist these invitations to hopelessness or resentment by remembering that God knows. He knows you intimately, and he will always treat you as a person.

Other people may overlook us, but God never does.

Abishag's story is told in 1 Kings 1:1-4; 2:13-24.

Ambition without Wisdom

ADONIJAH

Adonijah . . . put himself forward and said, "I will be king."
(1 Kings 1:5)

Adonijah really, *really* wanted to be king of Israel. After all, he was the oldest living son of David. He was handsome, perhaps regal in appearance—so much so that two of David's advisers (Joab and Abiathar) gave him their support. But David had already promised his throne to Solomon. Adonijah's dreams and plans were in vain.

That didn't stop Adonijah. Hopelessly caught up in his own world, he hired a band of royal footmen and chariots to "prove" he was the king. He even performed the official sacrifices expected of a newly crowned king and sent invitations for his own coronation. His charade almost worked, but his willfulness ultimately led to his own death.

Adonijah was overly willful. He could neither recognize nor work within limits. For whatever reason, he was unwilling to respect the wishes of others or to accept God's will when it contradicted his own. His self-centeredness led him to defy his father, deny God's sovereignty, and eventually die an early death.

Pursue your own plans within the will of God, not instead of or in spite of it. The limits he has placed on you will only make them flourish.

Our desires fit best within God's.

Adonijah's story is told in 1 Kings 1:5-53; 2:13-25.

A Friend Indeed

BARZILLAI

Show kindness to the sons of Barzillai. . . . They stood by me.
(1 Kings 2:7)

Troubles and trials have a way of revealing our friends. When his son Absalom betrayed him, David barely had time to escape alive. Some of his closest advisers abandoned him. The kingdom seemed lost, and David was barely ahead of those pursuing him. Into this nightmare appeared Barzillai and several others with food and coverings. Their help was simple, timely, and perfect.

Later, David tried to reward Barzillai by having him come back to Jerusalem with the king. But Barzillai was already eighty years old and too wise to make an unnecessary move. He was thankful and glad he had been in a position to help the king. When David was giving Solomon counsel before handing over the throne, he made it a point to tell his son to treat the family of Barzillai with special honor. David did not forget those who proved themselves true friends in his time of trouble.

What people in your life have given you help like Barzillai? Perhaps your needs weren't material, but they gave you encouragement and understanding at the moment when you thought you were completely alone. They didn't substitute for God; they reminded you *of* God. What have you done lately to demonstrate that you haven't forgotten the value of their gifts?

A friend in our trouble has been proven double.

Glimpses of Barzillai's life can be found in 2 Samuel 17:27-29; 19:31-39; and 1 Kings 2:7.

The Pursuit of Excellence

HIRAM

A man of great skill. (2 Chronicles 2:13)

One of the most remarkable buildings in all of history was the temple of the Lord built by Solomon in Jerusalem. The architect and on-site builder was Hiram (also known as Huram and Huram-Abi). Hiram transformed ideas, metals, stones, and wood into a structure of beauty.

Hiram came from Tyre, but his mother was a woman of Israel. His father was a metalworker. Perhaps his father sharpened his skills while his mother trained him in the faith of Israel. We can only guess that the quality of his work was a tribute to the God whose temple he was building.

Hiram was not intimidated by his formidable undertaking, though some of the individual pieces he cast for the temple were immense. But large or small, the descriptions of his work convey a tone of admiration for his skill. From pillars to pomegranates, from bowls to bulls, from pots to shovels, Hiram produced articles of beauty.

We not only honor God by allowing him to develop our character, but also by making the best use of the skills he has given to us. The pursuit of excellence can be an eloquent tribute to our Creator. How can your efforts today make a statement to others about your relationship with God?

Sometimes our faith can be shown through the work of our hands.

Hiram's work is recorded in 1 Kings 7:13-45 and 2 Chronicles 2:13–4:16.

Guaranteed: Sin's Consequences

JEROBOAM

I raised you up from among the people and made you a leader over my people Israel. (1 Kings 14:7)

Even clear warnings can be hard to obey. God's warning to Jeroboam came through a prophet who declared that God would soon divide the kingdom of Israel to punish David's unfaithful descendants. Jeroboam would have the opportunity to rule ten of the twelve tribes. God made it clear that Jeroboam's family would suffer the same disaster that David's grandson Rehoboam had met if they refused to obey him.

Years later, Jeroboam assumed his reign over the tribes that had thrown off Rehoboam's rule. He forgot the prophet's words and led his kingdom away from the God who had allowed him to reign. The consequences of this action, while not immediate, were devastating. His family was eventually wiped out, and the northern kingdom collapsed, never to be restored.

Sin's consequences are guaranteed in God's Word. When we do something directly opposed to God's commands, we often fool ourselves into thinking we've gotten away with it when there are no immediate consequences. But that is a dangerous assumption that can only do us more harm. Jeroboam's life should make us recognize our frequent need to admit our disobedience and ask God to forgive us.

Sin always brings consequences.

Jeroboam's story is told in 1 Kings 11:26–14:20. He is also mentioned in 2 Chronicles 10–13.

Small Acts of Faithfulness

AHIJAH

Ahijah is . . . the man who told me that I would become king.
(1 Kings 14:2, TLB)

Age was not a factor in Ahijah's usefulness to God. He spoke for God on two distinct occasions, illustrating a lifetime of faithfulness. First, Ahijah, called "a prophet from Shiloh," predicted that an aspiring common man named Jeroboam would become king over ten rebellious tribes of Israel. Apparently, Jeroboam saw this as little more than a confirmation of his own ambitions, for he did not pay attention to the warning included in Ahijah's prophecy. As king, he led the people into renewed idolatry.

Years later, faced with a sick child, Jeroboam recalled the truthfulness of Ahijah's prophecy. The aging prophet was pressed into service once again by the Lord. He informed Jeroboam that his sick child would die and his reign would come to a terrible end because of his disobedience to God. We know of only these two occasions when Ahijah carried out special duties, but each time he was faithful. The years that separated those assignments show that he remained ready.

Today may or may not include a memorable event in your life. The hours may simply be filled with the small acts of obedience that make up a faithful lifestyle. But whether or not you are in the spotlight of special service, make this day another for which God can call you a good and faithful servant.

Faithfulness results when obedience piles up, small act upon small act.

Ahijah's story is told in 1 Kings 11:26-40; 14:1-18.

Not-So-Wonderful Counselors

REHOBOAM

He disregarded the advice that the older men gave him. (1 Kings 12:8, NRSV)

Perhaps you have heard the old saying "Never follow a legend." That was Rehoboam's dilemma. His father was Solomon—the king renowned for his wisdom, wealth, and fame. Solomon's immense talent and vision made Israel the envy of the civilized world.

One small problem: To finance this state-of-the-art kingdom, Solomon had increased taxes to the point where the average citizen was near financial ruin. And so, the people of Israel hoped that Rehoboam would relieve their misery.

Rehoboam listened to his subjects and then sought the advice of the elders who had served his father, Solomon. Their counsel was to lower the tax rate. Rehoboam dismissed these advisers and asked his friends for their advice. They replied, "Tell them, 'You thought things were tough under my dad? Well, you haven't seen anything yet!'" Unfortunately, Rehoboam followed the advice of his foolish friends. The result was an immediate split in the kingdom.

Clearly, it is not enough to merely seek out advice. We must consider the source of the counsel, and then we must weigh it against the truth of the Scriptures.

Do you have an older, wiser Christian in your life who provides you with godly counsel? If so, talk with that person when you need advice. If not, ask God to put a wise counselor or two in your life.

Wise people follow wise advice.

The story of Rehoboam is told in 1 Kings 11:43–14:31 and 2 Chronicles 9:31–13:7.

Vanishing Faith

ABIJAH

His heart was not right with God. (1 Kings 15:3, TLB)

An armed confrontation with King Jeroboam (of Israel) brought the crisis into Abijah's life. His army of Judah was half the size of Israel's forces. To make matters worse, Jeroboam demonstrated his tactical superiority by surrounding Abijah's army. Faced with such overwhelming odds, Abijah acted on what he knew about his God, rather than on what he had learned from his father, Rehoboam. He stated that God's reputation was at stake in the conflict between Israel and Judah. Army sizes didn't matter; what mattered was who was on God's side. Abijah's fiery speech hit the bull's-eye, and his army gained a crushing victory.

That victory on the battlefield, unfortunately, did not represent Abijah's true self at all. His speech, true as it was, constitutes the sum total of his good deeds. Sadly, King Abijah fits this description better: "His heart was not right with God."

A moment in the spotlight does not make a star. God is looking for people who will cling to him day in and day out, not only on occasions of emergency. How about you . . . right now?

Long-term faithfulness is what counts.

For more on Abijah, see 1 Kings 15:1-8 and 2 Chronicles 13:1-22.

Taking a Tough Stand

ASA

Asa called to the Lord his God and said, "Lord, there is no one like you to help the powerless against the mighty." (2 Chronicles 14:11)

The divided kingdom was still young when this great-grandson of Solomon took the reins of Judah. Already considerable pagan worship had crept into the culture, and Asa did his utmost to bring the country back to God. He was a courageous leader who stood up to fight the bully, Zerah of Cush, despite overwhelming odds.

When faced with opposing numbers that would bring goose bumps to Goliath, Asa knew where his strength lay: He asked God for help in a simple prayer, then moved forward. And when his scheming grandmother Maacah wanted to win points with a crowd of idol worshipers (2 Chronicles 15:16), Asa made the strong decision to strip her of royal privilege, putting devotion to God above family loyalty.

Asa had a clear vision of the direction he was taking Judah and pursued his policy in the face of danger and family opposition.

We can learn from Asa's simple, take-charge attitude: There's no room for compromise with pagan ideas or practice. When it comes down to it, take a tough stand for what you know God wants.

God gives courage to face a bully, to do what's right and good despite opposition.

Asa's bravery is recounted in 1 Kings 15:8-24 and 2 Chronicles 14–16. He is also mentioned in Jeremiah 41:9 and Matthew 1:7.

Love Grown Cold

ASA

Asa was so angry with the prophet . . . that he threw him into jail.
(2 Chronicles 16:10, TLB)

Something quite terrible but all too common happened to Asa in later life. He lost his heart for God.

Perhaps he let the prestige of his job go to his head. The job of being king tended to develop an exaggerated estimate of self-importance.

Perhaps the opposite occurred. Compared to David and Solomon, Asa was a minor league ruler. Perhaps he could see his reign fading into history's backwater and grew cynical about religious devotion.

Whatever the problem, Asa's respectable and God-fearing career was hurt by an alliance with the pagan Ben-Hadad of Syria, jolted by his imprisonment of the prophet who dared to call him back to faith (2 Chronicles 16:10), then wrecked by a foot disease and Asa's refusal to seek the Lord's healing strength. He died estranged.

We need to guard each other from Asa's fate. We need to support and encourage senior members of the church. We need to remember with prayer, visits, music, and human touch those once-vital believers who now reside in nursing homes and convalescent centers, lest the aged forget in their ailment and loneliness the sure promises of the gospel. Christians approaching their golden years need to nurture faith, to trust always in the goodness of God.

Faith needs nurture at every stage.

Asa's story is told in 1 Kings 15:8-24 and 2 Chronicles 14–16. He is also mentioned in Jeremiah 41:9 and Matthew 1:7.

Turning Back to God

JEHOSHAPHAT

So they turned to attack him, but Jehoshaphat cried out, and the Lord helped him. (2 Chronicles 18:31)

Jehoshaphat knew better than to make the mistakes he made. But he didn't allow his mistakes to get the best of him. His troubles began when he joined forces with evil King Ahab. Ahab wined and dined King Jehoshaphat in hopes of securing Judah's help in an enemy attack. However, God warned Jehoshaphat through the prophet Micaiah that their plans would not succeed. Jehoshaphat's decision to ignore the message and proceed into battle anyway was thus a willful act of disobedience.

Almost at once, he found himself the target of soldiers who mistakenly identified him as Ahab. He could have accepted this deadly fate, because he richly deserved it. But instead, he started shouting, and God miraculously saved him.

Unfortunately, few believers remember the extent of God's incredible mercy when they fall into sin. Instead of running to God for forgiveness and restoration, their guilt persuades them to run from him—a lingering instinct from the days in the Garden. While we must accept the consequences of our mistakes, Jehoshaphat's predicament shows us that turning to God is always the best recourse. No matter how greatly you have sinned, God is willing to forgive you.

God's infinite mercy can cleanse you of all sinfulness.

Jehoshaphat's story is told in 1 Kings 15:24–22:50 and 2 Chronicles 17:1–21:1.

Faithfulness in the Little Things

JEHOSHAPHAT

Later, Jehoshaphat king of Judah made an alliance with Ahaziah king of Israel, who was guilty of wickedness. (2 Chronicles 20:35)

When the challenges were obvious, Jehoshaphat turned to God for guidance and made the right choices. To combat widespread idolatry, he sent out officials to teach the Law to the people. He also called for prayer and fasting when Judah was threatened with war, and his faithfulness resulted in a great victory.

Jehoshaphat, however, was not so reliant on God in his day-to-day affairs. He allowed his son to marry Athaliah, the daughter of the wicked Ahab and Jezebel of Israel, who did her best to be as evil as her parents. Jehoshaphat was almost killed when, without asking God, he made an alliance with Ahab. Later, he got involved in an unwise shipbuilding venture with Ahab's son, Ahaziah—a venture that God shipwrecked.

We repeat Jehoshaphat's error when we fail to seek God's counsel in routine decisions. Because we lack the patience or trust to consult with him, we find ourselves making foolish choices that hurt ourselves or others. Perhaps you are facing no major crises today. Maybe it's just the same old routine. Have you paused long enough to give your day to God anyway?

Faithfulness to God comes from day-to-day obedience.

Jehoshaphat's story is told in 1 Kings 15:24–22:50 and 2 Chronicles 17:1–21:1.

The Blame Game

AHAB

When [Ahab] saw Elijah, he said to him, "Is that you, you troubler of Israel?" (1 Kings 18:17)

The labels we affix to people become a lens through which we see and view everything. The names you use can distort your judgment and eventually give you reason to think that wrong is all right. That was Hitler's strategy with the Jews, and Nebuchadnezzar's with the Israelite captives: Rename them; then exploit them for your own purposes.

Ahab had leadership potential, but his moral lens had become completely distorted. Wrong was right; right was whatever he wished. And the key person who could show Ahab his problem, Elijah, was the nation's chief troublemaker in Ahab's mind. Ahab's lifeline to God was thin and fraying. By placing on Elijah the label *troubler,* Ahab was cutting the cord altogether.

When friends confront us, we may call them disloyal. When parents urge us to mend a bad habit, we may call them conservative or "out of it." When a pastor counsels change, we may dismiss it with terms like *meddler* or *holier-than-thou.* And these labels may be hatchets whacking at the lifeline—God's towrope to keep us from floating adrift.

Put away the hatchet; quit labeling and start listening. Accept Christian counsel whenever it's given. Remain open to the corrective judgment of people who love you. Listen always to God's Word.

Christian counsel is our lifeline.

Ahab's story is told in 1 Kings 16:28–22:40 and 2 Chronicles 18–22. He is also mentioned in Micah 6:16.

The Pouting King

AHAB

He lay on his bed sulking and refused to eat. (1 Kings 21:4)

Do you sulk? When your plans are met with less than unanimous approval, when your preferences are rejected for other options, when promotions go to colleagues or dates to a roommate, do you pout?

Ahab failed to see setbacks as opportunities for toughness training. As a consequence, he was emotionally weak and easily manipulated by his aggressive, pagan wife, Jezebel. He acted like a baby his entire life.

When your plans hit a roadblock, do better than Ahab. First, trust God that the problem, rather than being a reason to sulk, is an opportunity for you to learn. Commit to solving the problem if it's important, abandoning it if it's trivial. Develop a plan, consult with trustworthy Christian mentors, and pray. Forge ahead, believing that God has good plans for you and will bless or block your efforts accordingly.

Every problem is an opportunity to grow, learn, and develop faith in God.

Ahab's story is told in 1 Kings 16:28–22:40 and 2 Chronicles 18–22. He is also mentioned in Micah 6:16.

A Life of Treachery

JEZEBEL

No one else was so completely sold out to the devil as Ahab, for his wife, Jezebel, encouraged him to do every sort of evil. (1 Kings 21:25, TLB)

Jezebel ranks as perhaps the most evil woman in the Bible. The book of Revelation makes her name synonymous with those who completely reject God (Revelation 2:20-21). Many pagan women married into Israel without acknowledging the God their husbands worshiped. But no one was as determined as Jezebel to make all Israel worship her gods. Her evil influence spurred the idolatry that would eventually destroy the northern kingdom.

Jezebel's plan to wipe out the worship of God in Israel led to her own undoing. Before she died, Jezebel suffered the loss of her husband in combat and her son at the hand of Jehu, who took the throne by force. She died in the defiant and scornful way she had lived.

Jezebel's bones were all that remained of her evil life. Her power, money, prestige, royal finery, family, and false gods failed to save her. In the end, her life of treachery crashed down around her. Power, health, and wealth may seduce you into thinking life will continue indefinitely. But death strips everyone of all external security. The time to set life's course is at the beginning. The end comes soon enough.

God's provision for our eternal life is the only guarantee we can rely on.

Jezebel's story is told in 1 Kings 16:31—2 Kings 9:37.

Bringing Injustice to Light

NABOTH

The Lord forbid that I should give you my ancestral inheritance.
(1 Kings 21:3, NRSV)

One of the cardinal rules of real estate is summed up in three words: location, location, location. Evil King Ahab owned many vineyards, but he wanted one that was located next to the palace in Jezreel. So when Naboth, the owner of the vineyard, respectfully refused his offer to trade for an even better property, Ahab turned angry and sullen.

King Ahab's wife, Jezebel, then schemed to take by force what Naboth would not willingly give up. The vineyard owner was publicly accused of having cursed God and the king, a crime punishable by immediate stoning. Jezebel arranged a ruthless betrayal, coercing Naboth's neighbors to speak against him, and the sentence was carried out. Naboth appeared to be just another simple person ground under the wheels of greed and power.

Yet God made the injustice public. Elijah was dispatched to meet Ahab just as the king arrived to gloat over his new acquisition. Through the prophet, God leveled a crushing indictment on Ahab and his family for their murder of Naboth and their theft of his property.

Naboth's tragedy can comfort us when we are treated unjustly and convict us when we mistreat others. Even when injustice appears victorious, we know a God who guarantees ultimate justice. We dare not treat God's holiness lightly.

God's character ensures that justice will win out.

Naboth's story is found in 1 Kings 21.

Knowing God above All

ELIJAH

Elijah walked up to the altar and prayed, ". . . Prove today that you are the God of Israel and that I am your servant." (1 Kings 18:36, TLB)

Elijah may be the most well known and dramatic of all the prophets in the Bible. His spiritual resume includes remarkably accurate predictions, raising the dead, and a single-handed showdown with idolatrous priests. Add to that an astonishing ride to heaven via a fiery chariot and an appearance with Moses during Christ's transfiguration.

The amazing miracles God accomplished through Elijah may dazzle us, but we would do well to focus on the relationship he and God shared. All that happened in Elijah's life began with the same miracle that is available to us—he was invited to know God. How else could he put himself in a life-threatening position with the prophets of Baal if he had not come to know God was trustworthy? How could he be God's messenger without spending time listening to God for the message?

Performing amazing miracles for God is admirable, but we should concentrate foremost on developing a relationship with him. The time we spend with God is far more precious to him than the things we do for him. The real miracle of Elijah's life was his very personal relationship with God. And that miracle is available to us.

God invites us to know him before all else.

Elijah's story is told in 1 Kings 17:1—2 Kings 2:11. He is also mentioned in 2 Chronicles 21:12-15.

The Anxious Prophet

ELIJAH

Elijah was afraid and ran for his life. (1 Kings 19:3)

Elijah reminds us of the fickleness of human emotions. After God worked an overwhelming miracle through him in defeating the prophets of Baal, Elijah panicked and fled because of one woman's threat to his life. As if he had forgotten God's power, Elijah felt afraid, depressed, and abandoned by God. He wanted to die. God bolstered Elijah with an audiovisual display of his power and revealed his presence to the troubled prophet in a gentle whisper.

Elijah, like us, struggled with his feelings even after receiving God's comfort. So God confronted Elijah's emotions and revealed a plan for action. He told Elijah what to do next. God also informed him that his loneliness was based in part on ignorance, for seven thousand others in Israel were still faithful to God.

God has given us a capacity for faith. Our faith can keep us from being controlled by self-defeating thoughts and irrational feelings. A strong faith in God can encourage us to continue in his work even when we experience fear and failure.

Daily exercise your ability to choose faith over feelings.

Elijah's story is told in 1 Kings 17:1—2 Kings 2:11. He is also mentioned in 2 Chronicles 21:12-15.

A Double Portion of Service

ELISHA

Elijah said to Elisha, "Tell me, what can I do for you before I am taken from you?" "Let me inherit a double portion of your spirit," Elisha replied. (2 Kings 2:9)

Few replacements in Scripture were as effective as Elisha. Elisha had a great example to follow in the prophet Elijah, even though each was called to a different role. The fiery Elijah confronted and exposed idolatry, while his counterpart, Elisha, quietly served the poor. Elisha spent less time in dramatic conflict with evil and more time caring compassionately for the suffering and sick. The Bible records eighteen encounters between Elisha and needy people.

Elisha's ministry reminds us that God does not call all believers to high-profile, headline-grabbing work. How easy it might have been for Elisha to downplay his contribution simply because he did not command the presence that Elijah did. He knew, however, that God counted the work of both men as equally and invaluably important. God has created you with specific gifts and abilities in order to serve him well. Are you comparing your abilities with others', or are you committing what you have to God's service?

God equips each believer uniquely to serve him.

Elisha's story is found in 1 Kings 19:16—2 Kings 13:20.

Faith in a Tight Spot

ELISHA

The officer assisting the king said, "That couldn't happen if the Lord made windows in the sky!" But Elisha replied, "You will see it happen." (2 Kings 7:2, TLB)

Elisha inevitably seemed to place the people he encountered in a tight spot. Possessing the brash ways of a prophet speaking on God's authority, he tested the faith of those he encountered. He offered a starving city hope, assured a lone servant victory over an army, and promised an aged woman she would mother a son. But Elisha knew that God's power relied on the faithfulness of those whose faith was being tested. They would be called upon to believe and see the unseen.

Elisha's career reminds us of the importance of trusting God's provision for the future. We may encounter Elishas in our everyday circumstances. God may use such people to put us in a tight spot—a place where our faith is challenged. Perhaps an employer's unexpected notice of pending cutbacks will challenge your belief in God's promises to care for you. Or maybe a loved one has become ill, and you wonder where God has gone. Your response during these difficult times will either boost or stunt your spiritual growth. Ask God for the faith to respond in complete trust concerning every aspect of your future.

Faith involves an attitude of expectancy.

Read about Elisha's interactions with others in 1 Kings 19:16—2 Kings 13:20.

Deceiving Ourselves

HAZAEL

"I would never do that sort of a thing." (2 Kings 8:13, TLB)

When Elisha told Hazael, a servant to the king of Syria, of the terrible things he would do to the people of Israel, Hazael objected. He believed (or wanted to believe, anyway) that he was a decent man; he wouldn't be the sort to commit such deeds. Yet the day after Elisha predicted that Hazael would become king of Syria, the servant shamelessly murdered King Ben-Hadad and replaced him on the throne. During his reign, Hazael was a constant threat to Israel and Judah. God allowed Hazael success in order to humble his own people. But God also held Hazael responsible for his sins, and his own family suffered for them.

Like Hazael, we may deceive ourselves or others into thinking we are incapable of blatant sin. We think we have the self-control to prevent ourselves from sinking so low. But often we are kept from sin by a lack of opportunity rather than our strength of character. God protects us from countless temptations that we are too weak to handle on our own. Instead of patting ourselves on the back for our goodness, we should take an honest look at ourselves and admit our sinful potential. We need to be reminded often that only God is capable of delivering us from evil.

We need God's strength to resist evil in all its guises.

Hazael's rise and fall are mentioned in the following passages: 1 Kings 19:15-17; 2 Kings 8:8-15, 28-29; 9:14-15; 10:32; 12:17-18; 13:3-25; and Amos 1:4.

Facing Unpleasant Facts

MICAIAH

But Micaiah said, "As the Lord lives, whatever the Lord says to me, that I will speak." (1 Kings 22:14, NRSV)

Why do humans seem to prefer to avoid the truth? It is almost as though the vast majority of people have consented to a conspiracy of deception. The rules of this arrangement are simple: "Forget the truth—tell me what I want to hear! And in return, I'll lie to you as well."

We see this perverted principle in the story of Micaiah, a prophet of Samaria. Unimpressed by King Ahab's yes-men, King Jehoshaphat of Judah wanted to hear from a true prophet of God before committing his armies to battle. When Micaiah's name came up, the evil Ahab made this classic statement, "I hate him because he never prophesies anything good about me, but always bad."

Nevertheless, Micaiah was summoned. Upon arrival he indulged in a bit of sarcasm and then announced his determination to speak the truth, no matter what. When Micaiah announced a depressing (yet true) picture of the immediate future, he received a sharp slap in the face and was sentenced to prison by the angry Ahab.

What about you? In your desire to be liked or to avoid unpleasantness, do you have a tendency to twist the truth? We do not honor God when we lie. In fact, when we distort the truth we unwittingly honor the father of lies, Satan himself! So, while others may find our fiction flattering, God finds it offensive. He is a God of truth. Determine today that you will be honest no matter what it costs.

We must speak the truth regardless of the consequences.

The story of Micaiah is found in 1 Kings 22:1-28 and 2 Chronicles 18:1-27.

A Legacy of Sin

AHAZIAH, KING OF ISRAEL

Ahaziah made the Lord God of Israel very angry. (1 Kings 22:53, TLB)

Ahaziah's life demonstrates what can happen to children of dysfunctional families. He inherited from his father, Ahab, and his mother, Jezebel, the most evil reputation of any royal family in Israel. Following his father's violent death, Ahaziah became king over a nation steeped in idolatry, dishonesty, and blatant rebellion against God.

Ahaziah immediately began to add his own mistakes to his unholy heritage. The kingdom stumbled when Moab declared its independence from Israel, exposing Ahaziah's lack of power. Next, Ahaziah invested in a fleet of merchant ships, hoping to create financial security. The fleet sank, along with the king's hopes. Then the king stumbled and fell from a palace porch, seriously injuring himself. Ahaziah added "idolatry to injury" by sending a servant to Ekron, a center for the worship of Baal-zebub, to find out if he would recover. At this point, God decided Ahaziah had been given enough opportunities to repent. Elijah intercepted the messengers with the news that God had declared the end of Ahaziah's life. Even then, Ahaziah gave no sign of repentance.

Our past may handicap us, but our own decisions condemn us. Understanding family problems and dysfunctions only becomes useful if we use the knowledge to make better choices. How often do you let your past influence your decisions? for better or for worse?

An evil past can be repeated or rejected for a better present.

Ahaziah's story is found in 1 Kings 22:51—2 Kings 1:18 and 2 Chronicles 20:35-37.

Miserable Monarch
JEHORAM, KING OF JUDAH

You have also murdered your own brothers, members of your father's house, men who were better than you. (2 Chronicles 21:13)

The reign of King Jehoram, son of Jehoshaphat, was a low point in the history of Judah. His reign was marked by sin and cruelty. He married a woman who worshiped idols; he killed his six brothers; he allowed and even promoted pagan worship. Jehoram's marriage to Athaliah, daughter of Ahab and Jezebel, was Judah's downfall, for Athaliah brought her mother Jezebel's wicked influence into Judah, causing the nation to forget God and turn to Baal worship (2 Chronicles 22:3). Yet he was not killed in battle or by treachery—he died of a lingering and painful disease (2 Chronicles 21:18-19). Punishment for sin is not always immediate or dramatic. But if we ignore God's laws, we will eventually suffer the consequences of our sin.

The people of Judah willingly followed Jehoram's errors. But by the time he died, they were sick of him. Scripture points out that his tomb was placed away from the respected tombs of the kings. The people had chafed under the consequences of Jehoram's sin but blamed their suffering on him rather than accepting their own responsibility.

Are you tolerating sin by blaming its presence on someone else? Don't take the easy way out—own up to your wrongdoing and get right with God.

When we join others in sin, we must also bear the responsibility for the consequences.

The reign of Jehoram of Judah is recorded in 2 Kings 8:16-24 and 2 Chronicles 21:1-20.

Presuming on God's Patience

JORAM, KING OF ISRAEL

He did evil in the eyes of the Lord, but not as his father and mother had done. (2 Kings 3:2)

Those who recorded the history of Israel noted that while things under Ahab and Jezebel's son Joram didn't get any worse, they didn't improve much, either. Joram clearly knew what God required of him as king, but he chose not to obey.

Joram clashed often with Elisha the prophet during his reign. Once, the combined forces of Joram and two other kings became stranded in the desert without water. Joram immediately saw God's vindictive action in their predicament. It was King Jehoshaphat, however, who called for the counsel of a "prophet of the Lord." Elisha informed Joram and the king of Edom that his own presence and God's help were meant for Jehoshaphat. The other kings were merely absorbing the overflow of blessings.

God also used Elisha to preserve the king and his army from the Arameans. But Joram missed the point. When famine and the armies of Ben-Hadad surrounded Samaria, the king decided Elisha should be blamed. The city and Elisha were rescued, but Joram was soon killed by Jehu.

Joram knew about God and had many opportunities to submit to the Lord. He resisted to the end. How often we, too, presume on God's patience! Choose to live this day conscious of God's presence.

Give recognition to God's work in your life.

Joram's reign is recorded in 2 Kings 3:1–9:26.

Using Us as We Are

YOUNG JEWISH SLAVE GIRL

Among their captives was a little girl who had been given to Naaman's wife as a maid. (2 Kings 5:2, TLB)

Life can take unexpected and painful turns. One little girl in Israel found herself a prize of war. She became a slave, the property of Naaman's family. And yet the story that unfolds is contrary to what we might expect. Instead of self-pity, we find her pitying her master; instead of wishing evil upon those who had captured her, she hoped for their well-being. She wasn't crushed by her misfortune; she rose above it.

Naaman, this little girl's master, was a successful Syrian commander. But he was also a leper. In Israel, a person with leprosy was shunned. Sufferers were forced to announce their uncleanness to anyone who came near.

In simple faith, a little girl suggested to her mistress that Naaman ought to see the prophet of God in Samaria. She was sure Elisha would be able to bring about his healing. There must have been a note of conviction in her suggestion, because Naaman took her seriously. Eventually, he was healed by God.

Sometimes, all we can do is point people toward God. Yet that in itself accomplishes a great deal. The faith of one child set in motion a chain of events through which God received glory. We should be alert to the same opportunities today. God can accomplish miracles with our small actions.

Young or old, God is willing to use us as we are.

The little Jewish girl is introduced in Naaman's story (2 Kings 5:1-27).

The Barrier of Pride

NAAMAN

*There were also many lepers in Israel in the time of the prophet
Elisha, and none of them was cleansed except Naaman the Syrian.*
(Luke 4:27, NRSV)

Naaman was a brilliant leader with a severe handicap. His successes on the battlefield did not erase the shame and isolation of
his leprosy. The depth of his desperation can be measured by his
readiness to accept the suggestion of a little Israelite girl who
served his wife. Naaman went to the king for permission to visit
Elisha the prophet.

Perhaps he thought Elisha would be impressed to have such a
celebrity for a patient. Elisha curtly dismissed the general with his
prescription: "Go, wash in the Jordan seven times, and your flesh
shall be restored and you shall be clean" (2 Kings 5:10). Clearly,
Naaman resented the treatment he received. Fortunately, he had
some clearheaded and devoted servants. His submission to the
simple treatment led to the healing of his wounds and scars.

As he did with Naaman, God will meet our needs, but not on
our terms. God is not impressed with our pride nor intimidated by
our demands. When we approach God with the intention of earn-
ing his acceptance and love, we are pursuing a hopeless plan. God's
prescription is painfully simple: repentance, followed by wholehearted acceptance of his free gift of salvation. Is your pride standing in the way of a restored relationship with God? Confess your
sin, and get right with him today.

Pride is often the last barrier between us and God's gifts.

Naaman's encounter with God is recorded in 2 Kings 5:1-27.

Deception's Reward

GEHAZI

Gehazi . . . thought, "My master has let that Aramean Naaman off too lightly by not accepting from him what he offered." (2 Kings 5:20, NRSV)

Some people live so close to the truth that they have to stumble over it before they really notice it. Gehazi, servant to Elisha, witnessed the fulfillment of one of Elisha's prophecies and saw him perform miracles and even raise the dead. However, we suspect that Gehazi did not appreciate the privilege of seeing God's amazing work.

When Elisha healed Naaman the leper, Gehazi saw a perfect opportunity to get rich by selfishly asking for the reward Elisha had refused. He even lied and tried to cover up his motives for accepting the money. What Gehazi received from Naaman was leprosy, not the payoff he had hoped for. He had to live with the permanent reminder of leprosy before he finally took God seriously.

Most of us have daily opportunities to see God's power, mercy, and faithfulness. When God uses painful measures to get our attention, it is often because we have turned a blind eye to the obvious signs he has given us. Decide to notice and express your gratitude for God's "fingerprints" in your world today.

Demonstrate your appreciation for God's work in your life.

Gehazi's life is recorded in 2 Kings 4:11–8:6.

Settling for Mediocrity

JEHU

Jehu said, "Come with me and see my zeal for the Lord." (2 Kings 10:16)

Jehu had the basic qualities that could have made him a great success. By many accounts, he was a successful king. His family ruled the northern kingdom longer than any other. God used Jehu to topple Ahab's evil dynasty and to rid Judah of Baal worship. He came close to being God's kind of king, but he recklessly went beyond God's commands and failed to continue the obedient actions that began his reign. Within sight of victory, he settled for mediocrity.

God gives each person strengths and abilities that will find their greatest usefulness only under his control. Outside of that control, they don't accomplish what they could, and they often become tools for evil. A natural talent in finances can become an avenue for greed. An outgoing and persuasive personality can be put to use promoting the wrong cause. One way to make sure this does not happen is to ask God to place you under his control. With his presence in your life, your natural strengths and abilities will be used to their greatest potential for the greatest good.

Our natural abilities and strengths find their greatest usefulness under Christ's control.

Jehu's story is told in 1 Kings 19:16—2 Kings 10:36.

A Lack of Heartfelt Obedience

JEHU

Yet Jehu was not careful to keep the law of the Lord, the God of Israel, with all his heart. (2 Kings 10:31)

Jehu was a man with big ideas but little spiritual resolve. His kingdom moved with excitement, but its destination was unclear. He fiercely eliminated Baal worship only to uphold the worship of calves his predecessor had set up. Despite all the good he accomplished, Jehu's reign was undermined by a crucial mistake: He did not follow God with all of his heart. He had become God's instrument for carrying out justice, but he had not become God's committed servant. He gave lip service to God while he worshiped the golden calves in his heart.

Likewise, we can be very active in our work for God and still not give him the heartfelt obedience he desires. To obey with all your heart means to give yourself fully to God—first in devotion to him and then to his service. And yet so often our efforts to know and obey God's commands can best be described as halfhearted. How do you rate your heart's obedience? God is more than willing to give you the power to obey him with all your heart. Just ask.

A lifetime of doing good is not enough if we fail to follow God with all of our heart.

Read more about Jehu's reign in 1 Kings 19:16—2 Kings 10:36.

Mother Didn't Know Best

AHAZIAH, KING OF JUDAH

His mother encouraged him in doing wrong. (2 Chronicles 22:3, TLB)

Ahaziah definitely came from bad seed. Both his father and mother murdered members of their families. And his grandparents Ahab and Jezebel were one of the most destructive and evil pairs in the Bible. Not only was he aware of his own evil history, he was also likely present when Elijah pronounced judgment on his wicked family.

So, when the people of Jerusalem enthroned him after his father, Jehoram, died, he had a choice. He could listen to the evil advice of his relatives or he could seek out the wisdom of God. He even had the prophet Elijah available to him if he had asked.

But Ahaziah chose to listen to his evil mother and her relatives in Israel for kingly advice. The consequences cost him his throne and his life. He was pierced by an arrow in a revolt, and his evil mother greedily assumed his duties.

When we are in a position of authority, it is wise to consider others' advice. However, it is equally wise to consider the source before we follow the advice. Think about what consequences have followed under the previous leadership of the advice-giver. God will supply his resources for godly persuasion, but the choice to take advantage of them is ours to make.

Consider the source before you follow the advice.

Insight into Ahaziah can be found in 2 Kings 8:25–9:16-28 and 2 Chronicles 22:1-9.

Killer Queen

ATHALIAH

She proceeded to destroy the whole royal family. (2 Kings 11:1)

Queen Athaliah and her parents, King Ahab and Queen Jezebel, rank as the most evil nuclear family in the Bible. Athaliah's folks ruled Israel. They established an alliance with Jehoshaphat, king of Judah, by giving her in marriage to Prince Jehoram. The Bible tells us that she was an evil influence upon her son when he assumed the throne after his father's death.

The peak of Athaliah's wrongdoing came long after Jehoram's death, when she received word that her son had been killed by Jehu in the same revolt which also saw the deaths of Athaliah's brother Joram, her mother, Jezebel, and at least seventy other half brothers and half sisters in Israel. Athaliah's appalling response was to put her own children and grandchildren to death. Not even her own flesh and blood would keep her from complete power. Her daughter Jehosheba's last act was to hide Ahaziah's baby Joash (her nephew) from Athaliah, ensuring one survivor from the line of David.

For seven years, Athaliah ruled ruthlessly as the queen mother in Judah. Meanwhile, her grandson Joash was growing up, hidden in the temple. When he was still a child, Athaliah was overthrown and killed. Her death marked the end of Ahab and Jezebel's immediate family. The evil they spawned was a shameful chapter in the story of God's people. They demonstrate that the family structure, a potential that can be the catalyst for great good, can also set in motion unspeakable evil. If we're not cautious, "natural" love and respect for one's family can be easily usurped by equally natural selfish ambition and personal gain. Families are worth guarding!

The sins of parents are often amplified by their children.

Athaliah's story is recorded in 2 Kings 8:25–11:20 and 2 Chronicles 24:7.

Resisting Evil in Small Ways

JEHOSHEBA

She hid the child from Athaliah so she could not kill him.
(2 Chronicles 22:11)

Jehosheba made an impulsive decision that changed the course of a nation. Ruthless Queen Athaliah, Jehosheba's mother (or perhaps stepmother), had planned to murder every prince in the royal family. Jehosheba was painfully aware that her own brother Ahaziah, the recently deceased king, had been the only survivor when his brothers had all been murdered years before. History was about to repeat itself in a gruesome way.

Jehosheba decided to rescue at least one of the children. She kidnapped her nephew Joash and hid him away in the temple with her husband, Jehoiada, a priest. For the next six years they became his parents in hiding. Unwittingly, Jehosheba would preserve the ancestral line from which Christ would be born.

This crucial moment in Jehosheba's life demonstrates an important lesson: Even when evil has the upper hand, we are still called to do good where we can. We may not be able to change everything, but if we can take even one positive action, we ought to do it. We don't know how great an effect a single act will have. Let God help you do the best you can with the opportunities before you.

Small acts done in obedience to God can have tremendous results.

Jehosheba's courage is recorded in 2 Kings 11:1-3 and 2 Chronicles 22:10-12.

The Tragedy of Borrowed Faith

JOASH

Joash did what was right in the eyes of the Lord all the years of Jehoiada the priest. (2 Chronicles 24:2)

Imagine becoming the leader of a nation at the tender age of seven! That's exactly what happened to young Joash. He succeeded the wicked Queen Athaliah as the ruler of Judah in about 835 B.C. Fortunately, this boy-king had a godly adviser, the priest Jehoiada. His influence can be seen in Joash's extensive plan to refurbish the temple. The new king made sure that sacrifices and burnt offerings were faithfully made to the God of Israel.

Then Jehoiada died. And almost immediately Joash abandoned his godly pursuits and plunged the nation into idolatry. When Zechariah, the son of Jehoiada, rebuked the king and the people for their waywardness, Joash ordered his execution. A short time later, Joash was assassinated by his own officials.

Joash epitomizes superficial spirituality. His decisions weren't based on deep-seated beliefs; rather, his was a borrowed faith. Like a chameleon, Joash changed to accommodate his surroundings. When Jehoiada was around, Joash behaved like a true believer. When his godly adviser was gone, Joash joined the crowd of unbelievers.

What about you? Do you act like a follower of Christ all the time, no matter what? Or does your commitment change with the circumstances?

One test of our faith is how we behave among unbelievers.

Joash's story is told in 2 Kings 11:1–14:16 and 2 Chronicles 22:11–25:25.

A Wise Mentor

JEHOIADA

He was buried with the kings in the City of David, because of the good he had done in Israel for God and his temple. (2 Chronicles 24:16)

Jehoiada the priest helped to save the life of Joash, the only survivor of an attempt to wipe out the male descendants of King David. He then became the child-king's mentor.

Six years later, Jehoiada organized the coup that removed Athaliah from the throne and replaced her with the rightful king. Joash took the throne at age seven and reigned forty years. Jehoiada acted as a chief counselor to the king during many of those years.

He and Joash led a significant renewal of the nation. The temple of Baal was destroyed, and God's temple in Jerusalem was gradually renovated. Although Jehoiada was honored when he died, his memory faded as the king's judgment waned. Jehoiada provided Joash with helpful counsel, but he couldn't compensate for the king's lack of internal stability. Joash was usually swayed by the latest counselor who had his ear.

Even the best advice must be received and followed if it is to be effective. Parents, teachers, and friends should remember that the wisdom they share can't be forced on another person. Your responsibility is to present the truth and warn of the consequences of disobedience. Others must choose to follow.

Give your best advice, and trust God to do the rest.

Jehoiada's ministry is recorded in 2 Kings 11:4–12:3 and 2 Chronicles 22:10–24:22.

Halfhearted Obedience

AMAZIAH

He did what was right, but sometimes resented it! (2 Chronicles 25:2, TLB)

Young Amaziah grew up in a court setting illustrated by a brief appearance of righteousness merely punctuating a history of idolatry and killing filled with intrigue, treachery, and killing. He watched his father, Joash, do well under the godly influence of the old priest Jehoiada, only to resort to idolatry and murder after Jehoiada died.

When Amaziah became king, he also kept alive an appearance of attentiveness to God, but his heart wasn't in it. He executed those who had assassinated his father. His early successes, which could have inspired humility, instead gave rise to arrogance. Furthermore, despite God's cautions, he challenged a reluctant Israel to a military confrontation and experienced the humiliating defeat God had forewarned. The remainder of Amaziah's reign was desolate. Like his father's case, Amaziah's own people plotted to kill him.

The pattern surrounding Amaziah's life affirms that hoping to obey God without heartfelt motivation is wishful thinking at best. Unfortunately, we all do a little wishing now and then. Do you often know what the right thing is but sometimes resent having to do it? Life with Christ can be so much more than a series of duties or obligations. Let God transform you from the inside out.

Integrity is obedience from the heart.

The story of Amaziah can be found in 2 Kings 14:1-23 and 2 Chronicles 25.

Sharing the Wealth

JEROBOAM II

He did evil in the eyes of the Lord and did not turn away from any of the sins of Jeroboam, son of Nebat. (2 Kings 14:24)

By worldly standards Jeroboam II, thirteenth king of Israel, was a successful monarch. He consolidated the northern kingdom, as Jonah had predicted (2 Kings 14:25). Jeroboam II cared little for God, yet under his skillful and aggressive statesmanship Israel enjoyed more national power and material prosperity than at any time since the days of Solomon.

The prophets Amos and Hosea, however, tell us what was really happening within the kingdom. Jeroboam and his government ignored the need for justice and compassion. As a result, the rich became richer and the poor, poorer. The people became self-centered, relying more on their power, security, and money than on God.

Jeroboam's dubious legacy reminds us that prosperity brings obligations. Having once been poor and despised, Jeroboam and his people should have seen the need to care for the needy and oppressed. Instead, they wallowed in luxury and turned their backs on the God who had restored them.

Keep in mind that God is responsible for the prosperity you enjoy—and share that wealth with others!

Are you generous with all God has given you, or do you keep it for yourself?

The story of Jeroboam II's reign is told in 2 Kings 14:23-29. He is also referred to in the books of Hosea and Amos.

A Moment of Foolishness

UZZIAH

But after Uzziah became powerful, his pride led to his downfall.
(2 Chronicles 26:16)

It's interesting how a little bad can overshadow a lot of good. A great golf round can be marred by a bad score on just one hole. An otherwise fun vacation can be ruined by one bad experience. A great race can be lost by a slight misstep near the end. A life begun well can be tarnished by the failure to end well. Such was the case with King Uzziah (sometimes known as Azariah).

Early in his reign, Uzziah sought the Lord. He enjoyed military success and gained fame for his innovative weaponry. He was an accomplished builder. The entire nation prospered for most of his fifty-two-year reign.

But late in life Uzziah became prideful. Forgetting that God was the source of all his success, Uzziah began to think that he was above the law. One day he brashly entered the temple, brushed past the priests, and attempted to burn incense before God. For this act of disobedience, God struck him with leprosy. For the rest of his life, Uzziah was disfigured and unclean, a visible testimony of his failure to remain faithful to God.

Uzziah reminds us of the sobering truth that a lifetime of good and wise living can be marred by a single moment of foolishness. Are you walking with God? Ask God for the grace to finish the race with humility and obedience.

Many people begin well, but not all will end well!

The story of Uzziah is told in 2 Kings 15:1-7 and 2 Chronicles 26:1-23.

Leaving the Job Unfinished

JOTHAM

But the places where gods were worshiped were not removed.
(2 Kings 15:35, NCV)

Although Jotham's official reign lasted twenty-five years, he actually governed longer. When his father, Uzziah, was forced into quarantine because of leprosy, Jotham performed the day-to-day functions of the crown.

Much good can be said of Jotham's time as king of Judah, but he failed in a most important area: He didn't destroy the high places of idol worship, although leaving them clearly violated the first commandment (Exodus 20:3). Apparently, Jotham preferred to build. He added to the architecture surrounding the lovely temple. He constructed cities, forts, and towers around Jerusalem. But his failure to remove the pagan worship places undermined the good he did. The consequences were fully realized in the life of his son Ahaz, who became one of Judah's most wicked rulers.

Like Jotham, we may live basically good lives and yet miss doing what is most important. A lifetime of doing good is not enough if we make the crucial mistake of not following God with all our hearts. God sometimes requires that certain habits or influences be removed from our lives. Our lives only have room for one god. A true follower of God puts him first in all areas of life.

Our obedience to God is sometimes measured by what we don't do.

The brief accounts of Jotham's reign are found in 2 Kings 15:4-5, 32-38 and 2 Chronicles 27:1-9. See also Isaiah 1–5 for a picture of Judah in Jotham's day.

The Root of Spiritual Illness

AHAZ

In this time of deep trial, King Ahaz collapsed spiritually.
(2 Chronicles 28:22, TLB)

The circumstances in the life of King Ahaz fall into the general categories of bad and much worse. When Judah suffered a debilitating attack from rival neighbors, his cry for help was answered by a foreign army, the Assyrians. Ahaz's cowardly leadership forced Judah into virtual slavery to Assyria.

Soon every evidence that Judah had once been a God-fearing nation was smashed, defaced, or tucked out of sight. Ahaz even presented his own children as an offering to the gods he hoped would rescue him and his nation from their disastrous situation.

Ahaz's life bears much similarity to our own potential to "collapse spiritually" beneath a load of failures and trials. Instead of repenting of any known sin and calling upon God for relief, we, like Ahaz, may entertain every other source of aid *but* God: our own abilities, money, harmful habits. The result is increased tragedy.

Difficulties and mistakes will either devastate our faith, or they will stimulate growth and maturity. The difference is made when we choose to humbly seek God's help, whatever the situation.

When you are facing trials, don't turn away from God; turn to him.

Read more about Ahaz's tragic life and reign in 2 Kings 16 and 2 Chronicles 28.

The Courage to Resist Sin

HEZEKIAH

Remember, O Lord, how I have walked before you faithfully . . . and have done what is good in your eyes. (2 Kings 20:3)

No more excuses; the time has come for change. Such was the resolution of King Hezekiah, who wanted to stamp out the idolatry of Judah. Hezekiah boldly cleaned house. Altars, idols, and pagan temples were destroyed. Even the bronze snake Moses had made in the desert was not spared, because it had diverted people from worshiping God. The temple, the doors of which had been nailed shut by Hezekiah's own father, was cleaned out and reopened. The Passover was reinstituted as a national holiday. Revival came to Judah.

The task of reform might have seemed overwhelming to Hezekiah. Few would have blamed him if he had deferred the call for awakening to another king and another time. Yet he acted boldly, knowing that God was entrusting him with this kingly responsibility.

We may feel powerless as we consider the problems of our communities: crime, prejudice, the homeless. We may be tempted to excuse our responsibility and "let someone else do it" in light of the magnitude of the problems. We need Hezekiah's resolve if we want the kind of society we pray for to become reality. What idols need to be torn down? Look for ways you can breathe God's life-giving Word into our dying world.

Look to God for the courage to resist sin.

Hezekiah's story is told in 2 Kings 16:20–20:21; 2 Chronicles 28:27–32:33; and Isaiah 36:1–39:8.

No Regard for the Future
HEZEKIAH

"The word of the Lord you have spoken is good," Hezekiah replied. For he thought, "Will there not be peace and security in my lifetime?" (2 Kings 20:19)

The past is an important part of today's actions and tomorrow's plans. The people and kings of Judah brought sorrow and ruin upon themselves when they forgot that their God, who had cared for them in the past, also cared about the present and the future. He still demanded their continued obedience.

Although Hezekiah responded admirably to contemporary problems, he did little to ensure that his reforms would last. His foolish display of wealth to a Babylonian delegation made Judah a likely target for aggression. When Isaiah criticized Hezekiah for his lack of prudence, the king was merely relieved that any evil consequences would be delayed until after he died. The lives of three kings who followed him were deeply affected by Hezekiah's accomplishments and weaknesses.

The past affects your decisions and actions today, and these, in turn, affect the future. There are lessons to learn and errors to avoid repeating. Today, reflect on a past shortcoming and consider how the lessons you've learned will benefit you now and tomorrow.

Lean on God's wisdom to avoid repeating the same mistakes.

Hezekiah's story is told in 2 Kings 16:20–20:21; 2 Chronicles 28:27–32:33; and Isaiah 36:1–39:8.

Changing the Hardest Heart

MANASSEH

The Lord was moved by his entreaty and listened to his plea.
(2 Chronicles 33:13)

Despite being the son of godly King Hezekiah, Manasseh lived a most ungodly life. He was a confirmed idolater, and as king, he introduced sorcery, witchcraft, and the consulting of mediums to Judah. He put carved images of other gods in the temple of the Lord. He built an altar to Molech and encouraged parents to sacrifice their children there. According to tradition, it was King Manasseh who ordered that the prophet Isaiah be sawn in half!

After repeated warnings, God judged the evil king. He raised up the Assyrians, who took Manasseh into captivity in Babylon. There a surprising thing happened. Manasseh cried out humbly to God for help! Apparently his pleas were sincere, for God restored him. Upon returning to Jerusalem, Manasseh began purging every vestige of idolatry from the land and started a habit of offering sacrifices to the one true God.

The story of Manasseh's transformation should encourage us. God's grace is greater than any sin we commit. His forgiveness reaches to the lowest depths. He can change even the hardest heart. You also can find forgiveness and a fresh start by turning away from your sin and to God.

It's never too late to start obeying God.

King Manasseh's story is found in 2 Kings 21:1-18 and 2 Chronicles 32:33–33:20. He is also mentioned in Jeremiah 15:4.

A Blueprint for Action

JOSIAH

When the king heard the words of the Law, he tore his robes.
(2 Chronicles 34:19)

As a young man of twenty-six, Josiah, king of Judah, instituted a campaign to repair and refurbish the temple. During the renovation process, Hilkiah, the high priest, discovered a scroll in the temple. What books of the Law this long-lost document contained is not known. What is recorded is Josiah's response upon hearing God's law.

King Josiah tore his clothes! In the ancient Near East, this was a way of expressing deep grief or remorse. Why was Josiah so upset? Because as he heard the holy standards of God's law, he immediately realized that the nation of Judah had totally neglected God's commands.

It's important to note that Josiah didn't just feel bad and let it go at that. He immediately began making decisions, issuing directives, and taking actions in order to comply with what God expected of his people. His response was both immediate and radical.

Is that how we react when we hear God's Word preached or when we read the Scriptures for ourselves? Do we instantly seek to apply the truth to our lives? Or do we procrastinate and rationalize with thoughts like *That's true, and one of these days, I'm going to stop/start doing that*? Determine today that with God's help you will obey instantly and completely.

God didn't give us his Word to increase our knowledge but to change our lives!

Josiah's story is found in 2 Kings 21:24–23:30 and 2 Chronicles 33:25–35:26. He is also mentioned in Jeremiah 1–3.

Tearing Down the Idols

JOSIAH

[Josiah] broke down the sacred poles and the carved and the cast images. (2 Chronicles 34:4, NRSV)

Josiah had been on the throne of Judah twelve years when he began a crusade to eradicate idolatry from the land. The Scriptures tell us of the determination of the young king. He was intense. He was zealous. He was thorough. To put it bluntly, Josiah was a one-man wrecking crew! Josiah understood the ageless truth that God will have no rivals. He realized that as long as the nation of Judah flirted with false gods, they would never know the blessings of the one true God.

Christians in modern cultures often think of idolatry as quaint ancient curiosity or a superstitious practice found only among primitive peoples. Wrong! Idolatry thrives today in the most sophisticated societies on earth.

An idol is anything or anyone that comes to take the place of God in our lives. If we give our devotion and commitment and energy to a human relationship, a job, a possession, a skill, or an activity, rather than to God, we are living just as idolatrously as the pagans of old.

Ask the Spirit of God to show you anything in your life that has come between you and your heavenly Father. Then ask God for the courage to do whatever it takes to remove the obstacle.

Tear down the idols in your life, with God's help.

Josiah's story is found in 2 Kings 21:24–23:30 and 2 Chronicles 33:25–35:26. He is also mentioned in Jeremiah 1–3.

Taking a Risk for the Truth
SHAPHAN

Shaphan read from [the book] in the presence of the king.
(2 Kings 22:10)

It has always been a bit dangerous to serve kings and high officials. King Zedekiah had Jeremiah thrown into prison for predicting the fall of Jerusalem. King Nebuchadnezzar ordered that all his advisers be executed when they couldn't interpret his dream.

Shaphan, King Josiah's secretary, was given the Book of the Law that had been found in the temple while it was being repaired. For decades during the rule of evil kings, the Book of the Law had been lost. How would King Josiah react to hearing the contents of this book? It could either cost Shaphan his life or start a spiritual revival in the nation.

Delivering the truth is sometimes a risk. How will the hearers respond to what you tell them? We are commanded to "speak the truth in love" (Ephesians 4:15). The challenge is to tell the truth even when it may not please the hearers.

When Shaphan read the Book of the Law to King Josiah, the king repented and led the nation back to God. Delivering God's Word to your friends and family can change the direction of their lives for eternity.

How beautiful are the feet of those who bring good news!

Shaphan's story is told in 2 Kings 22:1-12 and 2 Chronicles 34:8-20.

Experiencing Revival

HILKIAH

I have found the Book of the Law in the temple of the Lord.
(2 Kings 22:8)

Hilkiah served as high priest under Josiah, one of the few godly kings of Judah. The young king initiated a sweeping reform of the nation's religious life. Idols and pagan temples were torn down. Eventually, Hilkiah received orders to oversee the restoration of Solomon's temple, which had fallen into disrepair.

Buried in the trash, Hilkiah found a treasure—a scroll containing the Law of God. Misplaced for years, the missing Scripture was indicative of the spiritual condition of the people. They had lost God's Word. An entire generation, including the king, was ignorant of God's commands. Josiah tore his clothing in deep concern after hearing the Scriptures.

Hilkiah experienced the privilege of guiding a revival. Under his leadership a great Passover was celebrated. This reintroduced the people to vital worship. In his lifetime he witnessed the restoration of the Law and temple to their previous place of respect.

We still find it easy today to drift from the input of God's Word and the expression of worship. The importance of the Bible and worship in our lives gives a good indication of the state of our relationship with God.

The Word is the food of spiritual life, and worship is its heartbeat.

Parallel accounts of Hilkiah's ministry are recorded in 2 Kings 22:1–23:24 and 2 Chronicles 34:1–35:19.

Preparing for the Right Moment

HULDAH

So Hilkiah and those whom the king had sent went to the prophet Huldah. (2 Chronicles 34:22, NRSV)

King Josiah was stunned when his crackdown on Judah's idolatry led to the discovery of a scroll containing the law of God. He decided to consult with a prophet because there were dreaded consequences described in the Law for those who failed to obey. Although other better-known prophets could have been consulted, Josiah turned to the prophetess Huldah. Even though his written Word had disappeared from Judah, God made sure that a person who could profess his wisdom was available at this critical time.

Huldah was the wife of the king's valet, or "keeper of the wardrobe." She confirmed the truth of the scroll: The idolatry of the people would bring painful consequences. But she added a note of grace for Josiah. His personal repentance and humble work of reformation had afforded the people extra time for peace during his reign.

This story contains the only mention of Huldah's life. She had a key opportunity to testify to God's truth, and she didn't miss it. Huldah's secret was simply quiet preparation and obedience to God's way. The most basic spiritual successes start with this formula.

Prepare yourself for the opportunities God is waiting to provide for you.

Huldah's brief appearance is recorded in 2 Kings 22:14-20 and 2 Chronicles 22:19-28.

Royal Rebel against God

JEHOIAKIM

Jehoiakim was twenty-five years old when he became king . . . but his reign was an evil one. (2 Chronicles 36:5, TLB)

Many good kings had children who refused to follow God. Perhaps they neglected the religious instruction of their offspring or delegated it to someone else. Maybe they were preoccupied with political and military affairs. But whatever the reason, faithfulness to God was clearly not hereditary!

Josiah followed God, but Jehoiakim, his son, was evil. Jehoiakim continued the lamentable tradition of royal rebelliousness against God. He killed the prophet Uriah (Jeremiah 26:20-23). While he ruled, Judah became a pawn in the power struggle between Egypt and Babylon. Jehoiakim cast his lot with Egypt against Babylon. This proved to be a crucial mistake. Nebuchadnezzar crushed Jehoiakim's rebellion and took him to Babylon. Eventually he was allowed to return to Jerusalem, where he died.

A parent who believes God's truths has no guarantee that his or her children will share those beliefs. Children require loving, intimate training. They must be taught about faith, and parents dare not leave that task for others to do. Make sure you practice, explain, and teach your faith.

Good parenting includes training our children to obey God.

Jehoiakim's reign is recorded in 2 Kings 23:34–24:6; 2 Chronicles 36:4-8; and Jeremiah 22:18-23.

Going with the Flow
JEHOIACHIN

This man [is] . . . a man who will not prosper in his lifetime.
(Jeremiah 22:30)

Although his name means "God will establish," Jehoiachin's character brought about the opposite result. God unseated Jehoiachin from the throne after three months. Jeremiah's scathing imagery captured God's disgust: "If you . . . were a signet ring on my right hand, I would still pull you off" (Jeremiah 22:24).

Jehoiachin became king when he was eighteen years old. He spent his childhood in the court of his godly grandfather Josiah. But eleven years of evil practices by his father, Jehoiakim, quickly undid the reforms of Josiah and returned Judah to idolatry. Jehoiachin simply endorsed the prevailing evil of his family.

After a three-month reign, Jehoiachin was taken prisoner by Nebuchadnezzar, king of Babylon. He spent the next thirty-seven years under arrest. At age fifty-five he was released within the Babylonian court as a pitied prisoner of war. From then on he ate at the royal table.

Family patterns can be difficult to break. But Jehoiachin had no excuses; he had the memory of Josiah and the message of God's judgment and mercy. Bad family habits that aren't replaced with good ones tend to be repeated generation after generation. Will your contribution be a benefit or a hindrance to those who follow you?

Bad habits have to be ripped out from the root.

Jehoiachin's brief reign is recorded in 2 Kings 24:6-17; 25:27-30; 2 Chronicles 36:8-10; and Jeremiah 22:24-30.

Resting in a False Security

GEDALIAH

Then Jeremiah went to Gedaliah son of Ahikam at Mizpah, and stayed with him among the people who were left in the land.
(Jeremiah 40:6, NRSV)

Power, prestige, and popularity can arrive or disappear overnight. Gedaliah, son of a court secretary, found himself appointed as the largest fish in a very small pond. His sudden rise to power was due to Babylon's defeat and destruction of Judah. Jerusalem had been torn down to its foundations. Most of the people were deported to Babylon. But a handful of people were left behind as caretakers of the land. Gedaliah was appointed as their governor.

Apparently Gedaliah felt secure as the highest officeholder in the land. Instead of seeking God's direction, he trusted in the goodwill of Judah's conquerors to keep him safe. Yet Judah's enemies remained determined to wipe out God's people. Others like Ishmael, one of the surviving military leaders, resented Gedaliah for selling out to the Babylonians. The governor was aware of these threats, but he ignored them. The oversight cost him his life.

Depending on God's protection doesn't mean that bad things can't happen to us. But his safekeeping ensures that even suffering, failures, and death will fit into God's purpose for us. Jeremiah reminded us of this truth: "For surely I know the plans I have for you, says the Lord, plans for your welfare and not for harm, to give you a future with hope" (Jeremiah 29:11, NRSV).

Before all else fails, trust and love the Lord your God.

Gedaliah's brief career is recorded in 2 Kings 25:22-26 and Jeremiah 39:11–41:10.

Minister of Thanksgiving

JEDUTHUN

Jeduthun [was] . . . chosen and expressly named to render thanks to the Lord, for his steadfast love endures forever. (1 Chronicles 16:41, NRSV)

Although David was not allowed to build the temple in Jerusalem, he organized the people who would be needed to carry on worship there. Among those chosen for special duty were a group of men designated as ministers of thanksgiving. One of them was Jeduthun.

We know practically nothing of Jeduthun's life. He had six sons who also served in the temple. Jeduthun's family apparently specialized in music with the lyre, a small harp. Jeduthun also had the gift of prophecy. His understanding of God added insight to his thanksgiving, just as his thanksgiving heightened his understanding of God.

Jeduthun participated in the great dedication of Solomon's temple. He is associated in Scripture with three psalms (39; 62; and 77) and very likely composed music for their performance. These psalms demonstrate Jeduthun's familiarity with the big questions of life and his utter dependence on God.

What comes to mind when you think about God? Awe? Praise? Thanksgiving? Contemplation? Understanding? Intimacy? Fellowship? Obedience? Humility? Ask God to show you a new aspect of his character today.

There will always be more of God to understand and appreciate.

Jeduthun is mentioned in the following places: 1 Chronicles 16:37-43; 25:1-8; and 2 Chronicles 5:11-14.

How to Accomplish Great Things

ZERUBBABEL

This is the word of the Lord to Zerubbabel: "Not by might nor by power, but by my Spirit." (Zechariah 4:6)

When the Persians conquered the Babylonians in 539 B.C., the Persian king Cyrus gave the Jews exiled in Babylon permission to return to their homeland and rebuild their temple. Zerubbabel, a descendant of King David, was the man chosen to lead these exiles back to the Promised Land.

Under Zerubbabel's leadership, the people arrived in Judah and began the task. They built homes and laid a foundation for the temple. However, the rebuilding effort ground to a halt when Zerubbabel and his workers faced stern opposition from without and discouraging criticism from within. For sixteen years, the Jews looked daily at that desolate foundation, a constant reminder of their failure to finish the task assigned by God. It took the prophets Haggai, Zechariah, and Malachi to come along and challenge the people to complete the task. In a mere four years, the project was complete.

Why did Zerubbabel fail? Perhaps because he was easily discouraged. Or maybe because he was relying on his own strength and ability to get the job done. Rather than trusting in our own power, we need to remember the word of the prophet Zechariah to Zerubbabel: It is by the Spirit of the living God that we accomplish big and lasting things. Whatever you are doing today, draw on God's power.

We need the power of the Holy Spirit to do great things for God.

The story of Zerubbabel is found in Ezra 2:2–5:2.

Relying on the Word of God

ZECHARIAH THE PROPHET

Zechariah . . . prophesied to the Jews of Judah and Jerusalem in the name of the God of Israel. (Ezra 5:1)

The best way to judge preaching is not by how eloquent or clever the words sound, but by whose words they are. Are they God's?

Zechariah (together with Haggai) prophesied during the period of time when the Jews of Jerusalem were trying to rebuild their city. Catcalls from the neighbors had slowed the people down, so Zechariah's message was clear and forceful: Keep building! It's what God wants! You can do it! Too determined to let a little opposition spoil the Jews' resolve to finish what God had called them to do, Zechariah encouraged and helped the people. It made a big difference, too. The people listened to the words and were stirred to take action.

Common sense and experience-based wisdom have their place, but there's no substitute for the Word of God. Put another way, sometimes we get discouraged unnecessarily. We hear bad news, or face a setback, or think that all is lost, and we want to give up. We want to quit. We feel hopeless.

A good friend offers a reminder: God is still alive. His ways are going to prevail. Nothing is impossible with God. Don't let your friends lose sight of the hope we have in our eternal, all-powerful, loving God.

Encourage and help the discouraged.

Zechariah's story is told in Ezra 5–6 and in the Old Testament book bearing his name.

Growing in God's Word

EZRA

For Ezra had devoted himself to the study and observance of the Law of the Lord, and to teaching its decrees and laws in Israel. (Ezra 7:10)

The most effective leaders in the Bible likely had little awareness of the impact their lives had on others. They were too busy obeying God to keep track of their successes. Ezra fits that description.

About eighty years after the rebuilding of the temple under Zerubbabel, Ezra returned to Judah. He was given a letter from Artaxerxes, instructing him to carry out a program of religious education. As part of his prestigious assignment, Ezra pioneered the last spiritual awakening in the Old Testament. He may have even authored 1 and 2 Chronicles.

Ezra's accomplishments can be attributed to his diligent obedience to God's Word. He studied it seriously and applied it faithfully. Ezra affirms for us that personal achievement should be secondary to a personal commitment to live for God. Your growing relationship with God is always more profitable for you and your family than any pay raise, promotion, or position in social standing. What does your lifestyle reveal about your priorities? What changes could you incorporate, beginning today, to guard your time alone with God?

Our greatest accomplishment is a growing relationship with God.

Ezra's story is told in Ezra 7:1–10:16 and Nehemiah 8:1–12:36.

Protecting His Turf

SANBALLAT

Sanballat . . . [was] very angry that anyone was interested in helping Israel. (Nehemiah 2:10, TLB)

Sanballat opposed Nehemiah's efforts to rebuild the walls of Jerusalem. His opposition may have been provoked by racial hatred, greed, or jealousy. Whatever his motives, he was intent on stopping Nehemiah.

Sanballat and his friends ridiculed Nehemiah and his plan. He questioned Nehemiah's authority and motives. As the restoration work continued, he threatened them and tried to lure Nehemiah into a situation where his character would be discredited.

Before you write off Sanballat as an all-time bad guy, is there any "Sanballat attitude" in you? How do you respond when a new worker is assigned to your "turf" on your job or responsibilities? Do you welcome the new person with his or her new ideas and enthusiasm, or do you resent his or her presence as a threat to you?

Welcoming and supporting a new leader assaults our pride. Even the strongest Christians can feel the temptation to talk negatively and wish for the new leader's failure. If pleasing God is our overriding desire, we don't have to worry about who gets the credit for a job well done. We can be pleased to be a part of God's work—even if someone else plays a bigger role.

He who humbles himself will be exalted, and he who exalts himself will be humbled.

Sanballat's story is told in Nehemiah 2; 4; and 6.

An Unholy Alliance

GESHEM

I am doing a great work and I cannot come down. Why should the work stop while I leave it to come down to you? (Nehemiah 6:3, NRSV)

Nehemiah faced a huge logistical problem in rebuilding the walls of Jerusalem. But that wasn't his greatest concern. Three men were determined to keep Nehemiah from rebuilding the demolished walls. They were Sanballat and Tobiah, two local leaders, and Geshem, an Arab with clout. These men are remembered in Scripture principally for their evil motives and unsavory tactics: intimidation, threats of physical attack, and ridicule.

Whenever we set out to follow God's directions, we can expect to run into the same reactions Nehemiah faced. The names and situations will change, but God's opponents always share the same objective: to keep us from doing what God wants us to do.

We need to remember how Nehemiah countered his opposition: He prayed, planned, and kept on working. Even the threat of death did not keep him from carrying out what he knew God wanted him to do. How often do we give up before much weaker opposition? Rely on God's resources as you plan your defense against the enemy's opposition.

We set ourselves up for defeat when we try to face problems without prayer.

Geshem, Sanballat, and Tobiah's infamous deeds are recorded in Nehemiah 2:17–6:14.

A Life of Prayer
NEHEMIAH

Let your ear be attentive and your eyes open to hear the prayer your servant is praying before you day and night. (Nehemiah 1:6)

In 445 B.C. Nehemiah led a group of Jewish exiles from Persia back to Jerusalem for the purpose of rebuilding the city's broken-down walls. Despite strong opposition from without and extreme discouragement from within, the Jews accomplished this monumental task in only fifty-two days! What was Nehemiah's secret? How was he able to get such a disorganized, disillusioned bunch of people to accomplish such a remarkable feat?

Some cite his leadership and organizational skills. Others laud his ability to motivate. But perhaps the real key is found in Nehemiah's prayer life. The story of Nehemiah reveals a man who was intimate with God and highly dependent on his Creator.

When discouraged and depressed, he prayed (1:4-11). When under attack, he prayed (4:4-5, 9). When weak and powerless, he prayed (6:9). When happy, he spent time thanking and praising God (chapter 12). Even in the midst of his busy schedule, he carried on a running conversation with God (2:4).

What about you? Is prayer a regular part of your daily life? Do you rely on God during hard times? Do you regularly thank and praise him for his blessings? Spend some time today thinking about Nehemiah, and let his example motivate you to a life of power . . . through prayer.

The secret to a life full of power is a life full of prayer.

Nehemiah's story is found in the book that bears his name.

Taking the Wisest Course of Action

NEHEMIAH

But we prayed to our God and posted a guard day and night to meet this threat. (Nehemiah 4:9)

From the start Nehemiah's effort to rebuild the walls of Jerusalem met with opposition. His enemies were Sanballat the Horonite, Tobiah the Ammonite, and Geshem the Arab. These men tried everything to slow down or stop the work. They mocked Nehemiah and his builders. They accused the Jews of treason. They even threatened physical violence.

Nehemiah met each verbal attack with patience and prayer. Then, when he heard rumors of an impending military attack, Nehemiah not only prayed, but he prepared for action—posting guards and arming his workers. Often workers finished their tasks with one hand while holding a weapon in the other.

Nehemiah's response is a great example for us. Prayer should be the first thing we do when facing trouble; however, it is not the only action required of us. God expects us to do what we can. We must use common sense. We must do whatever we can do, trusting God all the while.

Are you facing a difficult situation in your life? By all means, pray! Then study the situation and consider what steps you can take to alleviate the problem. The Christian life is a joint venture. God works in us; yet, at the same time, we are expected to work out our own salvation (Philippians 2:12-13). Grasping this truth is crucial if we are to find success in walking with God.

When facing trouble, trust God and take the wisest course of action.

Nehemiah's story is found in the book that bears his name.

The Center of His Universe

AHASUERUS

Any man or woman who approaches the king . . . without being summoned the king has but one law; that he be put to death.
(Esther 4:11)

History's examples of human greatness seldom mirror God's definition. King Ahasuerus, also known as Xerxes the Great, may have ruled Persia in his day, but he was a minor figure in God's estimation. We know this to be true in part from the way he treated people.

Like many leaders of his time, Ahasuerus indulged his desires for women. As king, he simply drafted them into his harem. Sometimes they were gifts that sealed political treaties. Ahasuerus's treatment of women reveals the king's problem with royal self-centeredness. Most of us do not have the means to get all we want, but a king is able to spoil himself royally. Ahasuerus saw women, men, and even nations almost entirely as things to be used or discarded depending on how they pleased him. At one point he casually approved a plan to annihilate the Jewish people. Devaluing persons was part of his daily routine.

Whether or not we have the means to gratify our every whim, we can be just as self-centered as Ahasuerus. The way we treat others serves as a measurement. As you meet and work with people today, ask yourself how important they are apart from what they can do for you.

We reveal our self-centeredness by the way we treat others.

Ahasuerus appears throughout the book of Esther and is mentioned in Ezra 4:6.

A Part of God's Plan

VASHTI

But when the attendants delivered the king's command, Queen Vashti refused to come. (Esther 1:12)

Vashti lost her position as queen of Persia when she refused King Xerxes's command to display her beauty at a party for the king's guests. Her clash with the king gave opportunity for Esther to become queen.

While Vashti's strength of character earns our admiration, we also see God's sovereign hand at work in her situation, for Esther's resulting "promotion" enabled her to save her people, the Jews, from being massacred.

God works in the events of human history so that his will may be done, even in government. God had prepared Esther "for such a time as this" (Esther 4:14).

Can you see God at work for good even when you suffer for doing what is right? Resist the temptation to feel sorry for yourself. God may be using your circumstances for a purpose. Although you may not see the results immediately, you can be confident that God is at work for the best.

God's purpose transcends every king's decision.

Vashti's story is told in Esther 1:1–2:17.

Faith and True Security

ESTHER

I will go to the king, even though it is against the law. And if I perish, I perish. (Esther 4:16)

We treasure security, even though we know that security in this life carries no guarantees—possessions can be destroyed, beauty fades, relationships can be broken, death is inevitable. Real security, then, must rest on God and his unchanging nature.

Even though Esther had won King Xerxes's heart, she risked her life by attempting to see the king when he had not requested her presence. There was no guarantee that the king would even see her. Although she was queen, she still was not secure. But, cautiously and courageously, Esther decided to risk her position of honor, wealth, and prestige by approaching the king on behalf of her people. On the chosen day she went before him, and he asked her to come forward and speak. Esther's risk confirmed that God was the source of her security.

How much of your security rests on your possessions, position, or reputation? God does not intend for you to use such gifts for your own benefit. He asks you to serve him. Like Esther, you may risk your security to please God, but such risks will detach you from the false hope this world offers. Today, think of practical ways you can rely more firmly on the security only God can offer.

Serving God often demands that we risk our security.

Esther's story is told in the book of Esther.

Not Just a Coincidence

ESTHER

And who knows but that you have come to royal position for such a time as this? (Esther 4:14)

What others may call coincidence is known to wise believers as Providence. Esther could have rationalized her unique position in the palace as simply "happenstance" or "a roll of the dice." In fact, it seems she was initially tempted to downplay her role altogether: "I'm not the one to help the Jews. I don't have a chance." Her cousin and adviser, Mordecai, replied by reminding her of her particular place in the larger picture of God's plan. She realized that God had given her beauty, her nationality, her relatives, and her influence in the palace as crucial elements to be used in his service.

Have you considered lately that your neighbors, your career, and your fellow employees figure into God's design for your life? Are you aware of your untapped resources, past experiences, and personal contacts that could be used for God's purposes? Nothing about you is a coincidence—in fact, everything about you is vitally useful for accomplishing God's work. Set aside time this week to take stock of the potential assets you have yet to use in service to God.

What others see as coincidence, faith knows as Providence.

Read about Esther in the book named after her.

Working for the Good of His People

MORDECAI

He worked for the good of his people and spoke up for the welfare of all the Jews. (Esther 10:3)

The book of Esther reads like a great suspense novel. A foolish king. A beautiful young woman and her devoted relative. A power-hungry government official. A devious decree that causes thousands of lives to hang in the balance. An impossible plan. A plot twist. The demise of the bad guy. But don't get so caught up in the thrills and chills that you miss the lesson from the life of Mordecai.

Simply put, Mordecai was a positive influence everywhere he went. Even though Esther was only his cousin, Mordecai essentially adopted her and raised her as his own daughter. Later he was instrumental in helping his God-fearing Jewish "daughter" become the new queen of Persia. Once he helped thwart an assassination plot he overheard being planned at the city gate. Then, when the wicked Haman was exposed and executed, Mordecai became prime minister in his place. The Scriptures record that Mordecai spent the balance of his life "working for the good of his people" and speaking up for their welfare.

Do you approach life with that same determination? Is it your goal to make a positive difference in the lives of the people God has placed in your life? Do you use your position, your power, your possessions, and your "pull" to help others? You can make a huge difference today with a simple phone call, note of encouragement, or letter of protest. Will you exert an influence today?

Exert a godly influence wherever God has placed you.

The story of Mordecai can be read in the book of Esther.

Pride and Destruction

HAMAN

When Haman saw that Mordecai would not kneel down or pay him honor, he was enraged. (Esther 3:5)

The most arrogant people are often those who must measure their self-worth by the power or influence they have over others. Haman was an extremely arrogant leader. He hated all Jews because of their longstanding enmity with his own people. So when Mordecai refused to bow in submission to him, Haman wanted to destroy him. Mordecai's dedication to God and his refusal to pay homage to any man challenged Haman's self-centered religion. He became consumed with plotting Mordecai's arrest. But like others who opposed God, Haman's scheme led to his own downfall.

Our initial response to the story about Haman is to say that he got what he deserved. But the Bible leads us to ask deeper questions: Do I share some of Haman's traits? Do I desire to control others? Am I threatened when others don't appreciate me as I think they should? Do I want revenge when my pride is attacked? Haman's treachery should remind us that power corrupts. Christians are not exempt from its temptations. Ask God to create in you an attitude of mercy and humility.

God will exalt those who humble themselves.

Haman's story is told in the book of Esther.

What Hard Times Can Teach Us

JOB

Shall we accept good from God, and not trouble? (Job 2:10)

Calamity can ambush us. Life is going well until a phone call or letter or knock at the door suddenly turns our world upside down.

That's what happened to Job. He was a family man, a successful businessman, and a devoted follower of God. Then the roof caved in—figuratively and literally. In short order he lost his children, his wealth, and his health. It's hard enough to understand why terrible things happen; it's even more difficult to comprehend why bad things happen to good people.

Both the Scriptures and our experience tell us that trials can stem from several sources. We may suffer because of our own sinful actions. Or our difficulties may be due to the wrong choices of others. And sometimes, like Job, we undergo inexplicable natural disasters.

Suffering is never pleasant—even when we understand its causes. But even in the darkest night of the soul we can reap positive benefits from our pain. Hard times remind us of our frailty and need for God. Hard times can build character if we respond with trust and obedience. Finally, hard times can teach us how to comfort others faced with similar problems. God will uphold and reward all his children who endure suffering patiently and faithfully.

Suffering can work for our benefit and God's glory.

In addition to the book that bears his name, Job is mentioned in Ezekiel 14:14, 20 and James 5:11.

Being There

JOB

I have heard many things like these; miserable comforters are you all!
(Job 16:2)

When disaster fell upon Job, his friends Eliphaz, Bildad, and Zophar did what any friends would do. They dropped everything and came to sympathize with their devastated companion. For a solid week they said nothing. They simply made Job aware of their presence, weeping with him and suffering silently with him. But when Job began to question God and express the deep grief inside him, they forgot all about comforting and turned to correcting.

"Maybe you're in sin, Job," they speculated. "Your understanding of God is all wrong," they lectured. The more the accusations flew, the more heated the discussion became. Instead of sympathy, sarcasm flourished. And in the place of tenderness grew hot tempers. Even when God speaks at the end of the book, Job never gets the answers he is looking for.

But here's what we can learn from the book of Job about helping those who hurt: More than a Bible verse or a platitude or a Christian book or a sermon tape, those who are grieving need arms to hug them, ears to listen to them, shoulders to cry on, and hands to help them. Talking is not as important as simply being available. Even small acts of support can be a great comfort to those suffering loss.

Those who are hurting need your love, not your sermons.

Job's story is found in the book that bears his name; he is also mentioned in Ezekiel 14:14, 20 and James 5:11.

God Is in Control
JOB

The Lord said to Satan, "Very well, then, he is in your hands; but you must spare his life." (Job 2:6)

The opening chapters of the book of Job reveal much about the person and work of Satan. He is depicted as a real being. He has access to the Lord. He roams the earth. He has specific knowledge of those who love God. He questions the motives of God's servants and accuses them. He is given permission (within certain boundaries) to afflict the followers of God. He is ready, willing, and eager to cause suffering and grief.

Since Job never mentions Satan, it is possible that he was unaware of the devilish source of his suffering. Christians today, however, have the completed Scriptures. We know that Satan is real, and it is obvious that he would like nothing better than to wreck our lives. How are we to respond?

We can take comfort in the fact that God is in control. He defeated Satan at the cross and will soon crush him under our feet (Romans 16:20). So put on the armor of God daily (Ephesians 6) and be on the alert for the schemes of Satan. Also, realize that Satan uses sneak attacks much more often than full frontal assaults!

Satan is limited by the power of God and the faith of his saints.

You can read more about Job and the difficulties he faced in the book that bears his name as well as in Ezekiel 14:14, 20 and James 5:11.

Missing the Point

JOB'S WIFE

Curse God and die! (Job 2:9)

Job's wife suffered almost as much as Job did. Except for her health, she too lost everything—home, family, possessions. Her attitude and response exactly matched the one Satan had set out to evoke from Job—cursing God. How ironic that Satan achieved his goal in Job's sole surviving companion and not in Job himself.

Did Job's wife realize that she had surrendered to Satan's manipulative scheme? Did she feel her loss so greatly that she didn't care that she was wrong? Or did she respond to her calamity merely in a fit of emotion, which later passed, taking her bitterness with it? We don't know the answer to any of those questions. All we know is that she responded just as most people would have under the circumstances—she got angry at God and insisted that Job do the same. Most normal, commonsense people would have responded that way. Most people would have suggested the same thing. Most people would have done exactly as she did—missing the point, just as Job told her.

Every time we suffer, we also undergo a test of faith. Is God really in control? Is there any reason for this? Does any of this make any sense? If we let emotion take over, as Job's wife did, then we will indeed curse God. And we'll be just like her: bitter, angry, wrong.

Suffering tests our faith in God.

The story of Job's wife is told in Job 1:1–2:10.

Friendly Advice Worth Forgetting
ELIPHAZ, BILDAD, AND ZOPHAR

They set out from their homes . . . to go and sympathize with [Job] and comfort him. (Job 2:11)

Few people in history have experienced the kind of tragedy that crushed Job. He lost everything. His children were killed, his possessions and wealth were taken, his wife turned her back on him, and his health was broken, all in a matter of days.

Upon learning of Job's difficulties, his friends Eliphaz, Bildad, and Zophar came to comfort him. Shocked by Job's appearance, they wept for him and sat in silence for seven days.

Why did his friends remain silent for so long? One ancient Jewish tradition teaches that people who come to comfort someone in mourning should not speak until the mourner speaks. Job's friends were either demonstrating wisdom or were simply too stunned to speak.

The problem came when they opened their mouths. The more they tried to explain Job's suffering, the less they helped. God didn't want these men offering their well-meaning but misguided advice. God himself never answered Job's questions but instead challenged Job to trust, even beyond understanding.

Do you have a hurting friend? Avoid the mistake of Job's friends and resist the temptation to explain the suffering, to put a theological spin on it, to demonstrate the logic of it. Simply sit there. Show affection. Weep with those who weep.

Those who suffer need comfort, not explanations.

The story of Job's friends is told in the Old Testament book of Job.

Planting the Seeds

ISAIAH

And I said, "Here am I. Send me!" (Isaiah 6:8)

Trees and prophets share at least one important characteristic—both are planted for the future. Yet seedlings are often overlooked and prophets often ignored. Isaiah belonged in the latter category. Had they listened, the people of Judah could have saved themselves from the misery to come. Instead, they refused to believe him. Kings ignored his warnings, and the government accused him of treason because he disapproved of many national policies.

When he called Isaiah as a prophet, God did not encourage him with predictions of great success. In fact, God told Isaiah that the people would not listen. But he was to speak his messages anyway because eventually some *would* listen. God compared his people to a tree that would have to be cut down so that a new tree could grow from the old roots.

We who are part of that future can see that many of the promises God gave through Isaiah have been fulfilled in Jesus Christ. We also gain the hope of knowing that God is active in all of history, including our own. Therefore, be mindful of God's timetable as you patiently watch and pray.

Mighty works can grow through the seedlings of prayer and obedience.

Isaiah's story is told in 2 Kings 19:2–20:19.

A Life-Changing Experience

ISAIAH

I saw the Lord seated on a throne, high and exalted, and the train of his robe filled the temple. (Isaiah 6:1)

Certain experiences have the capacity to alter our entire life. Those who have had a brush with death, such as a close call in a traffic accident, often resolve to live with renewed appreciation and vigor. Isaiah's encounter with God, gloriously exalted in his temple, was such a life-changing experience. His message would flow from the vision that affected him so profoundly.

The book of Isaiah is a message of contrasts. The prophet's remarks were sometimes comforting, sometimes confronting. He feverishly details God's abandonment of Israel in one paragraph and lovingly consoles God's people in the next—all within the same passage.

Isaiah's intent was to point us to the only one capable of exercising perfect justice and perfect mercy—God himself. Sin separates us from God and brings us pain and suffering. But if we confess our sin and repent, God willingly forgives us. If your heart is heavy with sin you have yet to confess, a joyful reunion awaits you if you will ask God's forgiveness and return to him.

God alone is perfectly just and loving.

Read about Isaiah's encounter with God in Isaiah 6. His life story is told in 2 Kings 19:2–20:19.

The Prophet Who Endured

JEREMIAH

For I, the Lord, will be with you and see you through. (Jeremiah 1:8, TLB)

Endurance is a rare quality. Many people lack the long-term commitment, caring, and willingness that are vital to sticking with a task against all odds. But Jeremiah was a prophet who endured.

Jeremiah had to depend on God's love as he developed endurance. His audiences were usually antagonistic or apathetic to his messages. He was both ignored and hated. His life was often threatened. He saw both the excitement of a spiritual awakening and the sorrow of a national return to idolatry. With the exception of King Josiah, king after king ignored Jeremiah's warnings and led the people away from God. He saw fellow prophets murdered. He himself was severely persecuted. Finally, he watched Judah's defeat at the hands of the Babylonians.

Most people have felt like giving up at one time or another: in a relationship; during an overwhelming chore at home, school, or work; or during a persistent illness. But like Jeremiah, we are called to endurance, not despair. Instead of focusing your thoughts, prayers, and energy on getting out of a problem, draw on God's resources to get through it. God's love enabled Jeremiah to bear the worst humiliations; it can see you through your problems, too. Make endurance your theme throughout the trials of today.

God may not keep you from difficult circumstances, but his promise is to see you through them.

Jeremiah's story is told in the book of Jeremiah.

Sharing in the Suffering
JEREMIAH

Since my people are crushed, I am crushed. (Jeremiah 8:21)

World tragedy is painful to observe. However, by the time it reaches us, through a glance at a headline or a flip through the channels, it has lost much of its sting. Not so for Jeremiah. He lived in the midst of Israel's tragedies and received from God himself a revelation about the dreadful future awaiting his people. He was so deeply sorrowful for the fallen condition of Israel that he was known as the "weeping prophet."

Jeremiah's book is an emotional chronicle of a prophet who saw his nation beset by sin and cut off from God. Jeremiah was angered by the sinfulness of the people of Judah, but he had compassion for them, too. He realized that he was set apart from them by his work for God, but he still considered himself one of them. Anguish consumed the prophet as he anticipated the misery of his people, who would be dragged off to captivity.

We watch that same world still dying in sin, still rejecting God. But how often is our heart broken for our lost friends and neighbors or our lost world? Only when we have Jeremiah's kind of concern will we be moved to help. We must begin by asking God to break our hearts for the world he loves.

A heart beating with compassion begins as a heart broken by human need.

Jeremiah's story is told in the book named after him.

Sweet-Sounding Lies

HANANIAH

The Lord has not sent you, and you made this people trust in a lie.
(Jeremiah 28:15, NRSV)

False prophets draw a crowd because they tell people what they
want to hear. God's prophets unswervingly speak the truth. Hananiah, a false prophet, consoled his countrymen with sweet-sounding lies. In contrast, Jeremiah had long warned that punishment
for the sins of the nation was coming in the form of a conqueror.
Now he urged the nation to prepare for its fate.

Hananiah was sure he had a better idea. Perhaps he thought he
could change God's mind by announcing publicly a "better" plan
to save Judah. Surely God wouldn't pass up the opportunity to
endorse a last-minute, stunning defeat of the Babylonians. So
Hananiah contradicted Jeremiah's prophecy of humiliation and
broke the yoke Jeremiah had been wearing. Jeremiah responded by
reminding Hananiah what happened to false prophets. Within a
year, Hananiah was dead.

The temptation to place God in a compromising situation can
be powerful. Because we have good intentions, we sometimes
assume that God will bless our plans. We know from experience,
however, that God does not always behave the way we want. God is
not bound by our plans or by our limited understanding. He gives
us specific promises in his Word, but he also wants us to humbly
rely on his goodness to supply our needs.

Trust your plans to God's timing and wisdom.

The rise and fall of Hananiah are recorded in Jeremiah 28.

Faithful Scribe

BARUCH

While Jeremiah dictated all the words the Lord had spoken to him, Baruch wrote them on the scroll. (Jeremiah 36:4)

Baruch was one of those unsung biblical heroes—the secretaries. Through their hands and pens, inspiration became Scripture. It is clear that those whom God inspired by his Spirit frequently dictated to someone else what God moved them to communicate.

Not only did Baruch take dictation from Jeremiah, he also acted as the prophet's spokesperson. As such, he put his own life in danger. The insults, threats, and abuse which were heaped on Jeremiah spilled over onto Baruch. Chapter 45 of Jeremiah records a special memo to Baruch from God. Apparently Baruch had been feeling sorry for himself. His future seemed in doubt. He was equally at risk for being Jeremiah's secretary and for being a citizen of Israel if Jeremiah's prophecies came true. God's word to Baruch was very direct: "You're in safe hands with me" (Jeremiah 45:5).

Uncertainties in the world around us are frequently distressing. That is why certainties are important. There will be times, maybe even today, when you will not be able to trust what you see, hear, or feel. Remember God's memo to Baruch, and trust only what you know.

Remember in the storm what God told you during the calm.

Baruch's life and ministry are outlined in Jeremiah 36:1-32; 43:1-7; and 45:1-5.

Our Responsibility to Others

EZEKIEL

Go now to your countrymen in exile and speak to them. Say to them, "This is what the Sovereign Lord says," whether they listen or fail to listen. (Ezekiel 3:11)

During Israel's exile in Babylon, God called Ezekiel to be his prophet. God described Ezekiel as a watchman on the walls of the city, which was a fitting metaphor of his ministry. A watchman's job required unceasing vigilance. If he failed at his post, he and the entire city might be destroyed.

As a spiritual watchman, Ezekiel warned the people of coming judgment. If the people in Judah continued in their sins, they and their land and cities would be swallowed up by Nebuchadnezzar's armies. If they turned to God, however, they would be spared. God would hold Ezekiel responsible for his fellow Jews if he failed to warn them of the consequences of their sins.

Every man and woman is responsible to God, but believers often have a responsibility to warn others of the consequences of wrong living. If we are faithful, we may lead others to repentance and a restored relationship with God. This should motivate us to begin sharing our faith with others—by both word and deed—and to stop living callous, unconcerned lives. Are you ready today to keep watch?

Being entrusted with the Good News brings responsibilities.

Ezekiel's story is told in the book of Ezekiel.

Fit for God's Service

DANIEL

Daniel resolved not to defile himself with the royal food and wine.
(Daniel 1:8)

Best known for surviving the lions' den, Daniel was a remarkable young adult whose faith gave him unusual composure and personal discipline. He was the type of kid who would order a tossed salad in a fast-food hamburger joint, or close his eyes when R-rated violence flashed across the movie screen—a rare person with a gifted mind and a firm heart for God.

Daniel was also something of a scientist. His approach to the chief nutritionist in Babylon took the form of observation and experimentation (Daniel 1:8-15). Daniel proved his point not by sophistry or debate, but by simple evidence.

Daniel lived faithfully in an environment opposed to faith. Do people ridicule your Christian faith? Daniel felt it just as much. Yet he won respect and never flinched from his duty to obey God first and foremost. Daniel's obedience in a hostile situation began with his diet, extended through his education, and finished with his constant practice of prayer.

If you wonder where to start witnessing for God, follow Daniel's example.

Honor God by living faithfully in an environment opposed to faith.

Daniel's story is told in the book of Daniel. He is also mentioned in Matthew 24:15.

Trusting in God's Goodness

DANIEL

When Daniel was lifted from the den, no wound was found on him, because he had trusted in his God. (Daniel 6:23)

Most living lions seen by people today are the passive types restrained by cages in zoological parks. Babylon had its cage, too, and in the scariest experience of his life, Daniel was condemned to enter it. He did so with a prayer. God kept the lions at bay, and Daniel was freed the next morning.

Sometimes Christians do not get the rescue Daniel received. Cancer strikes with fatal results. A car accident claims a life. Prayers for healing or safety do not get the result we would like. Is the difference a measure of Daniel's faith and ours?

No. God hears prayers from even mustard-seed-size faith. Throughout the Bible we see that God grants mercy, but people still die. Tragedy and deliverance are both common themes. Daniel could not have presumed that his prayers or his faith obligated God to rescue him. Rather, whether hurt or spared, Daniel would trust in God's goodness every moment of his desperate night, just as he had trusted God every other night. In life or death, his savior was the Lord God.

When frightened or threatened, pray; then trust in God and in his goodness.

Our only comfort in life and in death is our faithful Savior, Jesus Christ.

Daniel's story is told in the book of Daniel. He is also mentioned in Matthew 24:15.

Refusing to Bow Down

SHADRACH, MESHACH, AND ABEDNEGO

We will not serve your gods or worship the image of gold you have set up. (Daniel 3:18)

As young men, Hananiah, Mishael, and Azariah were deported to Babylon. Given new names (Shadrach, Meshach, and Abednego, respectively), they were ordered to forsake their Hebrew heritage and faith in the God of Israel. But they refused to compromise.

When Nebuchadnezzar erected a statue of himself for his subjects to worship, the Hebrew trio staunchly refused to bow. They trusted God to save them from a royal sentence of death by fire, and they assured the king that even if God did not spare their lives, they still would not cave in.

This was a bold stand. Not only did the men have faith in a big God, but they drew strength from each other. As most students of the Bible know, God not only spared them from death in the fiery furnace but went through the experience with them!

When you are faced with a situation in which holding to your convictions may result in unpleasant consequences, how do you respond? Do you back down? Or do you stand up and stand firm? For extra strength to fight the temptation to compromise, find one or two committed Christian friends who can hold you accountable and encourage you to continue to do what is right.

A person of conviction refuses to compromise—regardless of the consequences.

The story of Shadrach, Meshach, and Abednego is found in the book of Daniel.

Humbled by God

NEBUCHADNEZZAR

Now I, Nebuchadnezzar, praise and glorify and honor the King of Heaven. (Daniel 4:37, TLB)

Nebuchadnezzar was the Babylonian king who subdued and took captive the people of Judah. As the ruler of a vast empire and the most powerful army on earth, Nebuchadnezzar was an arrogant man. Success has a way of doing that—too much of it can go to our heads and make us think we're more important than we really are.

Nebuchadnezzar's pride reached its zenith when he fancied himself to be a god. He had a ninety-foot-tall statue of himself created and ordered all of Babylon to worship it. When the Hebrew exiles Shadrach, Meshach, and Abednego refused to bow to this idol, Nebuchadnezzar had them thrown into a fiery furnace. Even when they came out of the blaze unharmed, Nebuchadnezzar realized only dimly that his greatness was a sham. Still, his pride remained.

Since he wouldn't humble himself, God humbled him. He caused Nebuchadnezzar to be insane for seven years, during which time he literally grazed like a cow on the palace lawn! At the end of that time, Nebuchadnezzar looked up to God and acknowledged his kingship over the universe. Then, and only then, was his health restored.

Learn from Nebuchadnezzar's mistakes! Beware of self-sufficiency. Don't take credit for the things God has done for you!

Proud people can either humble themselves or be humbled by God.

The story of Nebuchadnezzar is found in 2 Kings 24–25; 2 Chronicles 36; Jeremiah 21–52; and Daniel 1–4.

Weighed and Found Wanting

BELSHAZZAR

And you, his successor, O Belshazzar—you knew all this, yet you have not been humble. (Daniel 5:22, TLB)

Belshazzar was a man accustomed to pleasure. Living in a sumptuous palace that flowed with food and drink and teemed with concubines, he was used to getting whatever he wanted, whenever he wanted. So when he recalled the cups that had been taken from the temple in Jerusalem, he demanded that they be brought to his banquet so that he and his followers could drink to their idols.

Suddenly Belshazzar was confronted with a force he could not control: a hand writing strange words on the wall. After much anguish, he found Daniel, who interpreted the writing as a message of judgment. The prophet told the king that his empire would be torn apart and his life taken—all because he dishonored God and refused to humble himself. That very night, Belshazzar was assassinated.

Sooner or later, we will all come to the realization that terrified Belshazzar: We are powerless to control our own destiny. But will we shrink back as he did, reflecting on a life lived for self-gratification, or will we humbly turn to God and ask him to lead the way? Don't be lulled into a false sense of security because of your power, wealth, or status—give thanks to the God who shapes your destiny and lights your path!

In all your ways acknowledge God.

Belshazzar's tragic end is recorded in Daniel 5.

Extraordinary Obedience

HOSEA

I will take you for my wife in faithfulness; and you shall know the Lord. (Hosea 2:20, NRSV)

God told Hosea to marry a prostitute as a vivid illustration of God's love for a consistently unfaithful Israel. Hosea chose Gomer.

Hosea and Gomer had three children, though, because of her unfaithfulness, the children may not have been his. Later Gomer apparently did return to prostitution, for God now gave Hosea a different command: He was to love this woman who had deserted him. Her behavior had landed her in trouble, and Hosea had to purchase her freedom.

God often required extraordinary obedience from his prophets. God may ask you to do something difficult and extraordinary, too. If he does, how will you respond? Will you obey him, trusting that he who knows everything has a special purpose for his request?

God longs for us to be faithful to him.

Hosea tells his own story in the Old Testament book named after him.

Love without Conditions

GOMER

So Hosea married Gomer, daughter of Diblaim, and she conceived and bore him a son. (Hosea 1:3, TLB)

Hosea knew ahead of time that his wife, Gomer, would be unfaithful and that their married life would parallel God's relationship with the wayward nation of Israel. However, Gomer didn't have this insider's perspective. So what did she think and feel? What was her reaction when a holy man plucked her out of a life of prostitution and made her his wife?

She wasted no time in testing the limits of Hosea's love. She bore three children, but perhaps she couldn't say with certainty that they were his. During her infidelity, she apparently either sold herself into slavery or became another man's mistress in order to survive. But Hosea bought her back from her enslavement. Did this second chance mean anything to Gomer? We don't know. She must have been surprised by Hosea's relentless love for someone with her track record.

Probably the closest we come to feeling what Gomer felt are those times when we act unfaithfully toward God. Yet he continues to faithfully lavish his love on us. We know Gomer better than we might think, for she was what we are—sinners offered overwhelming grace! In what ways does this extravagant love and grace affect the way you look at yourself?

God does not love us because we are worthy, but in spite of our unworthiness.

Gomer's relationship with Hosea is found in Hosea 1–3.

The Proud Brought Low

OBADIAH

"Though you soar as high as eagles, and build your nest among the stars, I will bring you plummeting down," says the Lord. (Obadiah 4, TLB)

Obadiah was a Judean prophet and possibly a contemporary of Elijah. He possibly preached a message of judgment to the nation of Edom. Specifically, the Edomites were doomed to destruction for mistreating Judah, their northern neighbor.

What made Edom's actions even more reprehensible was the fact that the Edomites and Israelites weren't just neighbors; they were related! The fathers of Edom and Judah were Esau and Jacob, respectively. The countries should have been on friendly terms. Edom, however, constantly took advantage of Judah. When other nations attacked Judah, Edom either sided with the enemy or ignored pleas for help. Worse still, the Edomites would at times loot the Judean countryside.

And so God gave Obadiah a short but stern message for Edom. "You are proud, Edom. You think you are invincible. But be assured: I am going to bring you down, and lift Israel up." In 185 B.C., it happened. By the first century A.D., Edom had vanished from the map!

God humbles proud and wicked people. Hostility to him—or his people—will never go unpunished! If you are being mistreated because of your faith, remember that God sees your situation, and he will have the last word.

God brings low those who harm his people.

Obadiah's words are found in the Old Testament book that bears his name.

God's Patience with His Children
JONAH

Jonah ran away from the Lord and headed for Tarshish. (Jonah 1:3)

Few Old Testament personalities are as transparent as the prophet Jonah. We can see right through him. And most of what we see we don't like. He reminds us too much of ourselves: fearful, selfish, spiteful, and proud.

Jonah's call to service began disastrously. We don't know why he chose to flee from his assignment to preach to Nineveh, but we can guess that fear was the main motivation. Instead of staying put, Jonah imagined that if he put an even greater distance between himself and Nineveh, God would give up and choose someone else. But Jonah greatly underestimated God's determination that Jonah would fulfill his mission.

Encountering a violent storm on the way to Tarshish, Jonah at last realized that fighting God's will was useless. Rather than risk the lives of the other travelers, he insisted that he be thrown overboard, where he was swallowed by a great fish. But Jonah was not finished. God used this time of solitary confinement to encourage Jonah's repentance and recommitment. Three days later, Jonah was released, ready to begin the work he was called to do.

God's patience with us is amazing. Even though we run and rebel, he patiently corrects us and places us back on course. Even so, we should not test God's mercy. It is always better to do what he asks the first time.

God will do whatever it takes to bring us back to him.

Jonah's story is told in the Old Testament book of Jonah.

Desiring Mercy
JONAH

This change of plans made Jonah very angry. He complained to the Lord about it. (Jonah 4:1-2, TLB)

The outpouring of God's love upon the parched, sinful land of Nineveh stunned Jonah. After all, he had gone through a lot to give the message of impending judgment to the imperial city of Nineveh. And now God had relented, showing mercy on the very ones he had earlier condemned. Jonah didn't want the Ninevites forgiven; he wanted them destroyed.

Unfortunately, we often share Jonah's you-get-what-you-deserve manner of thinking. We show our disgust, even in subtle ways, with others who defy or ignore God's commands. Some people can seem so far gone in our estimation that we would be admittedly shocked to learn they were destined for heaven. Maybe we would even feel disappointed with God's decision.

Jonah's understanding of God's love was distorted. Is it possible that our view is similarly narrow? We must not forget that God devoted himself to us even when we, too, were a lost and hopeless cause. If we are honest, it is not justice, but mercy, we desire most for ourselves. And yet, like Jonah, we often tend to hold others to a different standard. Begin now to confess to God any familiar reflections you see in the mirror of Jonah's life.

God withholds the justice we deserve so we may have the mercy we do not.

Jonah's story is told in the book of Jonah.

Strong Faith for Tough Times
MICAH

But as for me, I am filled with power, with the Spirit of the Lord, and with justice and might, to declare to Jacob his transgression, to Israel his sin. (Micah 3:8)

Micah was a prophet during the reigns of Jotham, Ahaz, and Hezekiah. A contemporary of Hosea, Amos, and Isaiah, Micah faced the daunting task of preaching to a people who were drifting further and further from God. Because his culture was so corrupt, Micah needed special insight to fulfill his mission. What qualities stand out from his life?

He was filled with the Spirit (3:8). This gave Micah the power and boldness to speak truth—even unpopular, convicting truth—to the most powerful leaders of the nation.

He knew the difference between empty religion and true devotion (6:8). Micah recognized that outer actions mean little; God wants to change his people from the inside out. This fundamental truth permeated his life's message.

He trusted God in hard times (7:7). Despite the sad decline of his culture, Micah prayed and waited for God to work. This hope sustained him even in his darkest hours.

He understood the character of God (7:18-20). Micah knew that God, in his justice, must punish sin; however, he also knew that the Creator longs for a relationship with his beloved creatures.

We need to develop these same qualities if we are to live for Christ in a corrupt culture. Pick out one or two attributes from the life of Micah that are most meaningful to you and share them with a fellow believer today.

Godly leaders are needed in godless times.

What little we know about Micah is found in the prophetic book that bears his name.

Messenger of Doom

NAHUM

The Lord is good, a refuge in times of trouble. (Nahum 1:7)

Nahum was a prophet from Elkosh (a village of Galilee) who was sent by God to prophesy to the people of Nineveh. This was not the first time the Assyrians—a people with an unrivaled reputation for evil and cruelty—were confronted with God's truth. A century earlier God had sent another prophet (the reluctant Jonah) to Nineveh with a message of judgment. When Jonah delivered his prophecy, the Assyrians renounced their wicked ways and turned to God. The Lord mercifully spared this idolatrous nation.

Over time, however, the Assyrians reverted to their godless lifestyle, and so God summoned Nahum. This time there would be no mercy. The nation known for its pride and power would be completely destroyed.

Ironically, Nahum means "compassionate" or "full of comfort." But the prophet's message to the Assyrians was anything but soothing! They could only listen to his stern words and wait for the wrath of God to fall. However, for the godly remnant in Israel, Nahum's sermon was full of comforting reminders of God's power and justice.

The next time you see injustice or evil, remember that God will one day right every wrong and punish those who defy him. And remember that those who cling to him will be kept safe forever.

Hope awaits the humble; divine displeasure, the disobedient.

All that we know about Nahum can be found in the book that bears his name.

The Timetable of Heaven

HABAKKUK

The righteous live by their faith. (Habakkuk 2:4, NRSV)

Like many of the Old Testament prophets, Habakkuk—and any memory of his life—was outlived by the power of his message. But we can draw at least one conclusion from Habakkuk's writing: He was like us. Hard times forced him to ask God hard questions. Why isn't life fair? Why do evil people succeed while the innocent suffer? Why does God put up with so much mockery? Why does God seem so distant? Habakkuk expressed our doubts, but he also received answers from God.

What were God's answers to Habakkuk? Much as the Lord did with Job, God insisted on being trusted as *God,* not as the one we can compel to answer every question. God will not be held hostage by our doubts. God pointed out to Habakkuk that when we take the larger view of history and the world, we are more likely to see God in control. And when we experience the confusion and pain of daily living, we need to cling more tightly to God.

Habakkuk ended his prophecy with a prayer in which he stated his intention to trust. He realized that there would be times when the immediate evidence would challenge the presence of God. In those times of darkness, he would remember the God he had met in the light.

God will reveal his will, but not according to our timetable.

What little we know of Habakkuk is found in his book.

God's Loving Yoke

ZEPHANIAH

Beg him to save you, all who are humble—all who have tried to obey. Walk humbly and do what is right; perhaps even yet the Lord will protect you from his wrath in that day of doom. (Zephaniah 2:3)

Zephaniah was a prophet to Judah for nineteen years. He influenced King Josiah and his efforts to turn the nation back to God. Zephaniah's message was simple and clear: God will judge and punish the people for their disobedience, but he will also show mercy to all who are faithful to him.

That same prophetic message is still true today. We will be judged and punished for our disobedience to God. The punishment God brings to us isn't vengeful. It humbles us and purifies our desires. Through the disciplining process of judgment, we learn how much we were created to live in relationship with God and how foolish we are to ignore him.

Many Christians ride the spiritual roller coaster . . . drifting away from God and returning to worship and serve him when crises arise. But do you consider that the difficulties of our lives are often God's way of getting our attention and disciplining us? He still loves us and wants to purify us so that we can serve him. Decide today to submit to God's loving yoke of discipline.

His yoke is easy, his burden is light.

Zephaniah's story is told in the Old Testament book that bears his name.

The One-Year Prophet
HAGGAI

Is it a time for you yourselves to be living in your paneled houses,
while this house remains a ruin? (Haggai 1:4)

Haggai could well be called the "One-Year Prophet." God gave him
a very specific mission that required him to deliver four messages
over the course of a single year. In 520 B.C., Haggai spoke to Jews
who had been home from their Babylonian exile for nearly twenty
years. He criticized them for looking after their own comfort while
leaving the rebuilding of the temple unfinished.

Haggai used the condition of the temple as a metaphor to
describe the spiritual life of the people. Their relationship with
God was in shambles and needed to be restored from the bottom
up. Haggai assured the people that a healed relationship with God
would result in wonderful benefits that had been forgotten during
the years of neglect.

Haggai's message reminds us that the daily habits of our relationship with God (involvement in church fellowship and service,
as well as consistency in prayer and Bible study) need continual
attention. If you've been letting some of the disciplines of your
faith slide, ask the Lord to show you what effect this has had on
your fellowship with him.

Wonderful blessings accompany a restored relationship with God.

Both the book of Haggai and Ezra 5:1; 6:14 give us glimpses of
Haggai's ministry.

Responding to Adversity

JOSEPH, MARY'S HUSBAND

Because Joseph her husband was a righteous man . . . he had in mind to divorce her quietly. (Matthew 1:19)

Mary informed Joseph of the staggering news that she was pregnant. Her claims of angelic visits and her explanation that the baby inside her was the child of God may have soothed his mind a little bit, but still . . . the news hit him like a punch in the gut. What would people think? What would Joseph tell his family and friends? And the most disturbing thought—was Mary really telling the truth?

Joseph might have reacted in any number of ways. He could have publicly shamed Mary. He could have demanded that she be stoned as an adulteress. He could have disappeared in the night.

Instead, Joseph tried to find a solution that would please God and spare Mary any sort of public ridicule. Isn't that interesting? In the midst of a severe personal crisis, Joseph's primary thoughts were (1) *What does God want me to do?* and (2) *How can I best show mercy and kindness to Mary?* Ultimately God sent an angel to Joseph with the instructions to go ahead and take her as his wife.

Think back to the last crisis in your own life. How did you react? If a writer summarized your response in a sentence or two (like Matthew summarized Joseph's response above), how would that assessment read?

Ask God to cause you to become the kind of person who responds righteously to life's tough situations.

Adversity reveals much about our spiritual character.

Joseph's story can be found in Matthew 1:16–2:23 and Luke 1:26–2:52.

Urgent Obedience

JOSEPH, MARY'S HUSBAND

When Joseph awoke from sleep, he did as the angel of the Lord commanded him. (Matthew 1:24, NRSV)

Joseph had made up his mind. His fiancée was pregnant, and he was not the father. There was only one thing to do. He would divorce Mary quietly and get on with his life. But then he had a dream in which an angel of the Lord explained Mary's pregnancy and the importance of the child. Joseph listened and obeyed.

After the child was born, an angel told Joseph to leave Israel ASAP and go to Egypt to avoid violence at the hands of King Herod. Joseph listened and obeyed.

Imagine for a moment what would have happened if Joseph had ignored the clear revelation of God. Suppose Joseph had awakened from one of the dreams and tried to explain it away: *How can I be sure that dream was really from God? It certainly seemed urgent, but maybe I should just wait for more evidence.* Can you imagine the blessings Joseph would have missed or the dangers he would have encountered?

For us, obedience might not seem so urgent. We're not faced with world-changing events or life-and-death choices very often. But the principle is still true: God wants to guide us and bless us. But we can't know the full extent of his blessing unless we follow his lead.

What clear command of God do you need to obey today?

When we obey God, we experience his blessings.

Joseph's story can be found in Matthew 1:16–2:23 and Luke 1:26–2:52.

Stay and Follow

THE WISE MEN

They offered him gifts of gold, frankincense, and myrrh. And . . . they left for their own country. (Matthew 2:11-12, NRSV)

We know little about the "three wise men" who came to see the baby Jesus. In fact, some of what we "know" comes from legend, not Scripture. Despite what you may have heard, we don't know their names. Though we assume there were three, the Bible never says how many came, only that they presented three gifts. And they came to see Jesus some time after he was born—probably when he was a toddler, not an infant.

Why did the magi come? We really don't know that, either. They said they saw his star in the east and had come to worship him (Matthew 2:2). But as soon as they found him and gave him their gifts, they went back home, never to return. What did they get out of this trip? Did they ever think about Jesus again?

Many people, like the magi, honor Jesus. A few, unlike the magi, also follow him. That's not to disparage what the magi did or to say that we should not honor Christ, but to point out the difference between magi and disciples. The one pays his or her respects and leaves; the other stays, sits at Jesus' feet, and learns. Ponder this question today: Are you making occasional visits to fellowship with God, or do you take every opportunity available to be with him?

Don't just pay your respects to Jesus: Stay and follow.

The story of the wise men can be found in Matthew 2:1-12.

The Disease of Self-Centeredness

HEROD THE GREAT

When King Herod heard this he was disturbed, and all Jerusalem with him. (Matthew 2:3)

Herod the Great is remembered as a builder of cities and the lavish rebuilder of the temple. But he also destroyed people. Herod's title, king of the Jews, was granted by Rome but never accepted by the Jewish people. Consequently, his constant concern was to hold on to his ill-fitting crown at any price. When Herod heard that a new king had been born in Bethlehem, he ordered the death of all the male infants in the town in an attempt to abolish the threat to his throne. His suspicions and jealousy eventually led to the murder of his wife and several of his children.

Herod's appalling behavior reveals a full-blown case of self-centeredness. It is a disease that infects us all. In its initial stages, it seriously impairs one's ability to make wise decisions and can cause extensive damage to the family. Left untreated, the human heart is soon ravaged with corroded desires, resulting in a tragic prognosis for everyone involved. The antidote for this universal malady is a commitment to live for Christ and his ideals—to be renewed daily. The recovery rate is slow but certain. Have you renewed your commitment to him today?

Selfishness is a disease that only God can cure.

Notes about Herod the Great are found in Matthew 2:1-22 and Luke 1:5.

Released from Bondage

THE GADARENE DEMONIAC

What have you to do with me, Jesus, Son of the Most High God?
(Mark 5:7, NRSV)

Jesus brought out the best and worst in people. One of his most vivid encounters was with an unnamed man from Gadara who lived among the tombs near the Sea of Galilee. Others had long since given up on helping him. They hadn't even been able to control him. So they isolated him where he could hurt only himself. The demonic gang in him had almost accomplished their mission of destruction. But Jesus arrived unexpectedly.

Speaking through the man, the demons immediately betrayed their panic at having to face the Son of God. The tormentors found themselves suddenly in danger of torment. In a frenzy, they pleaded to be sent into a herd of pigs grazing nearby. We may not understand entirely why Jesus agreed to the destruction of the animals, but we can appreciate in that action the value Jesus placed on the life of that one human being.

Jesus didn't let the healed man accompany him in the boat, but he invited him to be a follower at home. Those who knew what he had been needed to see the change in him. And they needed to hear who had made the difference. Our last glimpse of the rescued man shows him amazing people in Gadara with his story.

The Son of God wants to have everything to do with us!

The Gadarene's story is told in Matthew 8:28–9:1; Mark 5:1-20; and Luke 8:26-39.

Seeing Jesus as He Really Is

MATTHEW

Many tax collectors and sinners came and were sitting with him and his disciples. (Matthew 9:10, NRSV)

Christians are capable of cooking up some elaborate evangelism programs. We bring in celebrity speakers and blanket our communities with tracts. We put up billboards and plaster bumper stickers on our cars. We televise our church services and hold up signs at athletic events.

God can (and does) use such methods to draw people to himself. But perhaps we've overlooked a more natural strategy for reaching out to the spiritually needy—creating nonthreatening situations in which our non-Christian friends and neighbors can see what Christ is really like.

That's what Matthew the tax collector did. After he decided to follow Jesus, he threw a party. He invited all his wild tax collector buddies, and he made sure Jesus and his disciples showed up. Instead of bringing his friends into a religious setting where they would be uncomfortable, Matthew brought the Good News into their world. Though these tax collectors and "sinners" were turned off by religion, they were attracted to and intrigued by Jesus!

Before you worry about reaching total strangers with the gospel, think about your non-Christian friends, neighbors, and coworkers. God has put these individuals in your life (and you in theirs) for a reason. Cultivate those relationships.

Evangelism means creating natural opportunities for your unbelieving friends to see Jesus as he really is.

Besides appearing throughout the Gospels, Matthew is also mentioned in Acts 1:13.

Attention to Detail

MATTHEW

The names of the twelve apostles . . . [included] Matthew the tax collector. (Matthew 10:2-3)

When Matthew listed the names of the twelve apostles in his Gospel, he also mentioned his former occupation—tax collector. This meant that Matthew had formerly gathered revenues from his own Jewish countrymen and turned them over to the hated Roman government. Since a standard practice of tax collectors was to overcharge people and pocket the excess, we can safely assume that Matthew was rich—and despised. Branded a traitor and treated like a leper, Matthew was an unlikely disciple.

Then Jesus came along. Not only did Jesus change his life, but he also chose Matthew to be one of his most trusted followers. It may seem odd for God to use a man with a shady past to advance his kingdom. But consider these facts: Matthew obviously had a knack for keeping records. In his career as a tax man, he had to be a keen observer, a careful, detail-oriented individual. What better individual to write an accurate history of the life of Christ!

The story of Matthew is an encouraging one. It reminds us that God is in control of the affairs of our lives. He has put together each one of us with an individual personality, special abilities, and unique experiences.

Have you surrendered your life—your past, present, and future—to God? Do so today, and watch him do something amazing in your life!

God can use your training and skills to make a difference for his kingdom.

Besides appearing throughout the Gospels, Matthew is also mentioned in Acts 1:13.

Turning toward the Darkness

HERODIAS

So Herodias nursed a grudge against John and wanted to kill him.
(Mark 6:19)

Herodias appeared on the stage of history as the wife of King Philip, who was actually her uncle. Later she exchanged one incestuous relationship for another when she left Philip to marry his brother Herod Antipas. When John confronted the two for committing adultery, Herodias formulated a plot to kill him. Instead of trying to get rid of her sin, Herodias tried to get rid of the person who brought it to public attention.

Herod arrested John the Baptist under pressure from his wife and advisers. Though Herod respected John's integrity, he was no match for his wife's ingenuity. Herodias managed to cause John's death by using her daughter Salome, who danced for Herod and his guests during a party. The king made a thoughtless promise to grant her any request. With the pressure of the public moment on her side, Herodias had Salome ask for John's head on a platter. Not wishing to lose face, Herod gave in to his wife.

Herodias chose a pathway of evil. We have no evidence that she ever veered toward the truth. But she had at least one crystal-clear moment to face it. John showed her the light, but she turned toward the darkness. Her life was an extension of a common human tendency to defend ourselves and our actions when confronted. How do you react to unwelcome truth?

Sins exposed may incite fierce opposition.

Herodias's part in history is recorded in Matthew 14:1-12 and Mark 6:14-29.

Lavish Gifts

MARY, SISTER OF LAZARUS

Then Mary took about a pint of pure nard, an expensive perfume; she poured it on Jesus' feet and wiped his feet with her hair. (John 12:3)

During the final week of his life, Jesus attended a dinner given in his honor. Right in the middle of the meal, Mary, the sister of Lazarus and Martha, broke open a bottle of nard and poured it over Jesus' head and feet. Nard was rare, costly, and reserved only for the most special occasions (like the ritual anointing of kings). This small vial of perfume, the Gospel writers tell us, was worth more money than the average laborer could make in a year!

As the aroma filled the air, several partygoers began grumbling. "What a waste!" they cried. "This money could have been put to better use!" But Jesus shocked the naysayers when he praised Mary's extravagant behavior and commended the love that prompted it.

Christians who tend to be very measured in their giving or in their service need this example from the life of Mary. Our Lord, because of who he is and what he has done, deserves more than token amounts and empty gestures. He is worthy of our most lavish gifts. We cannot thank him or love him or serve him or honor him too much.

Give God your best efforts and your most precious hours today. Use your most valued possessions for his glory. Such devotion not only pleases God but tells the world how great he is.

People in love do lavish things for those they love.

Mary's story is found in Matthew 26:6-13; Mark 14:3-9; Luke 10:38-42; and John 11:17-45; 12:1-11.

Phony Commitment

JUDAS

So now Judas came straight to Jesus and said, "Hello, Master!" and embraced him. (Matthew 26:49, TLB)

Scholars and laypeople have long speculated about Judas. Why did Jesus pick him to be a disciple? Why did he betray Jesus? What are we to think about the sorrow he felt after committing his treacherous act?

Most of these questions are beyond our ability to answer. But these facts are beyond dispute: (1) Judas was one of the twelve disciples; (2) Judas lived and traveled with Jesus for about three years; (3) Judas heard Jesus teach; (4) Judas witnessed the miraculous works of Christ.

To onlookers, Judas appeared to be a committed follower of Christ. After all, he was the treasurer of the group. Judas had to have been a true believer, right? Wrong! Jesus warned that one of his disciples was "a devil" (John 6:70), hinted that this evil follower was unforgiven (John 13:2), and later stated that he was "doomed to destruction" (John 17:12).

The sad story of Judas should remind us of a sober truth: It is possible to be deeply involved in Christian activities, to learn the lingo of the church, to look and act like a follower of Christ, and still be lost in your sins.

What about you? Your religious activity aside, have you ever come to Jesus on his terms and bowed before him as Savior and Lord? This decision is what separates those who know *about* Christ from those who truly know him.

Being associated with Christ is not the same as being committed to him.

The story of Judas Iscariot is told in the Gospels and in Acts 1:16-26.

The Wrong Agenda

JUDAS

The devil had already prompted Judas Iscariot, son of Simon, to betray Jesus. (John 13:2)

Judas, like so many other Jews, may have been looking for a military Messiah, a conquering king who would free Palestine from Roman oppression. Judas had watched the way Jesus enthralled the masses with his words. Certainly Jesus had the power—hadn't he performed great miracles?

And yet Jesus didn't seem to be interested in political or military liberation. He spoke instead of being a servant and turning the other cheek and being changed from within and taking up one's cross. What kind of talk was that for one with so much potential! And so, the argument goes, Judas tried to force Jesus' hand. He hoped that Jesus' arrest would wake this reluctant Messiah to his "true" calling, the overthrow of Roman rule. We all know, however, that Jesus did not deviate from his divine mission.

Perhaps the lesson for us in all of this is that we must be careful not to dictate to God. Rather than trying to manipulate him into implementing our agenda, we need to submit ourselves to his plan. When we think we know what is best, when we are most determined to get our own way, when we fail to consult God about what he wants—then we are most likely to make choices that will lead to sorrow and remorse.

Whose agenda are you pursuing today?

Submit your plans to God's scrutiny and direction.

The story of Judas Iscariot is told in the Gospels and in Acts 1:18-19.

Recipes for Success

CAIAPHAS

Caiaphas . . . spoke up . . . "It is better for you that one man die for the people than that the whole nation perish." (John 11:49-50)

No man was more intent on the arrest and execution of Jesus than Caiaphas. When the Sanhedrin seemed uncertain, Caiaphas rallied them. When Pilate wavered, Caiaphas insisted.

Caiaphas was an astute religious leader of the Jewish state. He survived in that volatile job for eighteen years, from A.D. 18 to 36. No one was better at placating the Romans and pacifying the Jews.

Caiaphas's big worry was a Zealot uprising that would bring the force of Rome crashing down on his people. He knew who held all the big sticks, and he also knew that his people, if stirred by revolutionaries, had the capacity to throw caution to the wind. That's why Caiaphas believed that executing one "troublemaker" was better than provoking Roman military action.

Pity Caiaphas. For all his learning, he failed to discern the truth. All the power of his personality and office was directed against God's Son, and he never saw it (or at least never admitted it). He was politically and religiously a huge success, but spiritually bankrupt. He had it all, and it was nothing.

Seek God first, and your life will have the meaning and purpose God intended.

Success can be the worst thing that happens to a person.

Caiaphas's story is told in Matthew 26:57-68 and John 18:12-28. He is also mentioned in Matthew 26:3; Luke 3:2; John 11:49; and Acts 4:6.

Confounding the Wise
CAIAPHAS

They were astonished. (Acts 4:13)

Two of the disciples, not outstanding men by any measure, went before Caiaphas to face questioning related to the healing of a crippled beggar near the temple courts. The people whom Caiaphas had sought to quiet down by Jesus' death were agitating again, carried away by "a miracle." How could this be? Who were these men?

Caiaphas got an earful that day from Peter and John. He had indicted and convicted their leader, yet these two disciples had the audacity to claim publicly that God had undone the Sanhedrin's plan, that Jesus was alive from the dead and directly responsible for the miraculous healing. What arrogant blasphemy! Surely these two must also die.

But this time even Caiaphas was stymied. The people were too excited by the miracle. The Sanhedrin lacked consensus, and thus had no legal basis to detain Peter and John. Caiaphas was left with an empty court, stunned by a power he had never comprehended, bewildered that his carefully conceived plans were unraveling through the words of simple fishermen.

Today, the gospel still surprises powerful, intelligent people who thought they had life all boxed, wrapped, and on the shelf. God's power stuns and stymies worldly wisdom. Be a student of God's wisdom.

The first lesson in wisdom is to know and reverence the Lord.

Caiaphas's story is told in Matthew 26:57-68 and John 18:12-28. He is also mentioned in Matthew 26:3; Luke 3:2; John 11:49; and Acts 4:6.

The Price of Indecision

PILATE

He took water and washed his hands in front of the crowd. (Matthew 27:24)

Pilate was in political hot water. As governor of Palestine, he was already in disfavor with the emperor (being assigned to govern the Jews was considered a demotion). Now the Jews were stirring up trouble again—some sort of religious matter involving a supposed miracle worker. Pilate did not want to get involved, but he had no choice.

His conscience (what was left of it, anyway) told him that this Jesus had done nothing to deserve death. Even his wife had strange dreams about this man, and she begged her husband to leave him alone. But the masses were calling for his hide. And so the choice was clear: justice or expediency? Pilate decided to pacify his critics. He may not have hammered the nails into Christ's hands and feet, but his cave-in to popular pressure served that very purpose. No matter how many times he washed his hands, he could not wash his guilt away.

When faced with tough situations, we often wrestle with similar temptations: to abstain from voting, to refuse to get involved, to make excuses, to remain silent. We do nothing and then convince ourselves that our passivity absolves us of guilt. And yet in doing nothing, we are doing something.

Ask God for the courage today to do what is right, regardless of the consequences.

Fearful inaction is as wrong as sinful involvement.

Pilate's story is found in each of the Gospels. He is also mentioned in Acts 3:13; 4:27; 13:28; and 1 Timothy 6:13.

Searching for the Truth

PILATE

"What is truth?" Pilate exclaimed. (John 18:38, TLB)

Standing before Pilate, Jesus probably looked like anything but a king. He was most likely bound, and he may have been beaten and bloodied. "I came . . . to testify to the truth," Jesus stated. "Everyone on the side of truth listens to me."

Pilate studied this curious teacher from Galilee and uttered his famous question: "What is truth?" We don't know if he was being sarcastic or if his query came from a heart hungry for real answers. Nevertheless, his question begins the most profound search upon which a human being can embark.

The irony of Pilate's question is that he didn't wait for an answer. Not only that, but he didn't look long enough at or listen hard enough to Jesus. Too bad Pilate didn't ask a few more questions. Perhaps then he might have recognized that the one on trial before him did not just know the truth, but he was, in fact, the Truth!

Is your life fully committed to the Truth? Are you seeking to know Christ? Are you listening to him? Are you convinced that he is who he claimed to be? Ask God to keep you from falsehood and to help you recognize, embrace, and live by the Truth.

To know the truth, we must come to know Christ.

Pilate's story is found in each of the Gospels. He is also mentioned in Acts 3:13; 4:27; 13:28; and 1 Timothy 6:13.

The Unexpected Reprieve

BARABBAS

Which one do you want me to release to you: Barabbas, or Jesus who is called Christ? (Matthew 27:17)

Did the echoes in the dungeon seem to emanate from hell? Did the convict shrink in terror at the sound of approaching feet? When they led him from his prison, did he follow quietly? Was he still rambling excuses when they left him in the street? Was Barabbas at Golgotha, drawn by curiosity? Did he whisper his repentance, tears streaming down his face?

It's hard to know how Barabbas may have felt about his role in Jesus' trial. He knew he had been the unlikely beneficiary of a Passover custom. And Barabbas was indeed known as a hero among many Jews. Yet as the guards led him from his prison, perhaps he remembered that Jesus had once been popular with many in this same crowd. So what did he think when the people chanted his name as their choice for whom they wanted released? The Bible account ends with Barabbas's release. But was he really free?

Barabbas's small part in the Gospel story makes a big point. He represents us. Like him, we have been declared guilty and worthy of death. The verdict has been rendered. Then, also like Barabbas, we hear the incredible news: Someone has taken our place. And yet, like him, we are not completely free until we respond to the one who offers total forgiveness. What is your response?

True freedom is found only in the blood of Jesus.

Barabbas's story is found in Matthew 27:15-26. He is also mentioned in Mark 15:6-15; Luke 23:18-25; and John 18:39-40.

Love with No Strings Attached

JOHN

This is love: not that we loved God, but that he loved us and sent his Son as an atoning sacrifice for our sins. (1 John 4:10)

What motivated John to write five books of the New Testament? What sustained him through those turbulent first years of the church when persecution was rampant—when eleven of his fellow apostles died violent deaths? What enabled him to cope with his own lonely exile on the isle of Patmos?

Perhaps the answer is found in an idea that John mentioned repeatedly in his writings. That recurring theme is love. The words *love, loves,* and *loved* are used more than fifty times in John's Gospel, and there are at least that many references to *love* in John's epistles. John was so amazed by God's unconditional love and acceptance that he even began referring to himself as "the disciple whom Jesus loved"!

It feels wonderful to be loved by another human, but when we catch a glimpse of the depths of the love of God, we are awestruck. His love comes with no conditions, no strings attached. And once embraced, it has transforming power, taking ordinary sinners like John and changing them into extraordinary servants of God.

Have you ever pondered God's infinite love for you? More than that, have you accepted the priceless gift of forgiveness and salvation that he offers?

God's love not only liberates us, it gives us a reason for living.

More insights from the life of the apostle John can be found in the Gospels, the book of Acts, and Revelation.

Transformed by God

JOHN

Jesus named them Boanerges, which means "Sons of Thunder."
(Mark 3:17, NCV)

Because the apostle John wrote so much about love, it's easy to imagine him as a bookish, soft-spoken man with a squeaky-clean reputation. Not so fast. Let's go back and check the biblical record.

John was a professional fisherman without formal education.

He and his brother James once wanted to call down fire from heaven on some unfriendly Samaritans.

On another occasion John and James schemed (without success) to get special favors from Jesus.

When Jesus was arrested, John fled along with all the rest of the disciples.

Not the most glowing resume in the world. But then something revolutionary happened in John's life. The scared, inconsistent, self-centered, hot-tempered disciple of the Gospels reappears in the book of Acts as a bold, devoted, unselfish apostle of love. So extreme was the transformation that even the Jewish leaders noticed.

That's the kind of change that is possible when we make the commitment to follow Jesus. He's not that concerned with where we've been or even with what we are. Instead, he sees us as we can be. And when we give our lives to him, he changes us (for the better) in mind-boggling ways.

If you let him, God will revolutionize your life.

Details about the life of the apostle John can be found in the Gospels, Acts, and Revelation.

Time for Trust

JAIRUS

Do not fear, only believe. (Mark 5:36, NRSV)

We don't know how many remedies Jairus tried in attempting to help his little daughter, but he certainly was convinced that Jesus was his last hope. His little girl was dying. Jairus desperately threw himself at Jesus' feet and begged for help. To his relief, Jesus agreed to come.

The next few minutes must have been agonizing for Jairus. The pressing crowds made progress difficult. Jesus stopped to heal a woman. Then Jairus heard his name being called. Someone arrived from his house with the crushing news—his little girl was dead. Their well-meaning but misguided advice was to accept the facts and get on with life. Jesus wasn't needed any longer.

Fortunately, Jesus overheard the news. But his words to Jairus must have encouraged and bewildered the father simultaneously: "This isn't time for fear but for trust." Jairus, Jesus, and three of the disciples found a grieving and unbelieving group who derided Jesus for saying that the girl was only sleeping. After escorting the mourners outside, Jesus spoke to the child and she awakened.

The words Jesus spoke to Jairus ought to echo frequently in our hearts. Fear always makes the outlook hopeless, but trust in God keeps hope alive. Those who trust in God often find they get back what they thought they had lost.

The antidote for fear is trust in God.

Jairus's story is told in Mark 5:21-43 and Luke 8:40-56.

Hearing without Listening
HEROD ANTIPAS

Herod was disturbed whenever he talked with John, but even so he liked to listen to him. (Mark 6:20, TLB)

Herod's illegal marriage to his brother's wife, Herodias, was public knowledge. One man made Herod's sin a public issue. That man was John the Baptist.

Herod liked John. But the truth about his sin was a bitter pill to swallow, and Herod wavered at the point of conflict: He couldn't afford to have John constantly reminding the people of their leader's sinfulness, but he was afraid to have John killed. Eventually Herodias forced his hand, and John was executed. Of course, this only served to increase Herod's guilt.

When Herod and Jesus met briefly during Jesus' trial, Jesus would not speak to Herod. Herod had proved himself a poor listener to John, and Jesus had nothing to add to John's words. Herod responded with spite and mocking. Having rejected the messenger, he found it easy to reject the Messiah.

For each person, God chooses the best possible ways to reveal himself. He is persuasive and persistent, but he never forces himself on us. To miss or resist God's message, as did Herod, results in tragedy. How aware are you of God's attempts to enter your life? Have you welcomed him?

Opportunities to experience God usually come to us in the form of choices we must make.

Herod Antipas's story is told in the Gospels. He is also mentioned in Acts 4:27 and 13:1.

Putting Pride Aside

SYROPHOENICIAN WOMAN

Now the woman was a Gentile, of Syrophoenician origin. She begged him to cast the demon out of her daughter. (Mark 7:26, NRSV)

Desperation had wiped clean any trace of sinful pride in this mother. She needed powerful help for her demon-possessed daughter. She broke through the cultural barriers to seek help from Jesus.

While Jesus' fellow Jews argued about his teaching and rejected him as the promised Messiah, this non-Jewish woman needed immediate help for her demon-possessed daughter. When Jesus explained that his primary mission was to his own people, she replied that she was ready to take whatever leftovers in time and attention he could give to her. Jesus recognized her humble faith and healed her daughter.

Today the people of former Communist countries are desperate and hungry for Bibles. They will wait in line for hours to receive even small portions of God's written Word. Meanwhile, in North America the Bible is widely available and generally ignored.

The first step to healing is realizing that we have no solutions to our problems and surrendering our stubborn pride to God. What has kept you from bringing your life with all its problems to Jesus? Today is the day to begin intently seeking God for his help.

The biggest obstacle to obtaining God's help is our own pride. The widest doorway is humility.

The story of the Syrophoenician woman is told in Matthew 15:21-28 and Mark 7:24-30.

Suffering and Endurance

JAMES

[Herod] had James, the brother of John, put to death with the sword. (Acts 12:2)

James was the first apostle to die for the sake of the gospel. His martyrdom was not an isolated event, but the culmination of other related sufferings he endured as Christ's disciple. When James was called to follow Christ, he forfeited the benefit of working in his father's fishing business. He was separated from his parents and would never enjoy a settled life with a wife and children.

As a disciple, James's life was marked by inconvenience and difficulty. Without a place he could call home, he followed Jesus from town to town, owning only the clothes he wore upon his back. But even with swollen feet and an empty stomach, James's joy outweighed his sorrow because he grew closer to Christ through suffering.

It is easy to say we are willing to suffer anything for Christ, and yet most of us complain when even little irritations come. If we say we are willing to suffer on a grand scale for Christ, we must also be willing to endure in little ways. Begin now to pray that God may use your suffering in a way that strengthens you and glorifies him.

The way to the kingdom is the way of the cross.

James's martyrdom is mentioned in Acts 12:2. His story is told in the Gospels.

A Heavenly Perspective

JAMES

"We want to sit on the thrones next to yours in your Kingdom," they said, "one at your right and the other at your left." (Mark 10:37, TLB)

Jesus singled out three of his twelve disciples for special training. James, his brother John, and Peter made up this inner circle. James enjoyed being in this elite group, but he misunderstood Jesus' purpose. He and his brother even tried to secure their role in the kingdom to come by asking Jesus to promise them each a special position. James had not yet grasped the nature of Jesus' mission; he could see only an earthly kingdom that would overthrow Rome and restore Israel's former glory. His understanding of God's kingdom would be transformed by Jesus' death and resurrection.

Like James, our expectations about life will be limited if this life is all we can see. And like him, we, too, must admit we can become consumed with securing a personal kingdom on earth. How long has it been since you withdrew from the distractions of this world, even for a moment, to think about heaven and your future life there? Take advantage of the opportunity to do so throughout the day, and let a heavenly perspective guide you in all your actions and decisions.

Reaching your potential on earth requires a heavenly vision.

James's story is told in the Gospels. He is also mentioned in Acts 1:13 and 12:2.

A Demonstration of Gratitude

BARTIMAEUS

Rabbi, I want to see. (Mark 10:51)

Bartimaeus had one handicap and one strength; he was blind and he was bold. To the crowd pressing around Jesus, Bartimaeus was a nuisance. The roads were lined with other such "nuisances": the lame, the sick, and the disfigured, begging for help. In this case, the blind man made sure he begged louder than most. They told him to be quiet, but Bartimaeus wouldn't cooperate. He kept shouting, "Jesus, Son of David, have mercy on me!"

When Jesus acknowledged Bartimaeus, the blind man leaped to his feet. In response to Jesus' question, Bartimaeus made his simple request, "Lord, I want to see." Jesus sent him on his way with the assurance that his faith had resulted in his healing. Sure enough, Bartimaeus gained his sight, but he didn't leave. Instead, he immediately followed Jesus.

The Lord did not make following him the prerequisite for mercy, but Bartimaeus realized that following Jesus was the best way to express his own gratitude for what Christ had done. How many examples of God's mercy in your life can you think of in fifteen seconds? How have you expressed your gratitude to God recently?

Gratitude goes beyond attitude to action.

Bartimaeus's story is told in Matthew 20:29-34; Mark 10:46-52; and Luke 18:35-43.

Following Wholeheartedly

SALOME

These used to follow him and provided for him when he was in Galilee. (Mark 15:41, NRSV)

Salome's obscurity doesn't mean she was inactive or unimportant. She was part of a group of women who supported Jesus and the disciples as they traveled around Galilee. Their persistent faithfulness may explain in part why Jesus didn't call any women to be among the Twelve. The men had to be specifically called to follow; the women were already following wholeheartedly.

It appears that Salome never wavered through the ordeal of Jesus' capture, trial, suffering, and death. When those who seemed to be his strongest followers were afraid to appear in public, Salome and other women boldly stood near the cross. Their faithfulness was rewarded when they made their way to Jesus' tomb on Easter morning, only to become the first to discover the glorious Resurrection! Salome and the others literally kept their eyes on Jesus, even when they couldn't understand what was happening.

Salome reminds us that we must, when all else fails, continue to trust! On a scale of one to ten, how quickly does your trust in God fade when trouble appears? What example from your own experience could you use to explain the principle that God does wonderful things for those who insist on trusting him? Resolve today to trust God, even when the outlook is bleak.

Keep your eyes fixed upon Jesus.

Salome is mentioned in Mark 15:40 and 16:1.

Acting in Spite of Fear

JOSEPH OF ARIMATHEA

Joseph of Arimathea . . . went boldly to Pilate and asked for Jesus' body. (Mark 15:43)

A crisis reveals true commitment. When the pressure is life threatening, those who don't have a clear reason for their faith give up. The disciples of Jesus demonstrated these all-too-human traits. They fled and hid, and some, like Peter, denied knowing Christ. But even in the chaos a few followers remained true. One of them was Joseph of Arimathea.

John's Gospel points out that Joseph was an undercover disciple until this point. He was afraid. But Mark describes his request for Jesus' body as "bold." It was bold because it challenged the appearance that all leading Jews were opposed to Jesus and because it placed Joseph's career at risk. Joseph stepped out of the shadows at a crucial moment in history.

We may be tempted to look down on Joseph's timid discipleship. But such an attitude is not fair to Joseph. All the disciples were afraid! Joseph did not stand out because he was afraid; he stood out because he acted in spite of his fear. He had every reason to keep his faith under wraps, but he chose to risk all to make his faith in Jesus known.

The big struggle for us is not to admit our fears. Those are usually pretty apparent. The challenge is to follow Jesus anyway. What fears keep you from being an effective disciple? Turn them over to God today.

Boldness for the faith is not a personality trait; it is a gift from God.

For accounts of Joseph's bravery, see Matthew 27:57-61; Mark 15:42-47; Luke 23:50-56; and John 19:38-42.

Talking about God

THEOPHILUS

It seemed good also to me to write an orderly account for you, most excellent Theophilus, so that you may know the certainty of the things you have been taught. (Luke 1:3-4)

What's in a name? Theophilus literally means "one who loves God." Luke wrote his Gospel to Theophilus, his friend and fellow believer of Greek descent, to describe the life of Jesus; he wrote the Acts of the Apostles to him to describe the life of the early church.

Apparently Theophilus's name also reflected his attitude and interests. He wanted to know about what God was doing in the world through the lives of other people.

What do you and your friends talk about when you are together? Talking about the weather, sports, our families, and our work is more than enough to exhaust our time. But how often do you talk with your family and friends about God and his work in the world and in your life?

God isn't a taboo subject or a private matter. We need friends who love God with whom we can talk about our spiritual interests. When you focus your conversation on God, you can be an encouragement to a friend. Find a way to talk about God with your friends this week.

Don't just discuss the news; talk about the Good News.

Theophilus is mentioned in Luke 1:1-4 and Acts 1:1.

The Doctor Has Good News
LUKE

I myself have carefully investigated everything from the beginning.
(Luke 1:3)

Luke was a medical doctor who experienced spiritual healing in his own life when he heard the gospel of Jesus Christ, probably from the lips of the apostle Paul. He later traveled with Paul and became a leader in the early church.

Doctor Luke's greatest achievements are the two New Testament books he authored under the inspiration of the Holy Spirit. Both books are marked by excellent style and are supported by comprehensive personal research. Clearly Luke approached his writing of church history with the same care that he approached his practice of medicine!

Unfortunately, many modern-day believers fail to serve God with excellence. They give their best time and efforts to other endeavors. Consider the man who willingly spends hours preparing a report for his supervisor and then throws his Bible study lesson together in 30 minutes. Think of the woman who wouldn't dream of missing her weekly tennis lesson but who is "just too tired" to get to church many Sundays. What kind of priorities are these?

If we are going to serve God—whether through writing as Luke did, leading a small group, teaching a class, or volunteering to keep the church building clean—we need to serve with excellence.

God is worthy of the best that we can offer.

Luke refers to himself in Luke 1:3; and Acts 1:1; 16–28. He is mentioned also in Colossians 4:14; 2 Timothy 4:11; and Philemon 24.

Unpredictable and Wonderful
ZECHARIAH

Zechariah . . . [was] upright in the sight of God, observing all the Lord's commandments and regulations blamelessly. (Luke 1:5-6)

Zechariah was an aged Jewish priest. He and his wife, despite a lifetime of praying, were childless. One day Zechariah's priestly division was on duty at the temple, and he was selected to burn incense before God.

While praying at the altar, Zechariah came face-to-face with the angel Gabriel, who announced some good news. The frightened priest learned that he and his wife were going to become first-time parents! Their child, John, would be a great man who would turn many in Israel back to God. Zechariah could not believe his ears—and because of this initial unbelief, he was struck dumb until the birth of his child.

The story of Zechariah reminds us of God's unpredictable and unusual ways. He often confounds conventional wisdom in accomplishing his ends. He chooses unlikely people. He disregards man-made customs and defies human reason. He overcomes staggering odds. His character is never inconsistent, but his boldness and knack for surprise often leave us marveling with delight.

Rejoice in the fact that your God is omnipotent. He can do anything! He is also good. Such a combination makes for real comfort. Whatever dilemma we find ourselves in, we can be sure that God is in control and at work for his own glory and our own good.

God's ways are distinctive . . . and wonderful!

The story of Zechariah is found in Luke 1.

God's Perfect Timing

ELIZABETH

But they had no children, for Elizabeth was barren; and now they were both very old. (Luke 1:7, TLB)

In societies like ancient Israel, in which a woman's value was largely measured by her ability to bear children, an aging couple without children often faced personal hardship and public shame. Elizabeth's childless years were a painful and lonely time; nevertheless, she remained faithful to God.

Life had probably settled into a well-worn routine when Zechariah silently announced the good news. What had been a faded dream was to become an exciting reality: Elizabeth would bear a son. She knew God had given her a gift she had not dared to hope for at her age.

The pieces of God's once puzzling plan began to fall into place. In another town, Elizabeth's niece, Mary, also unexpectedly became pregnant. Mary soon came to visit Elizabeth, and the women were instantly bound by the unique gifts God had given them. Knowing about Mary must have made Elizabeth marvel at God's timing. Things had worked out even better than she could have planned.

In our own lives, we need to remember that God is in control of every situation. Beyond any fevered planning and rushed efforts of our own, God's timing and plans are perfect. When did you last pause to recognize God's timing in the events of your life?

God's timing is worth waiting for.

Elizabeth's story is told in Luke 1:5-80.

Rejoicing with God's People

ELIZABETH

When Elizabeth heard Mary's greeting, the baby leaped in her womb, and Elizabeth was filled with the Holy Spirit. (Luke 1:41)

An angel sent out the birth announcements: Elizabeth was expecting! The exciting news overwhelmed her family and friends and initiated a series of delightful surprises. As Elizabeth whispered her praise to God for the baby she felt so strong and alive inside of her, the Holy Spirit revealed to her the biggest surprise yet: Mary would give birth to God's Son.

Thus Elizabeth exclaimed, "the mother of my Lord" when she saw Mary standing at her doorstep, beaming with excitement. Elizabeth was by now no stranger to the wonder of the impossible, so she believed Mary and rejoiced.

Even though she herself was pregnant with a long-awaited son, Elizabeth could have envied Mary, whose son would be even greater than her own. Instead, she was filled with joy that the mother of her Lord would visit her. Have you ever envied people whom God has apparently singled out for special blessing? A cure for jealousy is to rejoice with them, realizing that God uses his people in ways best suited to his purpose. The next time you feel a twinge of envy toward someone, remember how Elizabeth rejoiced. Make it your aim to enjoy that person's blessing.

Rejoice in good news, wherever you find it.

Read about Elizabeth's unexpected surprises in Luke 1:5-80.

Faithful Response

MARY

"I am the Lord's servant," Mary answered. "May it be to me as you have said." (Luke 1:38)

The gist of Gabriel's announcement was this: Mary, even though you're a virgin, you're going to have a baby.

How does a young bride-to-be explain that fact to her fiancée, to parents and in-laws, to friends and neighbors? No matter what Mary said, she had to know that people would talk. Her pregnancy was scandalous. The religious community would condemn her. The story would spread like wildfire. Gossips would have a field day.

How unfair! Both Joseph and Mary were devoted followers of God. They knew and God knew that they had been morally pure. But the world that loves to whisper didn't know and probably didn't care. How ironic! To God, Mary was chosen; to the world, Mary was cheap. She might have protested. Instead, she humbly submitted to the plan and purpose of God.

Mary's response to the surprising will of God is a great example for us. When we are confronted by situations that seem crazy or unfair, do we balk and complain? Or do we say, "God, I trust that you are in control, that you are good, and that you know what is best. If this is your plan for my life, then I accept it willingly"? Ask God today to help you develop confidence in his faithfulness in every situation.

How we respond to unexpected events is a good measure of our faith.

Mary is mentioned throughout all four Gospels. She is also mentioned in Acts 1:14.

Reflecting on God's Kindness

MARY

But Mary treasured up all these things and pondered them in her heart. (Luke 2:19)

Mary and Joseph had endured a whirlwind week. The arduous trip from Nazareth to Bethlehem for the census of Caesar Augustus. No vacant rooms anywhere. The birth of the child in a lowly, dirty stable. And then the visitation by the shepherds, wild-eyed with excitement, who told of seeing an angelic army in the heavens and jabbered nonstop about the baby, calling him "Savior" and "Messiah" and "Lord." Mary, the Scriptures say, soaked it all in. In her own mind, she gathered these images and experiences so that she could later recall them and contemplate their profound implications.

Luke's portrait of Mary is that of a pensive, reflective woman. Unlike many who are busy and distracted, Mary valued moments of quietness so that she could meditate on the works of God. It is probably this quality—this desire to fully appreciate all that God is and has done—that makes the difference between ordinary and extraordinary Christians.

The command of Psalm 46:10 is this: "Be still, and know that I am God." Unfortunately, many modern-day believers have a superficial knowledge of God because they are never still long enough to hear his still, small voice. What about you? How long has it been since you spent time quietly reflecting on God's workings in your life?

Use the solitude that God gives to reflect on the magnitude of what he has done.

Mary is mentioned throughout all four Gospels. She is also mentioned in Acts 1:14.

Rejoicing in Fulfilled Promises

SIMEON

Simeon took [Jesus] in his arms and praised God. (Luke 2:28)

Brooklyn Dodger fans used to rally to the cry "Wait until next year" as they rooted for their baseball heroes to win the World Series. Finally, in 1955, their hopes and dreams came true when the Dodgers beat the Yankees.

Simeon had a hope and a dream. God had promised that Simeon would live to see the promised Messiah. Each year as Simeon grew older, he must have wondered if this year would bring the fulfillment of the promise.

When he saw the baby Jesus in the temple with Mary and Joseph, God let him know that the promise had been fulfilled. Simeon praised God from the depths of his heart.

Waiting for God to fulfill his promises or answer our prayers can be a real test of our endurance and faith. We are tempted to stop praying or to settle for something less than God's best plan for us.

Don't lose confidence in God's promises each passing day. Your wait may be as long as Simeon's, but when you see it fulfilled you will have reason to rejoice as he did.

God is faithful. He keeps his promises.

Simeon's story is told in Luke 2:21-35.

The Rewards of Waiting
ANNA

She never left the temple but worshiped night and day, fasting and praying. (Luke 2:37)

Anna was a well-worn example of patient waiting. Her short marriage ended in widowhood. She spent the remainder of her eighty-four-plus years serving in the temple as a prophetess. She was there when Mary and Joseph brought the child Jesus to Jerusalem for the first time. She was probably one of those indelible memories from the early days of her son's life that Mary shared with Luke. Anna overheard Simeon's prophecy about Jesus and immediately added her own excited words of praise for the Savior.

Anna made the temple her home. Though he was writing about widows in the church several decades later, Paul seemed to be describing Anna when he wrote to Timothy, "The widow who is really in need and left all alone puts her hope in God and continues night and day to pray and to ask God for help" (1 Timothy 5:5). Anna discovered that God can make every passage of life meaningful and useful. The long years of widowhood were also effective years of worship and service.

Like Anna, we often patiently go about the daily routines of life. However, perhaps you are waiting for God to reveal a more exciting plan for your life. Ask God to show you the potential for even this time of seeming insignificance to become meaningful and effective service for him.

God can make every passage in life meaningful.

Anna's story is told in Luke 2:36-38.

Obeying When It Doesn't Make Sense

PETER

But if you say so, we'll try again. (Luke 5:5, TLB)

Peter, James, and John—colleagues in a commercial fishing business—were tired and frustrated. They had spent the entire night lowering and raising their nets into the Sea of Galilee. And they had nothing to show for their strenuous labors—not so much as a minnow.

As they cleaned and mended their nets on the shore, a crowd began to gather to hear Jesus, an itinerant teacher. The fishermen had heard him before, and his words intrigued them. As the audience grew and inched closer, Jesus retreated to one of the boats. After concluding his message, Jesus asked Peter to go fishing again! Peter might have thought, *What do you know about fishing, Jesus? You're just a preacher!* or, *We're exhausted. Maybe another time.* But he pushed his reluctance aside and headed out.

The results were astonishing—a greater catch of fish than Peter had ever seen in his life! What did it mean? Peter's head was spinning. But in that moment, he and his friends suddenly realized what they had to do. They left everything there on the beach and followed Jesus.

The same Jesus who suddenly and abruptly brought purpose and hope and help to Peter wants to do the same thing for you. Are you willing to "let down your nets," to do something odd or inconvenient in order to know Jesus better?

We must obey Jesus even when his commands don't seem to make sense.

Peter's life story is found in the Gospels and the book of Acts.

Standing against the Evil One

PETER

I tell you, Peter, the cock will not not crow this day, until you have denied three times that you know me. (Luke 22:34, NRSV)

After the Last Supper, Jesus told Simon Peter that he would deny being one of Jesus' followers. Peter was both shocked and offended: "Lord, I am ready to go with you to prison and to death!" No doubt, Peter meant these words. His intentions were honorable. And yet he was weak. Peter was completely unprepared for the trials that lay ahead. The faithful prayers of Christ were Peter's only hope.

Sadly, but not surprisingly, the events turned out just as Jesus had said they would. Peter was unable to stand up and speak the truth, even to a servant girl. With the words still on his tongue, Peter heard the arresting cry of a rooster. Looking across the courtyard into the sad but loving eyes of Jesus, Peter ran away and wept bitterly.

This episode from the life of Peter reminds us of several important truths: (1) Satan wants to wreck our lives and our relationship with Jesus; (2) in our own strength, we cannot stand against his attacks; and (3) when we repent, admitting our weakness and failure, we can once again strengthen our brothers (Luke 22:32). Ask God to protect you today from the temptations of the evil one. Trust him for the strength to respond as you should in trying situations. If you have failed, turn to God for cleansing and another chance.

Good intentions are not enough against great temptation.

Peter's life story is found in the Gospels and the book of Acts.

Feeding His Sheep

PETER

The third time he said to him, "Simon son of John, do you love me?
. . . [Then] feed my sheep." (John 21:17)

Much has been made of the question Jesus asked Peter three times:
"Do you love me?" Some pastors and teachers talk about how this
question intentionally parallels Peter's three denials of Christ.
Others stress the different Greek words translated *love* in this pas-
sage. Almost forgotten in all these discussions is the emphasis
Jesus placed on ministering to others.

"Feed my sheep," Jesus said each time Peter affirmed his love for
Christ. "If you really love me, you'll care for those who belong to
me." Notice that not once did Jesus ask Peter if he loved sheep.
The bottom-line motivation for ministry was, and is, a love for
Jesus Christ and a willingness to act. There is another message
here as well. "Even if you have failed," Jesus seems to be saying, "I
can still use you in the lives of others."

What about your life? Do you love Jesus? Are you proving your
love for him by serving others? Is your motivation in ministry to
show love for Christ? Anything less will not endure.

Are past failures haunting you and keeping you from seeking
Christ? Look at the lesson of Peter, and realize that God still wants
you to be a fruitful servant for him.

If we love Jesus, we will minister to others.

Peter's life story is found in the Gospels and the book of Acts.

Grudging Generosity

SIMON THE PHARISEE

One who is forgiven little, shows little love. (Luke 7:47, TLB)

Simon probably was quite proud of himself the day he asked Jesus to dine with him. After all, he was being a model of tolerance and goodwill, wasn't he? Not many Pharisees would have mingled with a controversial teacher who associated with sinners. Simon may have expected Jesus to be grateful for being admitted to the company of such a distinguished religious authority as himself.

The unexpected arrival of a prostitute exposed the hospitality of Simon for what it was: calculated and stingy. The lavish gift of perfume that the woman poured on Jesus' feet contrasted with the lack of courtesy Simon had shown to his guest. He had neglected the essential practices of wiping the dust off Jesus' feet, giving the customary kiss, and anointing his guest's head. Even after Jesus had called this to Simon's attention, we are left wondering whether the Pharisee felt any remorse for his unkind behavior.

It is too easy to write Simon off because he belonged to a group known for its hypocrisy. We can—and do—behave much the way Simon did when we assume smugly that God is pleased with our token efforts of service to others. Take time today to reflect on what you are doing for others. Are you motivated by the desire to look good in the public eye, or are you looking for the good you can do without thought of reward?

Service to others should be motivated by a love for God.

Simon's story is found in Luke 7:36-50.

Overflowing Gratitude

MARY MAGDALENE

Mary, called Magdalene, from whom seven demons had gone out . . ." (Luke 8:2, NRSV)

Many churches teach new Christians to share their spiritual story by using this simple formula: (1) Describe your life before you put your faith in Christ; (2) describe how you met Jesus; and (3) describe the changes in your life since trusting him.

Given those guidelines, here's how we could reconstruct Mary Magdalene's testimony: Before she met Christ, Mary was possessed by seven evil spirits, and, given the descriptions of demonic activity in the New Testament, we can only assume hers was a life of misery and madness.

At some point early in his ministry—we don't know precisely when or where—Jesus encountered Mary and freed her from the demons that had tormented her for so long. She was forever changed.

After this life-altering event, Mary Magdalene became a devoted follower of Jesus. She supported his ministry financially. She stayed with him at his crucifixion (when all the male disciples except John had run away). She was there at the tomb on the morning of his resurrection.

We find no trace of "I guess I ought to serve Jesus" or "I probably should give some money to the Lord" in the life of Mary. Instead we see the overflowing gratitude of one who grasped the blessings of her salvation. If your Christian life has become a dull routine of obligations and "ought-to's," ask God to help you recapture the joy of your salvation.

Appreciation, not obligation, should motivate our giving.

More about Mary Magdalene can be found in Matthew 27–28; Mark 15–16; Luke 8; and John 19–20.

Giving Thanks

SUSANNA

Some women went along, from whom he had cast out demons or whom he had healed; among them [was] . . . Susanna.
(Luke 8:2-3, TLB)

Several women accompanied Jesus and his twelve disciples as they traveled to the cities and villages of Galilee, announcing the coming kingdom of God. Susanna was one of three women Luke mentions who had been healed by Jesus and were helping to support his ministry financially.

Jesus gave these women the recognition and responsibility which was often denied them in their culture. Traveling together and learning with the disciples served as an example to all women that Jesus valued them. He taught them. In gratitude, they gave generously from their own money to support Jesus and his disciples.

In what ways has God helped you? In what ways has he healed you? How are you showing your appreciation to Jesus for all that he has done for you? Like Susanna, you can financially support churches and ministries that are spreading the message of Christ.

Giving is an appropriate way to say thank you to God.

Susanna's story is told in Luke 8:1-3.

Celebrity Servant

JOANNA

And Joanna . . . and many others . . . provided for them out of their resources. (Luke 8:3, NRSV)

The Bible treats celebrities with wonderful indifference. It practices what it preaches: The humble are raised up, while the proud are humbled. For people who are inclined to give fame and popularity entirely too much attention, Scripture provides a welcome antidote. The angels rejoice no more loudly when a celebrity repents than when an average person welcomes the Savior.

Joanna could have ranked as a celebrity among the early followers of Jesus. She had access to Herod's house. She might have been a person of some influence. Yet her important work took place far from the palace. She and other women helped meet the needs of Jesus and his traveling band. Luke merely mentions her, but what an honor to be mentioned in the company of Jesus!

And yet there is more. Joanna is mentioned one other time in Luke's Gospel. She was among those who heard and saw firsthand that Jesus was risen from the dead! Her persistent servanthood was rewarded with honor.

How could the basic intention of your life today best be summarized: a pursuit of service to God or self-service?

Those who are doing great things for God often go unnoticed.

Joanna appears in Luke 8:3 and 24:1-10.

The God behind the Healing

SUFFERING WOMAN

Who touched me? (Luke 8:45, NRSV)

How long did she follow Jesus in the crowd, hesitating? Did she avoid asking Jesus for help because she feared he would regard her as other Jewish men did, who refused to touch an "unclean" woman? Fully believing in his power to heal, yet not wanting to attract his attention, she struggled her way through the crowd and lightly touched the fringe of his garment.

Two things happened instantly. Her bleeding stopped, and so did Jesus. He wasn't angry, but he was firm: "Who touched me?" For a moment she thought she might slip away unnoticed, for Peter pointed out that many people were pressing in. But Jesus insisted that someone had tapped healing power from him.

The woman came forward, trembling. She had taken without asking. Would the gift have to be returned? Unmasked, she fell at Jesus' feet, sobbing her story. How relieved she must have been after he addressed her lovingly as "daughter" and assured her release from suffering.

No doubt the woman believed in the awesome power of Jesus and expected to be healed. What she didn't expect was the boundless love and assurance from the person behind the power. Behind every answered prayer and powerful miracle in our lives is a God who loves to surprise us with his love. Give thanks to God for the ways in which he has pleasantly surprised you recently.

When we turn to Jesus, we always get more than we expected.

The story of the suffering woman is told in Matthew 9:20-22; Mark 5:25-34; and Luke 8:43-48.

Caught Up in the Urgent

MARTHA

Lord, don't you care that my sister has left me to do the work by myself? Tell her to help me! (Luke 10:40)

Martha was a perfectionist. You know the type. They agonize over details. They write long to-do lists every day. They bustle about trying to make sure that everything is just so. They are fanatical about order. They detest mess. They compulsively plan and prepare. They are obsessed with not letting things slip through the cracks. People like Martha find it hard to relax—even on vacation. Their sense of worth is tied to what they do or how much they accomplish.

When Jesus came to visit, Martha's stress level shot through the roof. She wanted everything to be just so. But her priorities were clearly out of whack. The Lord of the universe was out in her living room, and she was back in the kitchen frantically concerned about cooking a good meal!

Jesus gently reminded Martha of this important truth: It is more important to spend time with God than to do things for him. God wants us more than he wants our busy activity.

Perhaps you suffer from "the Martha syndrome." You get so caught up in your service that you seldom spend time with the Savior. Make it your goal this week to take at least a few minutes each day to sit quietly in the presence of God. As you let God speak to you from his Word, you will see more clearly the things in life that matter most.

Don't let the urgent things in life crowd out the important things.

Details about the life of Martha can be found in Luke 10:38-42 and John 11:17-45.

The Thanks God Deserves

THE TEN LEPERS

Was no one found to return and give praise to God except this foreigner? (Luke 17:18)

Familiarity breeds contempt, the old saying goes. And perhaps that adage is applicable here in the story of ten men who were healed of leprosy. Luke tells us that this group begged Jesus to heal them, and he granted their request. Yet only one returned to thank him.

What about the other nine? One can speculate that they had heard it all before. They lived in a culture where God was talked about openly. They knew it was just and right to give thanks to God for his blessings. They knew that God was the source of all healing. Yet somehow it didn't register when the reality of those words became apparent. They were so caught up in their healing that they forgot to consider its source. By contrast, it was a Samaritan—an apostate half-breed—who gave thanks to God. It is to him that Jesus said, "Your faith has made you well"—implying that he was healed spiritually as well as physically.

In Christian circles, it is easy to slip into a comfortable pattern of "God talk." We can know all about evangelism, salvation, and discipleship but ignore the God who stands behind everything. Does your spiritual life run on a secondhand knowledge of God? Are you ignoring God's mighty works in your life? Today, pause to give him the thanks he deserves.

Familiarity with God is not the same as intimacy with God.

The story of the ten lepers is found in Luke 17:11-19.

Getting God's Attention

ZACCHAEUS

He wanted to see who Jesus was. (Luke 19:3)

Zacchaeus's approach to life involved compensating for his physical shortness by elevating himself in other ways. He was too short to be noticed, but as a rich tax collector he got plenty of attention. He came late to the parade and couldn't see over the crowd, so he climbed a tree. Zacchaeus wanted to see Jesus but suddenly found himself the object of observation.

As you pass through the world today, remember Zacchaeus in two ways. First, do you identify with his frustration at not being noticed? Do you sometimes wonder whether Jesus would have given you a glance if you had been in Zacchaeus's place? Remember that Jesus knew Zacchaeus's heart as well as he knew the man's name. Jesus knows you, too, and would never miss you in a crowd. Second, how many people will go unnoticed by you today? Make a special effort to notice as many as you can—use people's names; speak to people who don't expect it; show an interest in others' lives.

Read the rest of Zacchaeus's story for the delightful results of Jesus' interest. You may get some wonderful surprises by noticing others.

God doesn't overlook anybody.

Zacchaeus's story is told in Luke 19:1-10.

Keeping Your Eyes Open

CLEOPAS

Were not our hearts burning within us while he talked with us on the road and opened the Scriptures to us? (Luke 24:32)

If Jesus stepped into your life today without warning, how soon would you recognize him? What would give him away? Do you know him well enough to spot him under cover?

For Cleopas, it was the bread that gave Jesus away. That familiar way in which Jesus took the loaf, gave a prayer of thanks, then broke it. Unmistakable. Perhaps as he watched that simple act Cleopas finally noticed Jesus' hands—the nail wounds. It was the Lord.

But Cleopas and his traveling companion had failed to recognize Jesus right away. In fact, they had already spent several hours with Jesus, walking from Jerusalem to Emmaus. What would have happened if they hadn't extended simple hospitality to a fellow traveler at the end of the day? They would have been left with nothing more than an unusual story to share with their friends.

Once they recognized Jesus, he disappeared. They rushed back to Jerusalem to add their report to the growing evidence that the Lord was no longer dead. As they were sharing their tale, Jesus appeared again. Cleopas saw Jesus twice on Resurrection Day. How many clues about his presence will he place in your way today? Have you asked him yet to help you keep your eyes open?

Stay alert—watch for Jesus' appearances in your life today.

Cleopas's story is told in Luke 24:13-48.

A Hopeful Disciple

ANDREW

The first thing Andrew did was to find his brother Simon and tell him, "We have found the Messiah." (John 1:41)

Andrew knew a good thing when he saw it. He was the first person identified in the Gospels as a follower of Jesus. As soon as he met Jesus, he rushed to tell his brother Simon. Up to that time, Andrew had been one of John the Baptist's disciples. But when John pointed out Jesus as the Savior, Andrew became a follower of Christ. Later, when Jesus invited him to become a fisher of men, Andrew dropped his nets without a backward glance.

Another glimpse of Andrew's spontaneously positive outlook comes from an occasion when Jesus fed a multitude. Most of the disciples were initially stumped by the logistics. But Andrew, perhaps in jest, or in hope, essentially said, "Here's a kid with five loaves and two fish . . . but that's not much." It turned out to be more than enough.

Andrew seized the positive in life with both hands. Even when the positive outlook seemed like a long shot, like the bread, Andrew took a chance on it. As Andrew's life affirms, one person's bent on hopefulness can become a source of blessing for others. The world needs Andrews!

If you are not an Andrew yourself, try to spot one this week and give him or her a little encouragement. Being a hopeful person can sometimes be a lonely job!

Encourage a ray of hope whenever you can.

Glimpses of Andrew are found in Matthew 4:18-20; Mark 3:18; John 1:35-42; 6:8-9; 12:21-22; and Acts 1:13.

Pointing Others to Jesus

JOHN THE BAPTIST

When [John] saw Jesus passing by, he said, "Look, the Lamb of God!"
(John 1:36)

The ministry of John the Baptist evokes a number of images: his strange diet of locusts and honey; his odd clothing; his take-no-prisoners preaching style; his gruesome death at the hands of Herodias. But perhaps the most striking aspect of John's life is the way that he constantly pointed others to Christ.

In the desert he had the perfect opportunity to make a name for himself and enjoy a bit of celebrity. Instead, he talked about Jesus. As more and more people came to hear him, he could have tried to gather and keep a following. Instead, he encouraged folks to follow Christ.

When John's disciples expressed concern that the crowds were thinning out because people were following Jesus, John might have sulked or dreamed up a gimmick to win back the allegiance of the masses. Instead, he said, "He must become greater; I must become less." He understood that he was just a servant. Perhaps that is why Jesus said, "Among those born of women there has not risen anyone greater than John the Baptist."

Resist the temptation to promote yourself, your church, your brand of theology, or your Christian group. Instead, make the commitment to "make Jesus greater" by pointing others to him.

Your words and your deeds should point others to Jesus.

Read about John the Baptist in all four Gospels. He is also mentioned in Acts 1:5, 22; 10:37; 11:16; 13:24-25; 18:25; 19:3-4.

Honest Doubter

JOHN THE BAPTIST

When John heard in prison what Christ was doing, he sent his disciples to ask him, "Are you the one who was to come, or should we expect someone else?" (Matthew 11:2-3)

Things were not turning out the way John the Baptist expected. He had done his best to tell people that Jesus was the long-awaited Messiah. He had faithfully preached his God-given message of repentance. He had even chastised Herod for adultery and called on him to repent!

The next thing John knew, he was in prison. Loneliness and self-pity eventually gave way to doubt. *If Jesus really were the Messiah,* John likely reasoned, *God would never have allowed me to be locked up. I'm the messenger sent to prepare the way, so why am I here?*

And so John sent some of his disciples to Jesus to question him. "Are you really the Messiah?" they asked. Jesus was not offended. He simply reminded them of the evidence—his words and his works.

Even devoted people like John the Baptist have periodic episodes of honest doubt. They want to believe, and as soon as they are reminded of the truth, their faith is restored. Don't be devastated if you have momentary lapses in your faith. As Frederick Buechner once noted, "Doubts are the ants in the pants of faith. They keep it awake and moving." Just remind yourself of the things that you know are true, and you'll be OK.

Even the most faithful believers struggle with doubt.

John the Baptist's story is found in all four Gospels. He is further mentioned in Acts 1:5, 22; 10:37; 11:16; 13:24-25; 18:25; 19:3-4.

Working in Unexpected Ways

NATHANAEL

As they approached, Jesus said, "Here comes an honest man—a true son of Israel." (John 1:47, TLB)

Nathanael was a devout Jew from Cana in Galilee. Like so many other Hebrews who knew and obeyed the Scriptures, Nathanael was waiting for the arrival of the Messiah, who would bring salvation to Israel. One day, Nathanael was approached by Philip, a friend from Bethsaida. Philip was clearly excited as he told Nathanael that the Messiah was in their midst. He was a Nazarene named Jesus.

Nathanael was surprised and skeptical. Nazareth was the site of a Roman army garrison. How could the Messiah come from such a tainted town? Why not Jerusalem or some other Jewish city with better credentials?

Philip convinced Nathanael to come see for himself. Fortunately, Nathanael went and met Jesus for himself. A short conversation with Jesus was all Nathanael needed to convince himself that Jesus was, in fact, the long-awaited Messiah. Nathanael became a devoted disciple of Jesus.

Honest people don't form hard and fast opinions based merely on their presuppositions, their prejudices, or their past experiences. They know that things are not always what they appear to be, and that God often works in unexpected ways. Be hungry for the truth, but be willing to let God change your ideas about what he is like.

We must be careful not to put God in a box.

The story of Nathanael (also known as Bartholomew) is found in Matthew 10:3; Mark 3:18; Luke 6:14; John 1:45-51; 21:2; and Acts 1:13.

Growing in Boldness
NICODEMUS

He was accompanied by Nicodemus, the man who earlier had visited Jesus at night. (John 19:39)

When we first meet Nicodemus in the Gospel of John, he is coming to Jesus under cover of night. He is a Pharisee, one of Israel's prominent and respected religious leaders. He knows the Scriptures inside and out, yet he seems to be searching for something more. Nicodemus discovers that eternal life comes only when people put their faith in Jesus.

Exactly when Nicodemus became a follower of Christ, we do not know. But we can see definite signs of growth in his life. In John 7, as the Pharisees are having a heated discussion about what to do with Jesus, Nicodemus sticks his neck out: "Shouldn't we at least give him a hearing?" It's not exactly a ringing endorsement, but Nicodemus catches heat for even attempting to be fair.

Later, when the religious leaders have succeeded in getting rid of Jesus, Nicodemus and Joseph of Arimathea take a risky step: They ask for the body of Jesus so they can give it a proper burial. We have no record of either man suffering any consequences. But very likely Nicodemus was scorned, perhaps even shunned by the other Pharisees.

Nicodemus's spiritual pilgrimage was marked by slow but steady growth. He gradually became bolder in revealing his love and devotion for Christ. Can others see similar growth in your life? What is one action you can take today to identify publicly with Christ?

A sure sign of growth is a faith of increasing boldness.

The Bible mentions Nicodemus in John 3:1-21; 7:50-51; 19:39-42.

Reason for Rejoicing

THE MAN BORN BLIND

I was blind but now I see! (John 9:25)

Was he listening when the disciples asked Jesus, "Who sinned, this man or his parents, that he was born blind?" (John 9:2). Was he hurt by their insensitivity? Did they think blind people can't hear? Did he understand Jesus' answer? Was there something in that voice that gave him hope? What did he think when he heard Jesus spit? How did it feel to have mud rubbed on his eyes? Did he hesitate for even a moment at Jesus' prescription? Who helped him stumble his way to the Pool of Siloam? The Bible reduces it all to a sentence: "The man went and washed, and came home seeing" (9:7).

The miracle of this man's new sight gave the sophisticates fits. "He can't do that. He broke the Sabbath. He must be a sinner. This guy is crazy! You're crazy!"

The Pharisees had their own reasons for complaining, and today we have our own. We grump and complain at every injustice, every ache, every pain—even after it's over—as if God owes us better. Or it doesn't seem fair: Why *her* and not *me*?

But the man born blind held no grudges. He just rejoiced. Why can't we all do that?

Only grateful hearts can see God's miracles.

The blind man's story is told in John 9:1-38.

Obeying the Call

LAZARUS

Lazarus, come out! (John 11:43)

A scene like the one in Bethany that John describes is repeated around the world each day. A grieving family gathers at a graveside. Friends are silent, agonizing over what to say. Their downcast eyes and shifting feet provide more distraction than comfort. On this day, drawn by grief and duty, people came from Jerusalem and the surrounding area to pay their last respects to a citizen of Bethany.

Jesus' friend Lazarus was dead. His brief sickness overpowered the medicine available. Jesus had been sent for but failed to arrive in time. Death, on the other hand, failed to wait. The body was quickly wrapped and placed in a tomb. Four days later, Jesus arrived.

Lazarus was spoken about and spoken to, but we don't have a record of a single word he said. We do know that he listened to Jesus. Even when death separated them, Lazarus responded to Jesus' voice. We know because he came hobbling out of the tomb, still wrapped in the burial cloths. Jesus raised him from the dead!

When all is said and done, what really matters will be what God accomplished through us. We will not be able to take much credit. We have Christ's invitation to participate in his work, but we must not forget that he will do much more than we are able to know. Our obedience to Jesus' call will make the difference. Do you listen to Christ faithfully by reading his Word?

How are you responding to Christ's commands today?

Lazarus's role as an "active spectator" is recorded in John 11:1–12:11.

Time to Stop Doubting

THOMAS

"My Lord and my God!" Thomas said. (John 20:28, TLB)

The disciples were chattering excitedly about their visit with the resurrected Christ. Thomas listened to their eager claims, but part of him was still unconvinced. He voiced his doubts. For that moment of honest questioning, he was tagged with the unflattering nickname "Doubting Thomas." The label stuck. How unfortunate! Most of us probably would have responded in a similar way.

Just over a week later, Thomas got his wish. As the men gathered in a locked room, Jesus suddenly materialized. The Savior looked at Thomas and said, "Stop doubting and believe." Whatever uncertainty Thomas had gave way to immediate and total trust. "My Lord and my God!" he exclaimed. By his response, it is apparent that Thomas had wanted to believe. He was honestly searching for the truth. And when Jesus revealed himself, Thomas's doubts dissolved.

Temporary, occasional doubts are normal in the Christian life. They can even be a good thing if they motivate us to search harder for God. It is only when we languish in unbelief that we displease the Lord.

If you are struggling with doubts today, ask God to give you a fresh glimpse of Jesus. When he does, stop doubting and believe!

Honest questioning is a good thing; stubborn skepticism is not!

The story of Thomas is found in the Gospels. He is also mentioned in Acts 1:13.

Laboring Out of the Public Eye

MATTHIAS

The lot fell to Matthias; so he was added to the eleven apostles.
(Acts 1:26)

After Judas had killed himself and before the coming of the Holy Spirit at Pentecost, the followers of Jesus huddled in Jerusalem. Gathered in an upper room, they waited and prayed. At some point during these forty days, Peter addressed the group. He reviewed the sad defection of Judas and asked the disciples to choose a replacement. Peter cited both qualifications and a job description: Such an individual had to have been present during the entire course of Jesus' public ministry, and he would be responsible for being a witness of Christ's resurrection.

Two names were proposed—Barsabbas and Matthias. God revealed through the casting of lots that Matthias was the man. Matthias is not mentioned again in the New Testament. Various legends and traditions say that he either preached the gospel in Judea and was stoned by the Jews or that he was martyred in Ethiopia or Colchis.

From this scant description of Matthias we can glean these truths: (1) He had been a long-term, faithful follower of Christ; (2) being chosen to serve does not guarantee a position of prominence; and (3) whatever we are, whatever we accomplish, is all due to the grace of God.

Are you being faithful today in following Christ? Are you willing to serve in obscurity and do things that others may never know about? Do you feel resentful when others get more press or more praise? Remember the life of Matthias, chosen by God to labor out of the public eye.

The opportunity to serve results from God's grace.

The sketchy story of Matthias is found in Acts 1:15-26.

Disappointment Is Not Defeat

BARSABBAS

Show us which of these two you have chosen to take over this apostolic ministry. (Acts 1:24-25)

Judas was gone, and the apostles decided he should be replaced. They narrowed their choices down to two men (Barsabbas [Justus] and Matthias). Each of them met an important qualification: They had been followers of Jesus from the beginning. When lots were drawn, Matthias was added to the apostolic band. From then on, Barsabbas must have been known as the "almost apostle." The prayer and the lots ensured that the choice was not a popular or political one, but one in which God was involved.

Barsabbas may have been disappointed with the outcome, but he may just as well have been relieved. In order to have been identified as a possible candidate, he must have already been active in ministry. Perhaps God honored his willingness to serve by permitting him to serve in some other way.

Keeping our lives available to God may not mean we will be able to do everything we would like to do, or even what others would like us to do. Jobs will come and go; doors will open and close; opportunities will be presented or withdrawn. God is neither surprised nor caught off guard by such situations. He will continue to honor our willingness to be used in other ways. For what recent "disappointment" do you need to be mindful that God is in complete control?

The closed door of disappointment announces an open door of opportunity.

Barsabbas's story is told in Acts 1:23-26.

The Encourager

BARNABAS

Barnabas took [Paul] and brought him to the apostles. (Acts 9:27)

By any reasonable standard, it was a mismatch of wits that could have spelled disaster for the church. Saul (later Paul), the urbane intellectual, forceful Pharisee and Roman citizen, now claimed to be a Christian, and he wanted to meet the leaders at Jerusalem. Everyone except Barnabas smelled a plot. If Saul was faking it, the heart of the church would be vulnerable.

Barnabas cast worry to the wind and went into the city to meet this new brother in Christ. It was Barnabas's faith in the power of God that sent him. It was his willingness to believe the best of each person that won him a reputation as *encourager* throughout the early church.

We need such people today. Most folks in most churches do not know each other well and are unsure how to make friends. That's one of the reasons most church hallway conversation has to do with weather and sports—very safe. With a Barnabas in the church—an encourager of the saints—people begin to open up, conversation digs deeper, people begin to trust each other, and the mission of the church is recovered. What ailing brother or sister can you boost with a phone call or a gesture of acceptance, hospitality, or help?

Believing the best about people is really believing in God's power to renew a life—any life, all kinds of people.

Barnabas's story is told in Acts 4:36-37 and 9:27–15:39. He is also mentioned in 1 Corinthians 9:6; Galatians 2:1, 9, 13; and Colossians 4:10.

Taking Criticism the Right Way

BARNABAS

By their hypocrisy even Barnabas was led astray. (Galatians 2:13)

Paul's long-time friend and early mentor, the great encourager Barnabas, had followed the separatists' belief that Gentiles could not be full-fledged Christians. That was no part of the gospel, and Paul told him so. It must have been bitter medicine for Barnabas to realize that he had faltered at the point of his greatest strength.

In our areas of strength we expect only praise and admiration, yet we all need the corrective influence of a wider Christian community. No Christian can live isolated from the church's discipline, hard as it is to swallow—especially when it strikes so close to one's gifts.

Barnabas survived and prospered because he admitted his mistake. He took correction and went on. Community was strengthened, ruffled feelings soothed by grace, and mission strategy clarified. By any measure, the church would have been worse had Barnabas stormed off to pout and sputter about ingrates and malcontents.

There is no virtue in defending our mistakes or in finding fault with those who spot them. Far better to defer to the critics—or at least to give them a hearing. We can learn from each other without taking offense. Never become so proud of your talents that you cannot hear the voice of an honest critic.

Even the best aren't perfect . . . and they admit it.

Barnabas's story is told in Acts 4:36-37; 9:27–15:39. He is also mentioned in 1 Corinthians 9:6; Galatians 2:1, 9, 13; and Colossians 4:10.

God Is Not Deceived

ANANIAS OF JERUSALEM

Ananias, Satan has filled your heart. (Acts 5:3, TLB)

Almost any human group will include those who want to belong without the trouble of real commitment. The early Christian church had its share of those who failed to count the cost. Ananias and his wife, Sapphira, preferred to appear committed rather than to be genuine in their faith. They were under the mistaken notion that appearances are just as good as the real thing, but cheaper. Caught in the act of dishonest giving, they lost everything.

When he confronted Ananias, Peter made the problem very clear. The couple had owned their property and were free to sell or keep it as they wished. They were not obliged to give to the church, either. Ananias's sin came when he desired to gain prestige by making others think they had given the entire amount when they had only given part. Among those they intended to deceive was God. In their case, his punishment was quick and deadly.

How often would we be prevented from twisting the truth if we realized that beyond the people we may trick is a God we cannot deceive? Ask God to help you be a person of truth today.

God even knows when we lie to ourselves!

The story of Ananias is told in Acts 5:1-6.

Taking Sin Lightly

SAPPHIRA

The feet of the men who buried your husband are at the door, and they will carry you out also. (Acts 5:9)

The Internal Revenue Service would love to have the discernment Peter had the day he questioned Ananias and Sapphira about the amount of their gift to the church. How much would it be worth to know for certain if someone is telling the truth?

When Sapphira lied to Peter about the price of the land and the gift they were giving to the church, it wasn't a memory lapse or a slight exaggeration. She had full knowledge of what her husband was going to tell the leaders of the church. What she didn't know was that the consequences for lying were going to be severe and immediate.

When are you most tempted to lie . . . when you are trying to stay out of trouble or trying to save money? If you knew lying would bring severe and immediate consequences, would you let even an exaggeration come out of your mouth? If God chose to impose the same swift judgment on you that he did on Sapphira, how long would you last?

Whatever lies you have told, big or small, recent or old, can be forgiven by confessing them to both God and the people involved. Why wait until you are in the presence of God to tell the truth? Tell the truth right now, while God is giving you the opportunity that Sapphira didn't get.

Lying always costs us something.

Sapphira's story is told in Acts 5:1-11.

An Unlikely Advocate

GAMALIEL

If it is of God, you will not be able to overthrow them—in that case you may even be found fighting against God! (Acts 5:39, NRSV)

Christians owe a lot to Gamaliel. He trained one of the greatest defenders of the faith—a young man he knew as Saul of Tarsus. He equipped Saul with a thorough understanding of the Hebrew Scriptures. His student later spoke of Gamaliel humbly and with respect (see Acts 22:3).

Gamaliel may have been present at the trials of Jesus. However, he was not mentioned by name, nor was he apparently consulted. Later, during the explosive times following Jesus' resurrection and the birth of the Christian church, Gamaliel became a voice of reason. By that time, Peter and most of the apostles had been arrested. The Jewish council was intent on killing them as they had Jesus. But the previously timid disciples now refused to be cowed.

Gamaliel astutely observed that the popularity of the apostles would only be enhanced if they were martyred. He understood that fanaticism burns itself out, while the truth becomes stronger under pressure. He also considered the possibility that the apostles were speaking the truth and warned of the consequences of opposing God. His reasoning won the release of the Christian leaders. Perhaps he even understood more about Jesus than he revealed.

God finds his advocates in unusual places.

Gamaliel's wisdom is recorded in Acts 5:33-42; 22:1-5.

Chance Encounter?

PHILIP

Then the Spirit said to Philip, "Go over to this chariot and join it."
(Acts 8:29, NRSV)

Philip, the deacon and evangelist, saw God work in powerful
ways. Driven from Jerusalem because of persecution, Philip had
journeyed to Samaria and begun preaching about Christ. God
confirmed Philip's message with miraculous signs—exorcisms and
healings—and the Samaritans put their faith in Christ, finding joy.

Suddenly, right in the midst of this intense time of revival, God
summoned Philip to the desert. From a human perspective, this
might have seemed illogical: Why leave a place where many people
were finding God for a place where few people even live? And yet
Philip was obedient.

There, on the road to Gaza, Philip "just happened" to encounter
an Ethiopian government official. "Coincidentally," this man was
reading a scroll of Isaiah. "By chance" the man invited Philip into
his chariot to explain the meaning of the Scriptures, after which
the man embraced the truth about Jesus. After baptizing the man,
Philip was miraculously transported elsewhere. The Ethiopian
returned home, where, according to tradition, the gospel began to
spread throughout Africa.

God still works through chance encounters. The next time you
meet a stranger or get delayed in traffic or end up in a place you
did not intend to visit, pay careful attention to the Spirit of God.
You may be on the verge of a divine appointment with eternal
ramifications!

Chance encounters are really divine appointments.

Philip's story is found in Acts 6:1-7; 8:5-40; 21:8-10.

Shining for Christ

STEPHEN

But filled with the Holy Spirit, he gazed into heaven and saw the glory of God and Jesus standing at the right hand of God. (Acts 7:55, NRSV)

Stephen was a man of achievement. He was one of seven leaders chosen to supervise the food distribution to the elderly in the early church. He was an outstanding administrator, teacher, and debater. But he is chiefly remembered as the church's first martyr (person who dies for his or her faith).

More significant than what Stephen did, however, was how he lived. Acts describes a man who was full of God's grace and power, and full of faith. Twice we find references to the fact that Stephen was a man who was filled with the Holy Spirit, bearing the fruit of love, joy, peace, patience, kindness, goodness, faithfulness, gentleness, and self-control.

What we are is more important than what we do. Before we busy ourselves with serving God, we need to make sure that we are yielded to God. When we do give the Spirit of God the freedom to change us, we become walking billboards, testimonies to the life-changing power of God.

It's worth noting that as Stephen prepared to address the Jewish religious leaders, everyone in attendance noticed that "his face was like the face of an angel." In other words, Stephen's countenance was radiant! Do you shine for Christ in a similar fashion? If not, yield the control of your life to the Spirit.

It's obvious to all when we are filled with the Holy Spirit.

The story of Stephen is found in Acts 6:3–8:2.

No Action Is Insignificant

STEPHEN

Then [Stephen] fell on his knees and cried out, "Lord, do not hold this sin against them." (Acts 7:60)

Stephen's sermon to the Jewish ruling council started off like a pleasant review of Jewish history. But the more he preached, the more pointed his words became. By the end, Stephen was shouting, "You stiff-necked people. . . . You always resist the Holy Spirit!"

Enraged, the Jews began to stone Stephen. As he lay dying, he scanned the crowd (which included Saul of Tarsus) and prayed, "Lord, do not hold this sin against them." The whole episode seemed like such a waste. . . . Stephen, the gifted servant of God, dying before he could ever make an impact. But is that the whole story?

Stephen's last prayer was a plea that his murderers might find forgiveness. In other words, it was a prayer for their salvation! And, at least in the case of Saul, God heard and answered this request. Stephen's prayer contributed to Saul's conversion. And Paul went on to become God's leading spokesman for the Good News of Christ!

You may think you are leading a quiet, ineffective life. You may not see any tangible fruit. But continue to be faithful and continue to pray. Some small, "insignificant" action on your part may one day be revealed as a crucial turning point in salvation history. Without knowing it, you might play a role in the conversion of the next Paul or Martin Luther or Billy Graham! We never know what God may do through us.

Your prayers can change the world!

The story of Stephen is found in Acts 6:3–8:2.

A Matter of Serving

PARMENAS

Brothers, choose seven men from among you who are known to be full of the Spirit and wisdom. (Acts 6:3)

As the early church grew, so did its administrative work. One particular ministry that was requiring more and more oversight from the apostles was the care of widows in the church. The twelve disciples realized that in devoting too much of their energy to the physical needs of their church, they were neglecting its spiritual needs. So, they conferred and decided to delegate the feed-the-widows ministry to seven other qualified men.

The men selected had to meet exacting standards. It was stipulated that they be godly, wise men. Among those chosen was Parmenas, a man of whom we know very little. Various church traditions say that he was either martyred at Philippi during the reign of Trajan or that he become the bishop of Soli.

Assume for a moment that your church leaders decided to pick seven individuals to serve on a special ministry team. If the requirements for service were the same as those mentioned above—being wise and filled with the Spirit—do you think you would be nominated? Would your name even come up in the discussion?

Leadership in the church is not a matter of getting a position and then serving; it is about serving, period. If you are letting God work in you and through you, others will eventually notice. Even if they don't, God will. And that's what ultimately matters.

Those who yield to the will of God are useful to God.

Parmenas is mentioned in Acts 6:5.

The Source of Spiritual Fervor

PAUL

Never be lacking in zeal, but keep your spiritual fervor, serving the Lord. (Romans 12:11)

Paul was full of zeal. He was a passionate man who threw himself into everything he did. Before he met Christ on the road to Damascus, Paul (then known as Saul) zealously persecuted Christians. Then, after his conversion, we glimpse in Philippians 3 Paul's burning desire to know Christ more intimately. Throughout the book of Acts, we see Paul's intense commitment to take the gospel to the world. In Paul's letters we witness Paul's fervent effort to see believers grow up into "all the fullness of God."

What enabled Paul to maintain such spiritual fervor? He had been captured by the love of Christ. Jesus was real to Paul. He was not just a theological idea or a religious concept. Christ saved him and gave him a mission. Paul's life was consumed with the love of Jesus.

Remember how you felt the first time you fell in love? Remember how you wanted nothing else but to be with your sweetheart? Remember how you were willing to do anything—anything at all—for the sake of your beloved? That's a good if imperfect picture of the kind of passion with which we are to serve Christ. If you have "forsaken your first love" (Revelation 2:4), ask the Lord to help you regain a deep passion for him.

Our spiritual health is revealed by the things we get passionate about.

Paul's life story is told in Acts 7:58–28:31. Other details about him are found throughout the New Testament Epistles.

The Difference Praise Makes

PAUL

Say "hello" to Tryphaena and Tryphosa, the Lord's workers.
(Romans 16:12, TLB)

Few things in life motivate us like words of sincere praise. To be affirmed publicly is a tremendous reward. To be recognized for one's faithful service—especially by a respected leader—is a richly satisfying payoff.

The apostle Paul understood the importance of a well-timed word of encouragement. In every letter he wrote, he looked for godly attitudes and actions to commend. Here are just a few examples:

"Greet Apelles, tested and approved in Christ" (Romans 16:10). "I was glad when Stephanas, Fortunatus and Achaicus arrived . . . for they refreshed my spirit and yours also. Such men deserve recognition" (1 Corinthians 16:17-18). "Tychicus, [is a] dear brother and faithful servant in the Lord" (Ephesians 6:21). "Welcome [Epaphroditus] in the Lord with great joy, and honor men like him, because he almost died for the work of Christ" (Philippians 2:29-30). "Epaphras . . . is always wrestling in prayer for you" (Colossians 4:12).

Do you notice and applaud the efforts of others? Do you make a big deal out of their praiseworthy accomplishments? Make it your goal today to affirm everyone you interact with. Then watch what a difference a few words of praise can make!

Affirm your fellow workers in Christ.

Paul's life story is told in Acts 7:58–28:31. Other details about him are found throughout the New Testament Epistles.

The Thorn in the Flesh

PAUL

There was given me a thorn in my flesh, a messenger of Satan, to torment me. (2 Corinthians 12:7)

Christians through the centuries have speculated as to the nature of Paul's "thorn in the flesh." Was it—as various commentators suggest—a disease of the eyes, malaria, epilepsy, a stomach disorder like dysentery, or was it something else? We can't say for sure. We do know, however, that it caused him great discomfort. It was painful enough that he repeatedly asked God to take it away.

Yet Paul's prayers went unanswered. In time, Paul was able to recognize the hidden blessing of his debilitating condition. It kept him humble, forced him to depend on God, shaped his character, and turned Paul into a valuable role model for other Christians.

Do you suffer from unpleasant things that you wish God would remove? Perhaps you are struggling with a financial reversal, a lingering illness, a physical handicap, an unwarranted attack on your character, a relational breakdown that is beyond your control, a parenting dilemma, or a job crisis. If so, know that God understands your suffering. Depend on him to turn your thorn in the flesh into an opportunity to trust him more deeply and see his power more clearly in your life.

God's grace is more than enough for whatever problems you face.

Paul's life story is told in Acts 7:58–28:31. Other details about him are found throughout the New Testament Epistles.

Gifts for Hire

SIMON THE SORCERER

He offered them money, saying, "Give me also this power." (Acts 8:18-19, NRSV)

Simon the sorcerer thought he could buy God's power, as if it were some sort of potion that could be doled out to talented magicians. Peter rebuked Simon harshly and urged him to turn from his selfish and misguided plans. To his credit, Simon responded with a humble request for prayer.

We get the word *simony*, which refers to the sin of buying or selling spiritual things, from this man's market-driven attitude toward God. It is a great perversion of Christianity to use God for our own purposes rather than letting God use us for the accomplishment of his purposes.

Serving God is not a franchise operation. We don't pay a fee and get a proven product to market to others for personal gain. There are too many modern examples of people who are using God's name for their own fame and financial benefit.

Listen to your own prayers. Are you asking God to give to you and do for you for your own gain? Do you go to church expecting to get something for yourself or to give worship to God and encouragement and service to others? It can be a great temptation to use church, connections with certain people, or even God himself for our own ends. Or to think we can buy him. We can't.

God doesn't exist to serve us—we exist to serve him.

Simon's story is told in Acts 8:9-25.

309

A Responsive Heart
ETHIOPIAN EUNUCH

He was reading the prophet Isaiah. (Acts 8:28, NRSV)

The Ethiopian eunuch had more to think about than most people. An official in Queen Candace's court, he had charge of the entire Ethiopian treasury. But his stopover this day came about on a trip from Jerusalem, where he had visited not to negotiate a deal or to broker a settlement but to worship the God of Israel. During the trip back he had a little free time on his hands, and he decided to use it reading the Scriptures.

And that is where he speaks to us. He focused his attention on the passage in Isaiah that foretells the suffering of Christ. He read even though he did not really understand it. When the opportunity (through Philip) came to have it explained to him, he jumped at it. No wonder he became a Christian that day.

A man caught up in the political machinery would not have had time for Scripture reading. A man concerned with power and selfish interest would not have concerned himself with personal reflection. A man too calloused to hear the words of Isaiah 53 would not have cared about the Suffering Servant. But this man's heart responded when he heard about Christ. How often do you listen with your heart as you read the Scriptures, hear a sermon, or seek advice? Have an open mind; have a softened heart. Let the truth of what you hear capture your attention.

The Scriptures change soft hearts.

The Ethiopian eunuch's story is told in Acts 8:26-40.

Obedience Overcomes Fear

ANANIAS OF DAMASCUS

In Damascus there was a disciple named Ananias. (Acts 9:10)

"Not him, Lord; that's impossible. He could never become a Christian!" That was Ananias's response when God told him of Saul's conversion. One moment Ananias was pondering the possibility of his own imprisonment and death; the next, God was telling him to go help the man who held the warrant for his arrest. Ananias must have felt like running; but he decided to obey God anyway.

Until God knocked him from his saddle, Christians seemed to be at the mercy of Saul. Suddenly, he was blindly at their mercy. Saul's first experience in his new life was a soft touch and a stranger's voice calling him "brother." Ananias left a lasting impression on Saul. Later, when Paul told a crowd about his conversion, Ananias was the only person he mentioned by name.

Ananias was only in the spotlight for a moment. His role was small but significant. Even though God told him of his plans for Saul, Ananias probably did not appreciate the scope of the events in which he was participating. We usually fail to see what God can accomplish through our own "small efforts." Fortunately, we are not asked to understand the entire plan. We are simply asked to be faithful with our part. What "small" opportunities to practice obedience are already before you today?

Fear can highlight the importance of obedience.

The story of Ananias is told in Acts 9:10-19; 22:12-16.

Devoted to Good Works

DORCAS

She was devoted to good works and acts of charity. (Acts 9:36, NRSV)

Who makes a local church function well? We can usually think of several kinds of people who regularly make life in the local church miserable. But what kind of people provide balance? The pulse of the church can most often be found among those who quietly work at good deeds and obedient service—people like Dorcas.

True to her calling, Dorcas only appears briefly in the New Testament. She was a disciple of Jesus in Joppa. She was too busy to sit still in the spotlight very long. In fact, she probably didn't plan to get sick and found it a nuisance to discover she was dying. There was too much to get done to allow any time for dying.

When Dorcas died, Peter happened to be visiting in nearby Lydda. The Christians in Joppa sent him a message to come. Since they had prepared her body for burial, it isn't likely that they were expecting a miracle. They simply wanted to honor Dorcas by having Peter present at the funeral. When Peter arrived, Dorcas's wake turned into a wake-up call. How overwhelmed they must have been to receive back someone they were going to miss so badly.

Undoubtedly, Dorcas went back to her work. But Luke tells us many people came to believe because of what God did through her and to her.

Do you know a woman or man in your church who serves quietly and gladly like Dorcas did? Show your appreciation in some special way today.

The life of a true disciple always leaves behind a sweet sorrow.

Dorcas's story is briefly told in Acts 9:32-42.

The Quiet Revolution
CORNELIUS

He and all his family were devout and God-fearing; he gave generously to those in need and prayed to God regularly. (Acts 10:2)

Beneath the surface, there's a revolution going on. You might not see it when you walk through the office or hear it when the swing shift gets onto the assembly line, but it's there. In every walk of life, in every place where people do business, a spiritual revolution is transforming lives.

Cornelius was an early part of it. He did his job, but in a special way that told everyone he was different. He approached his men with discipline, but also with compassion. He imposed the power of Rome on the Jewish people around him, but with a keen eye toward fairness and reason. In Cornelius and among his family, the revolution was defining a new kind of person: a Christian.

Did Cornelius ever become a Roman general? Did his faith help or hurt his career? We do not know. But wherever Cornelius went, he was a witness to the revolution God started back in Genesis. He would never be *just* another centurion. His life had purpose that transcended rank and battle ribbon. His heart knew joy and peace in a new company of brothers and sisters, the church of Jesus Christ.

Be like Cornelius. Let God put his revolution in your heart.
God's transforming power changes lives.

Cornelius's part in the revolution is told in Acts 10:1–11:18.

God's New Community

CORNELIUS

The gift of the Holy Spirit had been poured out even on the Gentiles.
(Acts 10:45)

Cornelius's family was a test case of how far God was willing to go in changing people's hearts. Peter himself was unsure whether non-Jews had any share of God's attention. How could God give his blessings to such an unvarnished secularist as a Roman army officer? Such a person represented everything offensive: a sharpened sword, emperor worship, foreign occupancy. But a strange thing happened! God sent the Spirit powerfully on Cornelius and his family.

"Hey," they must have said, "God is blind to all those Gentile-Jewish distinctions that call one group good and the other bad. United in Christ and blessed by the Spirit, Gentile and Jewish believers are true brothers, however different their traditions and political bents." One in Christ! How surprising of God!

Today we know that other divisions are just as illusory in God's eyes: race and skin color, ethnic background, gender and social status. God has declared all people to be his people—none more than others by any measure of color or wealth. Still, many churches pretend that God prefers white to brown, rich to poor, man to woman. So the revolution begun in Cornelius's home still goes on—proving that God isn't finished with us yet.

Do not discriminate, dear brother or sister. It isn't kosher.

God is building a new community of brothers and sisters in the church, where love overcomes all barriers.

Cornelius's story is told in Acts 10:1–11:18.

Bad News and More Bad News

AGABUS

Agabus . . . had the gift of prophecy. (Acts 21:10, TLB)

Agabus holds the distinction of being one of the few prophets of New Testament times to have his name recorded in Scripture. We have two of his prophecies on record: He predicted a severe famine that would affect Judea, and he foretold Paul's imprisonment in Jerusalem. "I have bad news, and I have bad news," we might have heard him say.

But Agabus's prophecies were not intended as declarations of doom. Rather, they offered knowledge that could be used to prepare the right response. In the first instance, his prophecy stirred the church into a relief action for the believers in Judea. In the second, Paul's companions panicked while Paul rightly took the news as advance notice of God's plan for him; he declared his devotion to Christ and got ready to go. Everyone learned from that.

Should Agabus have held his tongue because of "what people might think"? Of course not! He delivered God's words because that was his God-given job. God gave him a prophecy; he *had* to hand it off.

Don't be timid about serving God with the gifts he's given you just because you see some natural barrier. Many people around you need your word of encouragement, act of hospitality, or whatever other gift you may have.

God works *among* **his people** *through* **his people.**

The story of Agabus is found in Acts 11:25-30; 21:10-17.

Expecting the Unexpected

RHODA

She was so overjoyed that, instead of opening the gate, she ran in and announced that Peter was standing at the gate. (Acts 12:14, NRSV)

We know nothing about Rhoda except for her delightful response to an unexpected event. She was among a group of Christians who gathered to pray for the release of Peter. Herod had already put to death the apostle James and promised to do the same to Peter. Christians felt helpless to do anything except pray, which they did persistently, even though hope of a miracle seemed slight.

Meanwhile, Peter slept soundly in his chains. An angel appeared in his cell, released the chains, and led the sleepy apostle out of prison. Once outside, Peter finally came fully awake and hurried to the home where the Christians were keeping the prayerful vigil.

When Peter rattled the outside gate, a servant girl named Rhoda came to answer. Hearing Peter's voice, she got so excited she forgot to open the door but instead ran inside to tell everyone.

Rhoda's oversight underscores how many times we only half expect God to answer our pleas. In fact, immediate answers usually astound us. But to those who persist in specific prayer, such answers are not surprising.

What discoveries have you made about prayer? When you pray, do you expect God to answer or to ignore your concerns? If you decide today that prayer will become a regular part of your life, start expecting the unexpected!

Pray without ceasing!

Rhoda appears in Scripture in Acts 12:1-17.

Giving Credit Where It's Due

HEROD AGRIPPA I

Immediately, because Herod did not give praise to God, an angel of the Lord struck him down. (Acts 12:23)

Early in his reign, Herod Agrippa I traveled on the fast track to fame among the Jews. But his own popularity proved to be deadly.

An unexpected opportunity for Herod to gain new favor with the Jews was created by the growth of the Christian movement. Eager to solidify his position and popularity with his Jewish subjects, Herod initiated the revival of the persecution of Christians. He pleased the Jewish leaders with his clever arrangement for the murder of James and the arrest of Peter. However, Herod made a fatal error during a visit to Caesarea during which he delivered a moving speech. Inspired, the citizens proclaimed Herod to be a god, and he willingly accepted their praise. At the same moment, he was struck with a painful disease and died within a week.

Herod may have been uncommonly evil, but his prideful disposition is universal. Most of us know what it's like for others to give recognition to our accomplishments. And we must admit, the affirmation makes us feel good. But Herod's story reminds us of the foolishness of wanting to receive the *credit* for our achievements. When others acknowledge your abilities, take the opportunity to acknowledge God as the source of your success.

There is great danger in accepting praise that only God deserves.

Herod Agrippa I's story is told in Acts 12:1-23.

Coming to Maturity

JOHN MARK

Get Mark and bring him with you, because he is helpful to me in my ministry. (2 Timothy 4:11)

It's very possible that even as Paul wrote these words a smile flashed across his face. Perhaps he thought back to the time when he regarded John Mark (also known as Mark) as a hindrance instead of as a helper. Shortly into their first trip, John Mark decided he had had enough of missionary work and returned to Jerusalem. It is not until Paul and Barnabas are making plans for their second missionary outreach that we discover how annoyed Paul was with Mark's departure. He refused to allow Mark to go on the next journey, choosing Silas instead.

Nothing more is said of John Mark until he is mentioned favorably by Paul in Colossians 4:10; 2 Timothy 4:11; and Philemon 24. Reading between the lines, we can only conclude that at some point John Mark must have demonstrated maturity, prompting Paul to give him a second chance. It is evident that Paul then came to depend on this young disciple who had let him down years before.

The lesson for us is a good one. Like John Mark, all young believers (whether they are kids at church or our own children— or even adults who are "baby" Christians) make poor decisions. In spite of the risks, we must show mercy and give these "failures" other opportunities to succeed. How can we do less? That is how God treats us!

Don't give up on someone in whom God is still working.

John Mark's story is told in Acts 12:25–13:13 and 15:36-40. He is also mentioned in Colossians 4:10-11; 2 Timothy 4:11; Philemon 24; and 1 Peter 5:13.

Overlooking Our Past

JOHN MARK

Barnabas wanted to take John, also called Mark, with them. (Acts 15:37)

Put yourself in John Mark's place. You were selected to be an assistant on the first missionary journey of the apostle Paul. You accompanied him and your cousin Barnabas (another leader of the church) as they preached the Good News of Christ. But then you got scared. Or you felt homesick. Or the schedule was too demanding. Whatever the reason, you left the team and returned to Jerusalem.

Later, when it is time for the second missionary journey and Barnabas mentions your name, Paul is adamant. "John Mark? No way! He's not coming! Not after what he did last time!" Your self-esteem sinks to your knees.

But Barnabas, in spite of your track record, goes to bat for you. "Give the kid another chance, Paul. He'll be OK this time, I know it." Paul won't budge: "I can't afford to take that risk."

Barnabas is equally persistent. "OK, Paul, if that's the way it's got to be, then John Mark and I will strike out on our own." You can tell his words aren't just for show. He means them. Then Barnabas says to you, "Well, John Mark, I guess we'd better go pack our bags. We've got a big job ahead of us."

We all need someone who will overlook our past foul-ups and who will encourage us to become the people God made us to be. Do you have someone who believes in you? If not, ask God to put a Barnabas in your life.

Encouragement supplies others with courage and hope.

John Mark's story is told in Acts 12:25–13:13 and 15:36-40. He is also mentioned in Colossians 4:10-11; 2 Timothy 4:11; Philemon 24; and 1 Peter 5:13.

Obscure Obedience

LUCIUS

Now in the church at Antioch there were prophets and teachers.
(Acts 13:1, NRSV)

Lucius may well have been one of the unnamed Christians from Cyrene who traveled to Antioch to plant a church there (see Acts 11:19-21), the first of its kind among non-Jews. Later, Lucius became a leader in the Antioch church along with Paul and Barnabas. He was one of those who recognized God's call for missionaries to advance the gospel. His church's prayerful response led to Paul and Barnabas's departure to evangelize the peoples of Europe and Asia.

For every well-known person within the church, there are many who must be content to live out their lives in obscure obedience. The direction of the church may come from strong leaders, but the strength of the church comes from strong followers. We may want to be praised like Paul, but we will probably receive little more mention than Lucius. Jesus never promised earthly recognition for his faithful disciples. He actually predicted the opposite. In any case, the chance for fame makes a very poor reason for obedience. The lives of Lucius and many other Bible people provide us with healthy models of simple obedience. They lived their answer to the question: *How faithful to God are you when no one else is watching?* How will you answer that question today?

Genuine discipleship continues even when the spotlights are turned off.

Lucius is mentioned in passing in Acts 13:1.

Blinded by Sin

ELYMAS

Will you not stop making crooked the straight paths of the Lord?
(Acts 13:10, NRSV)

Luke informs us that Elymas was the Greek name of a Jewish false prophet and magician called Bar-Jesus. A person sold out to evil, Elymas acted as an adviser to Sergius Paulus, the local Roman ruler in Cyprus. Paul and Barnabas ran into him on their first missionary journey.

When Sergius Paulus heard Paul and Barnabas and expressed an interest in the gospel, Elymas tried publicly to distort the message. Under the influence of the Holy Spirit, Paul exposed Elymas's evil character and predicted an immediate punishment from God. Elymas lost his sight at that moment.

We don't know if Elymas recognized his spiritual condition while he was blind. But the clear demonstration of God's power certainly opened Sergius Paulus's eyes of faith. As we strive to spread the gospel, we should not be surprised when opposition to our message appears. We may not have to confront someone as Paul did, but we can trust God to ensure that his message gains a hearing.

The gospel is able to overcome even the fiercest opposition.

Elymas's showdown with Paul and Barnabas is recorded in Acts 13:6-12.

Gifted Encourager
SILAS

Then Judas and Silas, both being gifted speakers, preached long sermons to the believers, strengthening their faith. (Acts 15:32, TLB)

Silas was a Roman citizen and a leader in the Jerusalem church. He had a prophetic gift that enabled him to speak and teach with clarity and power. He became a traveling companion and colleague of the apostle Paul and a writing secretary for Paul and Peter.

We can't duplicate or emulate most of Silas's accomplishments (unless we want to travel thousands of miles and go back in time about nineteen hundred years). However, we can, in the words of Acts 15:32, become people who encourage and strengthen others. Silas's life and words gave fellow believers in Antioch and elsewhere the courage to press on. Those who were slipping and struggling found the practical help they needed.

It is really a simple proposition. You can encourage and build others up, or you can discourage and tear others down. You have to choose which it will be. Why not make the choice to be an encourager? Without being preachy, you could remind a friend or family member of some scriptural truth. Complimenting, affirming, cheerleading, supporting, caring, showing interest—these are all other ways we can encourage and strengthen others in their faith.

In these discouraging times, we need more encouraging people.

The story of Silas is told in Acts 15:22–19:10.

Aim for Faithfulness

SILAS

With the help of Silas, whom I regard as a faithful brother, I have written to you briefly. (1 Peter 5:12)

Of all the words that could be used to describe a Christian, one of the best has to be the word *faithful*. Faithfulness means you're dependable or reliable. It means you're trustworthy, steady, and solid. It means others can count on you. You'll be there.

Peter wrote that Silas was a "faithful brother." Silas earned this description by going through thick and thin with the early church and by hanging in there through all the ups and downs of missionary life with Paul. Nothing deterred Silas—not rough terrain, choppy seas, imprisonment, persecution, threats, hostile crowds, or poor health. He plodded along, faithfully using his gifts and abilities, his time and energy, in every situation God gave him. Perhaps he remembered (and longed to hear) the words uttered by Christ, "Well done, good and faithful servant."

In our success-crazed culture, we think God is pleased with measurable results and large numbers and big programs. We like to use words like *victory* and *winning* and *excellence*. To be sure, these concepts have a place in the Christian life. But the one ideal that we ought to shoot for is faithfulness. If we plod along and carefully seek to do the will of God, we will bear fruit.

In what area of your life do you need to be more faithful today?
Faithfulness leads to fruitfulness.

The story of Silas is told in Acts 15:22–19:10.

Rising above Our Weaknesses

TIMOTHY

For the Holy Spirit, God's gift, does not want you to be afraid of people, but to be wise and strong. (2 Timothy 1:7, TLB)

The Scriptures make it clear that Timothy had a timid personality, though no one knows exactly why. His ministry may have lacked assertiveness due to his mixed family background (his mom was Jewish, and his father was a Gentile). Perhaps Timothy suffered a lack of self-confidence because of his relative youth. He may have been overawed by the confident, talented apostle Paul. Some have even speculated that Timothy's mission to the Corinthian church had not gone well, fueling his self-doubt.

Whatever the case, you'll notice that Paul never scolded Timothy for his timidity. He challenged him instead to concentrate on (1) using his gifts, (2) modeling his changed character, and (3) fulfilling his God-given responsibilities.

Those of us who struggle with a sense of inadequacy would be wise to follow the same prescription: (1) Quit becoming despondent over your weaknesses. Instead, discover your spiritual gifts. Do you know what they are? Are you using your God-given abilities to serve Christ and others? (2) As a Christian, God is in the process of transforming you. Let others see the changes God is making in your life. (3) Remember that God has made you an ambassador of heaven. God wants to work in and through you—and he will if you let him.

Don't let what you can't do interfere with what you can do!

Timothy appears in Acts 16 and in several of Paul's letters.

An Inheritance of Faith

TIMOTHY

I have been reminded of your sincere faith, which first lived in your grandmother Lois and in your mother Eunice and, I am persuaded, now lives in you also. (2 Timothy 1:5)

Given the scriptural evidence, it is not too difficult to trace Timothy's spiritual heritage. His family lived in Lystra, a region of Galatia. The son of a devout Jewish mother, Timothy had been exposed to the Hebrew Scriptures since early childhood. His father was an unbelieving Greek.

When Paul visited Lystra on his first missionary journey and preached the Good News that Jesus is the Messiah, Lois and Eunice—and possibly Timothy—put their faith in Christ. By the time Paul returned to Lystra on his second missionary journey, Timothy was mature enough to be invited to accompany Paul on his journey. Paul would later call Timothy his "true son in the faith" (1 Timothy 1:2). Even so, it is obvious that Lois and Eunice deserve at least some of the credit for Timothy's spiritual progress.

As parents we have no idea of the amount of influence we have in shaping our children's spiritual destinies. Family prayer times, spontaneous conversations about God during life's everyday moments, and reading our children Bible stories contribute to a spiritual foundation that can withstand the storms of life.

What family habit or tradition can you begin this week that will attract your child(ren) to your Christian faith?

The greatest gift a parent can give is an authentic and attractive faith.

Timothy appears in Acts 16 and in several of Paul's letters.

Household of Hospitality

LYDIA

Come and stay at my home. (Acts 16:15, NRSV)

Lydia's day may have started out like any other Sabbath as she made her way outside of Philippi to meet with other women to pray. She was probably already a convert to Judaism. As women and Gentiles, this group was not allowed to do much, but their gatherings by the river to pray to the God of the Old Testament must have been a significant break from their pagan surroundings. On this day, she met Paul and Barnabas, and through them she met Jesus Christ. She had been seeking God, and he drew her.

Lydia's response to the gospel was personal, profound, and practical. She opened her own life to Jesus. She then led her entire household in committing themselves to Christ in baptism. Then she insisted on having the missionaries make her house their base of operations.

We simply do not know what God has planned for each of our days. There is profound guidance in the old saying "Wherever you are, be all there." To the extent that Lydia understood God, she obeyed. She displayed a willing heart. When God showed her more, she immediately responded. Does your plan and schedule for today reflect your desire to respond to God wherever you may be?

Inviting others into your home is an appropriate way of responding to God's graciousness to you.

Lydia's story is told in Acts 16:11-40.

A Costly Investment

JASON

These men who have caused trouble all over the world have now come here, and Jason has welcomed them into his house. (Acts 17:6-7)

Jason found out quickly that being a Christian can be costly. He lived in Thessalonica and met Paul and Silas when they passed through on their second missionary journey. Within a matter of weeks the gospel took root among the Jews and Greeks in town. The number of believers began to grow rapidly. Among them was Jason.

When a riot started over Paul's preaching, an angry mob showed up on Jason's doorstep. Paul and Silas were out, so they took Jason and some other new believers into custody. He was accused of aiding and harboring men who were challenging the authority of Rome. The charges had little truth to them, but they stuck. Jason and the others had to post bond before they could go home.

Jason is one of many unsung heroes who faithfully played their part to help spread the gospel. When Jason opened his home, he couldn't have known what that gesture would cost. You may not receive much attention for your service for Christ (in fact, you may receive only grief), but God wants to include you in his work. Lives will be changed because of your courage and faithfulness.

Obedient service is a valuable investment, but it isn't cheap.

Jason's part in the gospel advance is recorded in Acts 17:1-9.

Responding to the Truth

DAMARIS

A few men became followers of Paul and believed . . . also a woman named Damaris. (Acts 17:34)

Centuries after Socrates and Plato, Athens continued to be a center of philosophical thinking. Alone in that great marketplace of ideas, Paul began to preach the gospel. Paul was eventually invited to present his case for Christianity in the official forum. Among the people who heard the apostle that day was a woman named Damaris.

Paul achieved two results with his message: a strong reaction and a small response. The majority of his listeners only reacted to his call for repentance and his claim that God had raised Jesus from the dead. Some sneered, and others decided to think about it another day. We don't know Damaris's reason for being part of the Areopagus audience, but she believed Paul's message. The fact that her name was mentioned by Luke probably means she became a faithful follower of Christ. She was also a charter member of the local church in Athens.

God's truth requires a response. Damaris was one of those who responded to the truth rather than reacting from her prejudices. Instead of postponing it until another time, her commitment was prompt and wholehearted. How would you describe your usual pattern of response to God's truth?

God's truth requires a response. How will you choose?

Damaris's story is told in Acts 17.

A Faithful Team

AQUILA AND PRISCILLA

They invited [Apollos] to their home and explained to him the way of God more adequately. (Acts 18:26)

This remarkable husband-wife team could easily be called the first small group leaders of the church. Their home was open to Paul, to Apollos, and to many others. They were learners and teachers, passing on the great treasure of the gospel, which had transformed their lives. They worked together in the tentmaking business, helped Paul earn his living for a while, and befriended the talented evangelist Apollos, teaching him what they had learned about the Lord. The story of these two Christians is so full of hospitality, cooperation, and excitement about the gospel that even a modern reader can feel the suspense.

Aquila and Priscilla were faithful to each other, to the Lord, and to Christian friends, wherever their travels took them. If we only had their audiotapes and books, we would certainly recognize them as world-class leaders in neighborhood evangelism, marriage enrichment, and encouraging others toward excellence. At least we have Paul's simple declaration of gratitude: "They risked their lives for me" (Romans 16:4), which does reveal world-class courage and love.

Try to emulate Priscilla and Aquila in your marriage and out-reach—and discover what an impact Christ can make through you.

Christian marriage is a partnership that enables a couple to serve God eagerly and love others generously.

The story of Priscilla and Aquila is told in Acts 18. They are also mentioned in Romans 16:3-5; 1 Corinthians 16:19; and 2 Timothy 4:19.

An Open Heart, an Open Home

JUSTUS

Then he left the synagogue and went to the house of a man named Titius Justus, a worshiper of God. (Acts 18:7, NRSV)

The apostle Paul frequently got mixed reviews when he visited a new city. His method was quite consistent. He began in a familiar place—the synagogue. Paul announced his message about Christ as the fulfillment of all that the Jews truly believed. Some responded, some resisted, while others openly objected. In Corinth, Paul met stiff opposition from local Jewish leaders and decided to try a different strategy of evangelism. He took up the offer of a man named Justus, who lived next door to the synagogue.

For the next eighteen months Paul taught and ministered from Justus's home. We could say that Justus had both his heart and his hearth in the right place. The strategic location of his house allowed Paul's message to reach Jews, even while he was gaining a hearing among the Greeks. Within a short time Crispus, the leader of the synagogue, became a believer in Jesus. So did many others.

Justus's hospitality was motivated by his relationship with God. His open home was an act of worship! He shows us that even those of us with little must give what we can. When we make the best we have available to God, the results are often wonderful! What opportunities are you aware of for worshiping God through acts of hospitality?

When we make ourselves available to God, we open up countless opportunities for service.

Justus's role in the spread of the gospel is recorded in Acts 18:1-17.

Leading by Example

CRISPUS

Crispus, the official of the synagogue, became a believer in the Lord, together with all his household. (Acts 18:8, NRSV)

Paul first visited Corinth during his second missionary journey. As was his practice, he began his ministry in a new city by making contact with the local Jewish synagogue. He obviously created a weekly stir, showing up every Sabbath with a fresh dose of the gospel. Eventually some of the Jewish leaders banded together in opposition to Paul, and a confrontation occurred. Their rejection left Paul free to turn his attention to the Gentiles.

One person caught in the middle of the conflict was Crispus, the leader of the synagogue. Paul's message had reached him. But when Paul was forced out of the synagogue, Crispus was faced with a choice: He could remain in the safety of his religious role or openly declare his belief in Jesus. His choice to believe became a family decision, and his household became followers of Christ, too. Paul even baptized him. Luke attributes to Crispus's public faith the rapid growth of the church in Corinth. His decision opened a way for others to trust Christ. People who step out in faith are rarely alone for long.

You may not know what difference it will make, but others will be watching your life today. Live for Christ.

Crispus appears in the events of the early church in Acts 18:1-17.

Suffering Is Not Wasted

SOSTHENES

They all turned on Sosthenes . . . and beat him. (Acts 18:17)

Sosthenes was the ruler of the Jewish synagogue in Corinth when the apostle Paul was there. On each Sabbath Paul would speak about Jesus, the Christ. Many Jews didn't like this. When they couldn't get the Roman magistrate to punish Paul, they turned on Sosthenes and beat him in frustration. Eventually this man became a believer.

We don't know if Sosthenes became a believer in Christ before or after that beating, but he is mentioned as a brother in Christ in 1 Corinthians 1:1.

Jesus promised his disciples that suffering for him would not be wasted: "Blessed are you when people insult you, persecute you and falsely say all kinds of evil against you because of me. Rejoice and be glad, because great is your reward in heaven" (Matthew 5:11-12).

What kind of persecution have you faced because of your commitment to Christ? While some Christians around the world often risk their lives living for Christ, most of us, as believers in North America, only risk losing our reputations when we publicly identify with Christ.

How can God use you as a witness with your friends and family? What fears do you have about clearly identifying yourself as a follower of Jesus Christ?

Acknowledge Jesus before men, and he will acknowledge you when you stand before his Father.

Sosthenes's story is told in Acts 18:17 and 1 Corinthians 1:1.

Serving with Heart and Mind

APOLLOS

He was a learned man, with a thorough knowledge of the Scriptures . . . and he spoke with great fervor. (Acts 18:24-25)

This brilliant public speaker and debater reminds us of how much we have lost since the early church:

The only public debate appropriate now is over policy, technology, and money. To debate about the truth of Christ would offend too many people.

Being "learned" is not so popular among Christians today. Better to be "trained" or "called." To be learned suggests a serious investment in developing the intellect. Such people raise too many questions, and our pastors are busy enough without that.

Great fervor seems out of line with our tendency to be respectable, mainstream citizens who are polite and tolerant. Fervor today translates to fanaticism, hate speech, and bigotry.

When Apollos looked out at an audience, he could see a proud, even arrogant crowd of thoroughly secular skeptics on the one side—the Romans—and on the other, deeply loyal Jews who, like himself, revered the Law, but unlike himself, knew nothing of the Messiah and the New Covenant. Those were tough crowds by any standards. Yet Apollos addressed them intelligently and passionately. He served the Lord with all his heart and mind.

Study widely and constantly, speak with conviction, and urge all people to find the truth in Jesus Christ.

Knowledge of and fervor for the Scriptures are good.

Apollos's story is found in Acts 18:24-28. He is also mentioned in 1 Corinthians 1:12; 3:4-6, 22; 4:1,6; 16:12; and Titus 3:13.

The Gods of Our Making
DEMETRIUS

Gentlemen, this business is our income. (Acts 19:25, TLB)

The idol business in Ephesus found itself in a slump. Silver symbols of the goddess Artemis were not selling. Demetrius, a well-known local silversmith, traced the problem to a traveling evangelist named Paul, who was convincing people that silver idols were just silver. Demetrius disagreed. Silver idols weren't just silver; they were also his livelihood. Besides, he argued to his fellow businessmen, their great goddess might be threatened if people came to believe that "man-made gods are no gods at all" (Acts 19:26).

The anger and arguments of the craftsmen revealed who their god really was—their own self-interest. Their religion was motivated by profit. Interestingly enough, a non-Christian city clerk demolished their case by calling their bluff. If Artemis (Diana) were really a goddess, she could certainly take care of herself!

The lesson to us is clear: If we find the focus of our faith threatened, we may be trusting in something less than God. We may have substituted ourselves, another person, or some *thing* for the one true God. The God who revealed himself in Jesus Christ doesn't need to be defended. Invest your faith in him alone.

The gods we make for ourselves are easily unmade.

Demetrius's attempt to corner the silver market is recorded in Acts 19:23-41.

Friendships Rooted in Faith

GAIUS, FRIEND OF PAUL

Gaius, who is host to me and to the whole church, greets you.
(Romans 16:23, NRSV)

At least two men mentioned in the New Testament were named Gaius, but the one we will consider here was Paul's companion.

Although many people became Christians while Paul was in Corinth, Gaius was one of the few he personally baptized. Later, just before his final trip to Jerusalem, Paul wrote the Roman church a letter while he was staying in Gaius's house in Corinth. When he left Corinth that time, Gaius probably traveled with him.

Luke notes (Acts 20:4) that Paul's companions were believers from many of the places where Paul had planted churches. They were going with Paul to deliver a large gift to the church in Jerusalem from many of the younger churches in Asia Minor. Paul and Gaius must have enjoyed a close relationship. Gaius undoubtedly looked for ways to serve Paul and other Christians.

We are deeply indebted to those who introduce us to Jesus Christ. Sometimes we should express our thanks with more than just words. We can serve those who have helped us as well as seek to pass on the Good News to others. In what ways have you thanked those who have had the greatest effect on your life?

The gospel harvest includes great friendships.

Gaius is mentioned in Acts 19:29; 20:4; Romans 16:23; and 1 Corinthians 1:14.

A Cheerful Giver

TROPHIMUS

[Paul] was accompanied by . . . Trophimus. (Acts 20:4)

Have you ever helped take the offering in your church? Paul recruited Trophimus to help take the church's offering. He didn't just have to carry a plate down the aisle; he was one of several men Paul designated to take the offering from their churches in Asia Minor (modern-day Turkey) across the Mediterranean Sea to Jerusalem.

Paul wanted the new churches he was starting in Asia that were made up of non-Jewish believers to help the church in Jerusalem (made up of Jewish believers) with its great financial needs. Trophimus was the representative from the church in Ephesus. Sending the men with the money gave the gift a personal touch and promoted unity among the believers from these diverse cultures. Trophimus was part of that human connection.

Recent natural disasters have left many churches today in great need of finances and physical repairs. You and your church could be a major encouragement to another needy church and other believers by giving some of what you possess.

It *is* more blessed to give than to receive. Find out what Trophimus learned when he presented the gift in Jerusalem. In addition to the blessing you will be to those in need, God may grant a blessing of joy and satisfaction to you.

God loves a cheerful giver.

Trophimus's story is told in Acts 20:3-5; 21:29; and 2 Timothy 4:20.

A Sound Sleeper
EUTYCHUS

Keep awake and pray that you may not come into the time of trial; the spirit indeed is willing, but the flesh is weak. (Mark 14:38, NRSV)

Every Christian, sometime in his or her life, ought to stand behind the pulpit during a worship service. The perspective is unforgettable. Inevitably, at some point in every service, one or more of the people in the congregation fall asleep. Watching them struggle to stay awake can actually distract a preacher! Poor Eutychus! We've all been in his seat.

It was Paul's last night in Troas, and the believers gathered in an upper room. The apostle had a lot to say. Midnight passed, and the oil lamps flickered hypnotically. Eutychus wasn't bored; he was just tired. Because the room was packed, he had chosen to sit on the windowsill. He drifted off to sleep and tumbled from his precarious perch. Luke notes that he fell three stories and was killed.

Fortunately for Eutychus, Paul was not a person to accept death lightly. He took the young man into his arms and declared, "Don't be alarmed. He's alive!" They all took a break for a snack, and then Paul continued to speak until dawn. Eutychus's narrow escape left a lasting impression on the believers in Troas.

God understands sleepiness, but he urges wakefulness!

Eutychus's unexpected adventure is recorded in Acts 20:7-12.

Every Deed an Act of Service
CLAUDIUS LYSIAS

It cost me a large sum of money to get my citizenship. (Acts 22:28, NRSV)

Paul owed his life three times over to a Roman soldier named Claudius Lysias. Twice in the temple grounds, Claudius guarded him from the crowd. Later, when Claudius was told of a plot against the apostle, he arranged Paul's escort to Caesarea under military protection.

Roman officers in Palestine did thankless work. They were hated by the local population and considered expendable by their superiors. They were expected to maintain order in a world they seldom understood. Claudius Lysias was not a Roman by birth but had reached the rank of tribune (commander) in the Roman army by sheer hard work and effective military discipline. He was a man who evidently took simple pride in doing his work well.

The Bible includes many examples of people through whom God worked but whose eventual relationship with God is not revealed. Claudius was one of those.

Remember in your dealings with people today that God might use you to touch someone else in ways you do not know. See everything you do as an act of service to God, and be grateful for the role he allows you to play.

Sometimes people serve God unaware of their special role.

Claudius's efficient work is recorded by Luke in Acts 21:27–23:35.

Avoiding the Good News
FELIX

When I find it convenient, I will send for you. (Acts 24:25)

Felix had been the Roman governor of Judea for six years when Paul appeared before him. He certainly would have known about the Christians ("the Way"), a topic of conversation among the Roman leaders.

Felix announced that he would wait to pass judgment, but within days he apparently became curious to hear more from Paul. Rather than defend himself again, the apostle instead preached forcefully to the governor. Paul's words fascinated the governor until they turned to "righteousness, self-control, and the judgment to come." Whether he knew it or not, Paul had exposed a very tender spot in Felix's conscience, for the governor had taken another man's wife. Felix abruptly ended the interview and kept Paul under guard. Instead of repenting, Felix brushed off Paul's troubling words in the hope that the apostle would offer a bribe for his release.

Many people will be glad to discuss the gospel with you as long as it doesn't touch them personally. When it does, some will resist or run. Don't assume you have failed in your witness if a person's conversion isn't immediately evident. Continue to spread God's Good News regardless of response.

God's truth will leave a mark on a person's life even if it is rejected.

Paul's encounters with Felix are recorded in Acts 23:23–24:27.

The Hope within Us

FESTUS

I was at a loss how to investigate such matters. (Acts 25:20)

Festus found himself in the middle of a legal firestorm. He replaced Felix as the Roman governor of Judea in late A.D. 59 or early 60. Festus practiced a more fair-minded version of Roman law and treated Paul more justly than Felix had.

Shortly after Festus arrived, he was confronted by Jewish leaders anxious to bring Paul to trial. Instinctively, the new governor stalled them until he could hear from Paul. Upon arriving in Caesarea, Festus immediately ordered Paul's trial to resume. As soon as Festus gave him the opportunity, he made a formal appeal to be heard by Caesar. It was Paul's right as a Roman citizen. Festus was required to send him on to Rome.

Festus was unclear about the difficulties surrounding Paul. The charges against him sounded like religious hairsplitting. Paul seemed to be babbling about someone named Jesus who had died and then come back to life. To Festus, Paul seemed like a reasonable man until it came to this Jesus. He certainly wasn't the first to find the Christian way puzzling and farfetched. Jesus still gets the same reception today. Christianity offers a startling contrast to the struggle for power, success, and wealth that consumes the world. But, like Paul, we should be ready at any time to give an account of the hope within us.

Will anyone hear you name the name of Jesus today?

Festus's dealings with Paul are recorded in Acts 24:27–26:32.

Missed Opportunity

HEROD AGRIPPA II

Agrippa said to Paul, "Do you think that in such a short time you can persuade me to be a Christian?" (Acts 26:28)

Each generation of the powerful Herods had a confrontation with God, but each failed to realize the importance of the decision. Herod Agrippa II's opportunity came during his official visit to Jerusalem to meet with Festus, the Roman governor. Paul, who was imprisoned, was allowed by Festus to present his case before the king. Herod heard the prisoner's animated testimony but considered the message mild entertainment. He found it humorous that Paul actually tried to convince him to become a Christian.

Like so many before and after, Agrippa II stopped within hearing distance of the kingdom of God. He listened to the gospel but decided it wasn't worth responding to. Unfortunately, his mistake isn't uncommon. Many who read his story also will not believe. Their problem is not that the gospel isn't convincing or that they don't need to know God. It is that they willfully choose not to respond, with little concern for the eternal consequences of such a decision.

What has been your response to the gospel? Has it turned your life around and given you the hope of eternal life, or has it been a message to resist or reject?

There are no guarantees of tomorrow's opportunity to respond to the gospel.

Herod Agrippa II's story is told in Acts 25:13–26:32.

Bad Blood

HEROD AGRIPPA II

A few days later King Agrippa arrived with Bernice for a visit with Festus. (Acts 25:13, TLB)

Like great-grandfather, like grandfather, like father, like son—this tells the story of Herod Agrippa II. His life is an insightful study in family dynamics and dysfunctions. This is most evident in Agrippa II's interpersonal relationships. He followed the moral weaknesses of his great-grandfather (who murdered his own wife and children) and his great-uncle (who committed adultery with his brother's wife). It was the choice of the youngest Herod to become involved in an incestuous relationship with his sister, Bernice.

While he was not responsible for the bad decisions of his predecessors, he was undoubtedly influenced by this heritage of evil. Regardless, his ultimate destiny and course in life were never beyond his control. He could have broken the cycle of abuse and shame that had pervaded his family.

Many people, like Herod Agrippa II, inherit the effects of a family chain of harmful influence—whether it is abuse, alcoholism, or even greed and a quick temper. But it is our willful choice to allow ourselves to become the next link in the chain. You can take a stand against any family pattern of behavior you do not want to perpetuate. Ask God that a new and hopeful family heritage will begin with your life.

You may feel the effects of a family chain of dysfunction, but you do not have to become the next link.

The Herod family history is recorded in the Gospels and Acts. Herod Agrippa II's story is told in Acts 25:13–26:32.

Hearing Problem
BERNICE

This man is not doing anything that deserves death or imprisonment.
(Acts 26:31)

The apostle Paul was a persuasive speaker, but he did not convince all his listeners. Bernice was part of the second highest-ranking audience before which Paul presented his defense. She was with her brother Herod Agrippa II when Festus invited them to evaluate this outspoken Jewish/Roman prisoner who had recently appealed his case to Caesar. Bernice was apparently convinced of Paul's innocence, but failed to apply his message to her own life.

We know from sources outside the Scriptures that Bernice led a shameful life. She lived with her brother in what appears to have been an incestuous relationship. She outlived one husband and abandoned another. Later she was the mistress of Titus, who eventually became emperor. She moved in the high society circles of her time yet rejected or ignored the opportunity to find peace with God that came so close to her through Paul.

We don't know whether Bernice considered what Paul had to say, only that she passed up her golden opportunity.

God may well bring a life-changing opportunity into your life today. Or he may simply nudge you toward a more honest, patient, or self-controlled lifestyle. In either case, are you listening?

We hear God speak when we are listening.

Bernice's story is told in Acts 25:13–26:32.

Influencing the Authorities

JULIUS

They transferred Paul and some other prisoners to a centurion of the Augustan Cohort, named Julius. (Acts 27:1, NRSV)

Once he became a messenger for Christ, Paul spent a great deal of time in prison. While under arrest, an unusual relationship developed between Paul and a centurion named Julius, who had received orders to escort several prisoners to Rome. Julius and Paul may have known each other during the two years the apostle was detained in Caesarea. Julius showed kindness and trust toward Paul from the start, even allowing him to visit friends along their route.

When the ship ran into bad weather, Paul warned Julius of danger and loss. Yet Julius felt pressure to accomplish his mission, and others convinced him to journey on to a better port. Paul's warning proved true, and the ship sank. Only the passengers survived.

During the shipwreck, the soldiers planned to kill the prisoners rather than run the risk of having them escape. But Julius overruled the plan. He wanted to protect Paul. From then on, Luke's account indicates that Julius allowed Paul a voice in the decision making. We can easily imagine that Julius met Christ through Paul.

Every person we meet gives us an opportunity to be faithful to Christ in our words and actions. How do you show your faith to those whom God has placed in authority over you?

No relationship is accidental.

Paul and Julius's adventure is recorded in Acts 27:1–28:16.

A Proven Disciple

PHOEBE

She has been a benefactor of many and of myself as well. (Romans 16:2, NRSV)

Paul provided us with his most mature summary of the Christian faith when he wrote his letter to the Roman church while in Corinth. It remains one of the most widely studied books of the New Testament. Yet for several weeks the single, handwritten copy of this letter probably traveled under the personal care of a woman who was a courier for Paul. Her name was Phoebe.

Though she was not mentioned anywhere else in the New Testament, Paul warmly praised her to the church in Rome. She was a deacon of the church in the Corinthian suburb of Cenchrea. She was a proven disciple, providing financial support for Paul and other believers. He encouraged the Roman Christians to extend whatever assistance Phoebe might need. Paul was confident that Phoebe would find like-minded believers during her visit to Rome.

Paul's introduction of Phoebe reveals his confidence in her character. What traits do people mention when they introduce you? To what degree are you a dependable person? Have you practiced the kind of trustworthiness that makes others desire to introduce you to their friends? Who's counting on you today?

God wants to fashion you into a person of character.

Phoebe is introduced to us by Paul in Romans 16:1-2.

The Value of Encouragement

QUARTUS

Erastus . . . and our brother Quartus send you their greetings.
(Romans 16:23)

Quartus would be an ideal character for a historical novel. We know a handful of details about his life (there's the history), and we can imagine the rest (there's the novel).

Here's what we know for sure: (1) Quartus's name means "a fourth"; (2) he was a Christian; and (3) he lived in Corinth (where Paul wrote the book of Romans). We also have ancient church traditions that say that Quartus was one of the seventy-two disciples mentioned in Luke 10:1 and 17 and/or that he later became the bishop of Berytus.

Beyond this smattering of evidence we know nothing about Quartus . . . except this: When he heard that Paul was writing a letter to the Christians in Rome, Quartus said, "Tell them I said hello."

What did this greeting mean to the Roman Christians? Here are a few possible reactions:

"Our brother Quartus? You mean Quartus has become a Christian? That's fantastic! Praise God!"

"Quartus sends his greetings?! That means he's still alive. It means God healed him! How wonderful!"

"So old Quartus is still serving the Lord. Great!"

We'll never know for sure how Quartus's greeting affected these Christians. But in all likelihood, his message was encouraging. Think of someone in your own life today who could use encouragement. Drop that person a note or give them a call. A few words can make a big impact.

Take advantage of brief opportunities to encourage others.

Quartus is mentioned in Romans 16:23.

Refreshing Believers
STEPHANAS

Such people deserve recognition. (1 Corinthians 16:18)

Stephanas and his family were the first to convert to Christ when Paul came to Corinth. Paul baptized them himself. In the closing chapter of 1 Corinthians, Paul aimed the spotlight at this relatively unknown ordinary guy (and his like-minded cohorts) and asked the Corinthians to please pat him on the back because "Stephanas . . . refreshed my spirit." He was a hero.

Stephanas was the kind of person who said what he said and did what he did to serve others. This is what it meant for him to serve his Lord. This is what it means for us, too.

Consider who has ever encouraged you. Such people deserve recognition. Think of a way to shine the spotlight on them.

Consider whom you can encourage. You can be a source of timely encouragement to others. Take time this week to write or call someone who has been important to you. Perhaps there is some tangible way you can help them. Your words and service to them will refresh their souls.

Encouragement is a gift everyone can afford to give.

Stephanas's story is told in 1 Corinthians 1:16; 16:15-18.

A Dedicated Worker

TITUS

I left you in Crete [to] straighten out what was left unfinished.
(Titus 1:5)

Some of the best and most capable people have a low profile. Not celebrities, not famous, not loud, they make their mark in quiet ways. And those who know and rely on them could hardly live without them. Such was the case with Titus. For someone who received a major New Testament letter, we know remarkably little about Titus's background. All we know for sure is that he was Greek.

But Titus made a profound impact on the early church. To this faithful and skilled man of God the apostle Paul entrusted great responsibility—responsibilities that even Paul's favored Timothy could not handle. In fact, Titus was such a strong and dedicated Christian that Paul relied on him for many critical tasks.

When the Jerusalem church was still unsure whether non-Jews could be Christians, Paul used Titus as a prime example of a believing Gentile. When Timothy could not get the Corinthians to accept Paul, Paul sent Titus to "straighten out what was unfinished." Titus's most challenging assignment was to oversee the immature Christians of Crete, an island where immorality ruled.

Titus, in other words, was a reliable servant of God. The early church took root and grew to a large extent because of Titus's influence. Can people count on you? Can your pastor count on you? They need you.

The church relies on dedicated workers.

Titus's story is told in 2 Corinthians 2:13; 7:6-16; 8:6, 16-24; 12:18; Galatians 2:1-5; 2 Timothy 4:10; and Titus 1–3.

Our Expectations and God's Plans

EPAPHRODITUS

He almost died for the work of Christ, risking his life to make up for the help you could not give me. (Philippians 2:30)

When the Christians in Philippi heard about Paul's imprisonment, the news must have been especially significant to them. They surely remembered Paul's brief stay in their own city jail, when a midnight songfest had concluded with an earthquake that cracked the prison open. They decided to say thanks by sending Epaphroditus to help Paul.

Epaphroditus arrived in Rome bringing gifts from the Philippians. Unfortunately, he soon became very sick and almost died. Word got back to Philippi of his illness, and that fact distressed Epaphroditus. He may have felt that his mission had failed. But Paul saw matters differently. He was deeply thankful for Epaphroditus's visit and urged the Philippians to welcome him home with joy.

Our plans don't always match God's objectives. Epaphroditus wasn't able to accomplish all he set out to do. But his effort had cheered Paul, who described the gifts he received as "a fragrant offering."

Faithful disciples allow God to determine how and when they will serve.

Epaphroditus and his ministry were mentioned by Paul in Philippians 2:25-30; 4:14-19.

Restoring Unity in the Church
EUODIA AND SYNTYCHE

I urge Euodia and I urge Syntyche to be of the same mind in the Lord.
(Philippians 4:2, NRSV)

Human relationships share a striking characteristic with pluto-nium: We don't recognize the energy stored in the bond until it is split. The destructive power released in an atomic reaction resembles the injury and fallout created by the splitting of a strong human relationship.

Euodia and Syntyche were two women whose zeal for the gospel had been eclipsed by a personal dispute. In an otherwise upbeat letter to the Philippians, Paul felt it necessary to admonish these Christians to settle their differences. This was obviously a public conflict, and Paul confronted it publicly. He challenged other believers to get involved for the good of all.

Hardly a church gathers around the globe that has not experi-enced the pain and division created by a feud like that of Euodia and Syntyche. The fallout injures those directly and indirectly involved. Trying to help sometimes means getting hurt. But a will-ingness to get hurt surely characterizes the example of Jesus. Chris-tians should take risks if their goal is to promote unity in the body.

Have you prayed for the Euodias and Syntyches you know today? Perhaps some of your own relationships could be included in that prayer.

Personal grievances must be put aside for the sake of our Chris-tian brothers and sisters.

Paul addresses himself to Euodia and Syntyche in Philippians 4:2-3.

Hometown Hero

EPAPHRAS

You learned it from Epaphras, our dear fellow servant, who is a faithful minister of Christ on our behalf. (Colossians 1:7)

During his third missionary journey, Paul made a significant visit to Ephesus. There he found a group of disciples who were living by the message of John the Baptist. They had repented and been baptized but had not yet heard about Jesus or the promised Holy Spirit. As soon as they did hear, they believed. Among those twelve men was probably Epaphras.

Though Epaphras may have been converted in Ephesus, he returned to Colosse, his hometown. Paul credits him with founding the church that eventually met in Philemon's house. Epaphras later visited Rome and told Paul about the problems in the Colossian church. This prompted Paul to write his letter to them.

Paul was impressed by Epaphras's deep concern for the Christians in Colosse. He described that concern as "wrestling in prayer." Epaphras's faith was other-centered. He carried the gospel to his hometown and then committed himself to a long-term caring relationship with those people. Even when he wasn't with them, his care continued.

What contacts have you maintained with other Christians over the years? Today, make it a point to at least pray for those significant people you know as the home-folk.

Do long-term relationships show up on your prayer list?

Epaphras is mentioned in Colossians 1:7; 4:12; and Philemon 23.

Always Finishing the Job
TYCHICUS

Tychicus will tell you all the news about me. (Colossians 4:7)

Do you stay in the theater to read the credits that roll at the end of a movie or take time to read the introduction of a book? Often you see listed acknowledgment and appreciation for a special person who tirelessly ran errands and provided service for well-known celebrities.

Tychicus provided that kind of help to Paul. He delivered at least two of the New Testament letters Paul wrote. He was always carrying messages and representing Paul. While Paul had the gifts to preach and write, Tychicus exhibited the priceless quality of simply being a reliable helper. Paul could send him on any task, confident that he would complete the job.

Few people are given the public spotlight, but everyone in it depends on the dedication of reliable helpers. It is the product of commitment, attention to detail, trustworthiness, honesty, and perseverance.

Can people count on you? Are you a helper? When people think of you, does your reliability stand out? It means keeping your promises and persevering until the job is done.

A lifetime of reliability is better than ten minutes of fame.

Tychicus's story is told in Colossians 4:7-9 and 2 Timothy 4:9-13.

Exceptional Commitment

ARISTARCHUS

My fellow prisoner Aristarchus sends you his greetings.
(Colossians 4:10)

Those who traveled with Paul did not paste exotic city stickers on their luggage; rather, their bodies bore scars of suffering. In Ephesus, an angry mob couldn't find Paul immediately, so they vented their anger on Aristarchus and Gaius. Aristarchus, a Thessalonian native, submitted to the life of a prisoner in order to accompany Paul to Rome. Later, he apparently spent time in chains with the apostle in Rome.

We have no record that Aristarchus was ever sent on any special missions by Paul. But he may have been the representative of the Thessalonican church in the team that took the collected money from the various Mediterranean churches back to Jerusalem to help the mother church. In any case, it appears that Aristarchus's main ministry was to Paul himself. The suggestion that he stayed in the background isn't as important as the fact that he was always there. He could be counted on, without requiring special attention or grabbing the limelight.

Being a devoted servant such as Aristarchus takes more commitment than many disciples have been willing to give. Most of us would rather be in charge than in chains. Where in your church or circle of Christian friends can you do quiet, supporting work like Aristarchus did?

A disciple is marked by exceptional commitment in and out of the spotlight.

Aristarchus is mentioned in each of the following contexts: Acts 19:29; 20:4; 27:2; Colossians 4:10; and Philemon 24.

An Oasis of Ministry
NYMPHA

Give my greetings to . . . Nympha and the church in her house.
(Colossians 4:15)

Nympha (or Nymphas in the King James translation) was a Christian whose home was used as a gathering place for believers. While this person's gender remains a mystery, his or her generosity does not. This person allowed a congregation of believers to meet and worship in his/her home. This was a normal practice since separate church buildings did not become common until the third century.

Hosting a church was a major commitment. It meant clear, public identification with a new, questionable, and radical religious faith. It meant accommodating large numbers of people weekly, with many men and women coming and going all the time. It meant little privacy and, no doubt, a lot of extra cooking and cleaning.

Whoever Nympha was, he/she deserves to be commended for such a hospitable attitude. It just goes to show that we all don't have to be preachers or teachers or evangelists to play a significant role in the building of Christ's church.

Do you make your home available for the work of the kingdom? Is it a place where other believers can come and find warmth and love and encouragement? Make the commitment today to transform your home into an oasis of ministry. Your life will become crazy and unpredictable . . . and you'll find more joy than you can possibly imagine!

The Christian faith and hospitality go hand in hand!

The one reference we have to the life of Nympha is found in Colossians 4:15.

Shipwrecked Faith

HYMENAEUS

Some have rejected these and so have shipwrecked their faith.
(1 Timothy 1:19)

Several leaders of the church in Ephesus had been seduced by false teaching. Among these leaders, Paul specifically mentioned Hymenaeus.

According to Paul, Hymenaeus made two mistakes that shipwrecked his faith: He rejected both the faith itself and the need for a good conscience. Apparently Hymenaeus wasn't bothered by what his teaching was doing to his own life or the lives of others. The results were so disastrous that Paul had been forced to take drastic action. He told Timothy that he had handed Hymenaeus "over to Satan to be taught not to blaspheme" (1 Timothy 1:20). Paul hoped that Hymenaeus would come to his senses by experiencing the consequences of his mistakes.

Two or three years later, when Paul again wrote to Timothy, Hymenaeus was still spreading falsehoods. No wonder his efforts were destroying the faith of others.

Today there are still many who treat the teachings of Christ lightly. To them, faith boils down to little more than personal preferences. But a faith that has no conscience or that is not anchored to the truth is a ship sailing to disaster. How would you describe the seaworthiness of your ship of faith? Can it handle the rough seas of temptation, or does it need to return to port for repairs?

An active conscience needs to be anchored to the Word of Truth.

Hymenaeus is mentioned by Paul in 1 Timothy 1:18-20 and 2 Timothy 2:14-19.

Passing On Our Faith

EUNICE

I have been reminded of your sincere faith, which first lived in your grandmother Lois and in your mother Eunice and, I am persuaded, now lives in you also. (2 Timothy 1:5)

Some of us have grown up in families that instilled values and behavior that benefited us greatly as we grew into mature men and women. One of Paul's disciples, Timothy, received such an upbringing. He received the gift of life twice from his mother. She gave him birth and then showed him what a life of faith could be.

Timothy's mother and grandmother, Eunice and Lois, were early Christian converts, possibly through Paul's ministry in their home city, Lystra (Acts 16:1). They had communicated their strong Christian faith to Timothy, even though his father was probably not a believer. Despite this division within the home, his mother instilled in him a character of faithfulness that carried into adulthood. Eunice was one of those behind-the-scenes saints who will eventually be recognized in heaven as one of the true heroes of the faith.

Don't hide your light at home: Our families are fertile fields for receiving gospel seeds. It is the most difficult land to work, but it yields the greatest harvests. Let your parents, children, spouse, brothers and sisters know of your faith in Jesus, and be sure they see Christ's love, helpfulness, and joy in you.

If our family can't see our faith, is it real?

Eunice is mentioned by Paul in 2 Timothy 1:5.

Going Out of the Way to Help

ONESIPHORUS

Please say hello for me to . . . those living at the home of Onesiphorus.
(2 Timothy 4:19, TLB)

Paul and Timothy shared a strong and effective relationship. Thousands heard the gospel because of their collaboration. But theirs was never a closed friendship. As they traveled, preached, and planted local churches, Paul and Timothy also built a team of diligent fellow workers. Among them was Onesiphorus, who had been a vital link between the imprisoned Paul and the outside world.

Onesiphorus arrived in Rome at a crucial time for Paul. Many of his associates had left him. But Onesiphorus tracked him down, overlooked his humiliating circumstances, and offered him real encouragement, ministering in the same way he had in Ephesus. Paul expressed to Timothy his profound gratitude for this servant. Apparently, Onesiphorus kept alert to any opportunity through which he might be of service.

Discipleship involves our willingness to respond when people ask for help. Onesiphorus carried this attitude further. He went out of his way to help. His sensitivity to those in need is a quality all Christians should desire. Do your opportunities for service come because others ask or because you actively seek them out? Ask God to make you more aware of the needs around you each day.

Once you start looking for places to help, you'll find them everywhere!

Onesiphorus is recognized by Paul in 2 Timothy 1:16-18; 4:19.

A Source of Refreshment
ONESIPHORUS

May the Lord show mercy to the household of Onesiphorus,
because he often refreshed me and was not ashamed of my chains.
(2 Timothy 1:16)

In 2 Timothy, the last letter that Paul ever wrote, he listed some of the people who meant the most to him. One obscure name that sticks out is the name Onesiphorus. Who was he? Listen to the way Paul described his friend:

(1) Onesiphorus was a constant source of refreshment. Perhaps he brought food. Certainly he provided emotional and spiritual support—so much so that Paul was strengthened by his visits.

(2) Onesiphorus was not ashamed of Paul's troubles. Paul had many fair-weather friends—people who had turned on him or deserted him. Onesiphorus, on the other hand, was a foul-weather friend. Rather than avoiding Paul, he sought him out. He took the risk of visiting Paul in prison (a gutsy move that might have caused trouble for Onesiphorus and his family!).

(3) Onesiphorus helped Paul minister in Ephesus in "many ways." Obviously he was a kind, generous, and willing servant.

What kind of friend are you? Do you refresh others? When you leave a friend's company, is your companion likely to feel replenished or drained? In four verses, Onesiphorus shows us what a true friend is like. Ask God to give you a friend like that—and to make you one!

When times get tough, true friends rush in!

The story of Onesiphorus is found in 2 Timothy 1:16-18; 4:19.

Sincerely Wrong

PHILETUS

Among them are Hymenaeus and Philetus, who have swerved from the truth. (2 Timothy 2:17-18, NRSV)

Philetus may have known many of the believers in Ephesus. He seems to have been well versed in Scripture and able to debate theology and doctrine with anyone. He had strong convictions and sincerely argued his beliefs. But being sincere is not enough. It is possible to be sincere and wrong at the same time.

Philetus and his cohort Hymenaeus were upsetting believers with a "new" theology that denied the scriptural teaching of a bodily resurrection. Such a view struck at the very heart of Christianity, since the faith rests squarely on the evidence of the empty tomb! Because such beliefs and teachings were (and are) so dangerous, Paul warned others to steer clear of Philetus.

Within the Christian faith, there is plenty of room for contrasting viewpoints. For example, godly men interpret the Bible's teaching on the end times differently. But when it comes to the essentials—the reliability and authority of the Scriptures, the deity of Christ, and salvation by grace alone, to name just three—there can be no disagreement. Anyone who denies or trifles with the key articles of the faith is headed for trouble.

Creeds and doctrine may seem boring, but they are vital to all Christians. Ask your pastor to recommend a good, nontechnical theology book for laypeople. Then learn why a good grasp of doctrine is so important.

Being sincere is not the same as being correct.

Philetus is mentioned in 2 Timothy 2:14-18.

Loving the World

DEMAS

Demas, because he loved this world, has deserted me and has gone to Thessalonica. (2 Timothy 4:10)

Jesus described four different responses to the gospel in what we call the Parable of the Four Soils (Mark 4:1-20). Demas was among those represented by the third kind of soil, "Still others, like seed sown among thorns, hear the word; but the worries of this life, the deceitfulness of wealth and the desires for other things come in and choke the word, making it unfruitful" (Mark 4:18-19). Demas chose the world and may have lost his soul.

Our picture of Demas emerges in brief glimpses. He joined Paul sometime before the apostle's first visit to a Roman dungeon. The letters to the Colossians and to Philemon include his name among Paul's companions. But neither his role nor character were described. Only the length or difficulties of Paul's second imprisonment revealed the depth of Demas's commitment. When the going got tough, he quit. Hardship eventually did for Demas what it does for every believer—it forced him to recount the cost. When following Christ seems easy, the world has little to offer us. But when difficulties come along, life away from Christ takes on a whole new attraction. Part of the tragedy in Demas's case was that he lost himself and deserted others he could have helped. They could have helped him, too.

The going will get tough; don't quit.

Demas is mentioned three times: Colossians 4:14; 2 Timothy 4:10; and Philemon 24.

Growing in Christ
PHILEMON

Confident of your obedience, I am writing to you, knowing that you will do even more than I say. (Philemon 21, NRSV)

Philemon was a wealthy citizen of Colosse. The church in that city gathered in his home. It was to this man that Paul wrote concerning a slave named Onesimus who had run away. Onesimus was now a believer, but still a slave. Onesimus may have feared for his life, for a master had the legal right to kill a runaway slave. Paul wanted to assure both his friends that their relationship in Jesus Christ meant that reconciliation and restitution were possible.

Because Paul was an apostle, he could have used his authority to force Philemon to deal kindly with his runaway slave. But Paul appealed instead to Philemon's Christian commitment. He wanted Philemon's heartfelt obedience. To make his case more convincing, Paul gently reminded Philemon of his personal obligation to him. He was confident that Philemon would see Onesimus's return as a reminder of God's mercy in his own life.

Can others count on the consistency of your character? As you have grown in the Christian faith, have others trusted you with greater responsibilities and expectations? Do you forgive others completely? If not, determine today to address the issues that are hindering the growth of spiritual fruit in your life.

As our intimacy with Christ deepens, his unchanging character traits will emerge in us.

Our knowledge of Philemon comes from Paul's letter to him.

Running Back to the Problem
ONESIMUS

Where can I go from your spirit? Or where can I flee from your presence? (Psalm 139:7, NRSV)

God must have a special love for runaways. From Adam and Eve's attempt to elude God to Jacob's escape from his brother, from Moses' retreat to the desert to that inner circle of disciples who fled when Jesus was captured, the Bible abounds with runaways. Perhaps the best-known runaway, however, was a slave named Onesimus.

We are not told why Onesimus ran away from Philemon's house. Eventually he and Paul were united in Rome. There Onesimus became a follower of Jesus. His spiritual depth prompted Paul to call him a "faithful and dear brother" (Colossians 4:9).

Eventually Paul and Onesimus decided it was time for the runaway slave to return home. Paul wrote to his friend Philemon, assuring him that Onesimus would now serve him wholeheartedly. At the same time Paul challenged Philemon to look upon his former servant as a brother. When God confronts runaways, he often sends them back to the very place they ran from in the first place. As God transforms your life, you may also need to confront your past. Do you need to forgive others or be forgiven? Do you need to resolve a painful situation? Don't keep running—rely on your relationship with Christ for the courage to face what you used to run away from.

God will give us the confidence to face our fears.

Onesimus is mentioned in Colossians 4:9 and is the subject of Paul's letter to Philemon.

Faith Leads to Action

JAMES, BROTHER OF JESUS

I saw none of the other apostles—only James, the Lord's brother.
(Galatians 1:19)

James was one of Jesus' siblings who found it difficult to accept the identity of his brother. In fact, he did not believe until Jesus went to the cross. When Jesus rose from the grave, one of those he singled out to see was James.

James won a reputation in the early church for his wisdom. He was very practical. His gift of discernment, which meant that he had to be convinced of the Resurrection, became a powerful asset in the young church, and James quickly became recognized as a leader. He chaired the first church council mentioned in Acts 15 that settled the crucial issue of how Gentiles would be treated in the church. James reminded the group that God was clearly working among non-Jewish believers and that Scripture supported their inclusion. His advice won the day.

Later, James demonstrated the extent of his wisdom in the short New Testament letter that bears his name. Those with any doubts about the practicality of Christianity need look no further than James. For James, faith was action. Browse through this letter, keeping in mind that the thoughts were written by someone who watched Jesus closely for almost thirty years. To what degree would you be called a "doer of the word"?

True faith always results in godly action.

Our picture of James comes from the following passages: Matthew 13:55; John 7:3-8; Acts 15:1-21; 21:17-18; 1 Corinthians 15:7; and the book of James.

Authority Problem

DIOTREPHES

Diotrephes . . . likes to put himself first [and] does not acknowledge our authority. (3 John 9, NRSV)

The explosion of Christianity within the Roman world swept many different kinds of people into the church. Some arrived with their own plans. Some even tried to make a personal kingdom out of those who had been called into God's kingdom. Diotrephes and others had to be identified and confronted by the true leaders within the church. John had to deal with Diotrephes.

All we know about Diotrephes is that he wanted to control the local church in which he was a leader. His rise to leadership has not been recorded, but we do know that he enjoyed being in charge. He slandered his fellow leaders and refused to recognize their God-granted authority. He also set a bad example by refusing to welcome traveling Christians. Reveling in his own dictatorship, he even excommunicated those who opposed his control and offered hospitality. Diotrephes was one self-inflated person!

Sins such as pride, jealousy, and slander are still present in the church, although they may not be as blatant as in the case of Diotrephes. Well-intended concern can easily slip into subtleties of slander, and resentment can simmer unrecognized among members of the same Sunday school class. Unchecked, such sin continues to grow. Ask God to help you search for the seeds of self-centeredness within your own heart.

A true Christian leader is a servant, not an autocrat!

The record of John's confrontation of Diotrephes is found in 3 John 9-11.

The Ministry of Hospitality

GAIUS, FRIEND OF JOHN

Dear friend, you are doing a good work for God. (3 John 5, TLB)

One day Gaius received a letter from John the apostle. We now know the letter as 3 John. The scroll was probably handed to him by a man named Demetrius, a highly respected Christian. John's brief letter contains what little we know about Gaius's leadership in the early church.

John prayed for Gaius's physical and spiritual well-being. He also noted Gaius's effective service of hospitality. Apparently Gaius's church was located in a town along a trade route. They often hosted traveling teachers and missionaries. John remarked about the reputation that Gaius was gaining as a generous and hospitable host. People who stayed in his home left rested and equipped for their work. The apostle clearly wanted to encourage someone who was such an example of faith in action.

Hospitality is a ministry all believers should practice (see Romans 12:13). We may not be particularly comfortable in that role, but we will surely improve with practice. Make it a point to identify someone in your church who already lives like Gaius, and learn from that person.

Every believer can minister through hospitality.

Gaius's ministry of hospitality is recorded in 3 John.

Contender for the Faith

JUDE

Jude, a servant of Jesus Christ and brother of James. (Jude 1, NRSV)

We know very little about Jesus' brother Jude. Like his other siblings, Jude had found it hard to believe that his older half brother was God's Son. His doubt was understandable. Jesus' family members weren't always sure he was God's Son, but they *were* sure they *weren't* divine. And even though the authority and power of Jesus was plainly evident, they were not willing to call themselves his followers.

Jude at first likely rejected the claims of his half brother but later became convinced that Jesus was Lord. The brief letter he eventually wrote reflected his personal odyssey to the truth. He urged Christians to "contend for the faith" (Jude 3, NRSV). Jude, who now treasured that faith above all else, was anxious to prevent false teachers and immorality from snuffing out the life of the church. Undoubtedly he recalled the folly of his youthful skepticism and was determined to bolster the faith of young believers who may have been troubled by their own doubts.

It is often the person who has wrestled long and hard with the claims of Christianity who emerges with a strong faith and transformed life. Jude was slow in acknowledging the claims of Jesus, but his letter leaves no doubt that he developed into a loving, mature Christian, eager to serve God with his whole life. If you are struggling with the tough questions of the faith, take encouragement from Jude's life.

If we sincerely seek God, we will find him.

For more on Jude (also called Judas), see Matthew 13:54-58; Mark 3:31-35; 6:1-6; and the letter of Jude.

TOPICAL INDEX

NAME INDEX